AAA GUIDE TO THE NATIONAL PARKS

♦ A Comprehensive

Travel Guide

to the National Parks

of the United States ♦

Copyright © 1997 by American Automobile Association

Library of Congress Cataloging-in-Publication Data
AAA guide to the national parks/American Automobile Association:
compiled by Kim Sheeter.
p. cm.
ISBN 1-56251-245-5
    National parks and reserves — United States — Guidebooks. I. Sheeter, Kimberly. II. American Automobile Association. III. Title: American Automobile Association guide to national parks.

This book is available at special discounts for bulk purchases for sales promotions, premiums, fund-raising, or educational use. For details contact:

AAA

1000 AAA Drive
Heathrow, FL 32746
Tel. 407-444-7615
Fax 407-444-7508

Printed in Canada
Book design by Meredith Rushing & Amy McIntyre; Rushing & Associates Design, Inc.
Cover design by AAA Marketing Services
Maps by American Automobile Association
Writers: Sara Roen, Michael Sheeter

CONTENTS

MAP OF THE NATIONAL PARKS

Planning a Successful Visit

The national parks are increasingly popular. The most visited park, Great Smoky Mountains National Park, attracted more than nine million visitors last year. To ensure that campsites and special tours will be available when you visit, plan ahead. Contact the park about reservations, permits, regulations, activities and services.

If you are going to visit one of the more undeveloped parks with fewer facilities, also contact the local chamber or commerce or state division of tourism for information about lodging and activities in communities surrounding the park.

To get a general idea of the range of services and activities at a park, check the matrix provided in this book.

The National Park Hospitality Association offers a guidebook to help visitors plan their visits to the park. Call 202-682-9507 to request the **National Parks Visitor Facilities & Services** guide.

Fees and Permits

Many parks charge fees for entrance, camping, specific activities, tours and boat launch. Fees vary.

The National Park Service is increasing fees at 50 parks, including some areas at which fees have not been charged in the past. The fees range from $2 per person to $20 per car. In most cases, persons 16 and under are admitted to the parks free of charge.

All operating seasons, hours, entry fees and camping fees are subject to change – and in fact do change frequently. We strongly suggest you check with Park Headquarters to get the latest information before arriving.

If you plan to fish in a national park, you must have a state fishing license.

Special Permits

There are three passes available at parks that charge entrance fees. They are:

- ♦ Golden Eagle Pass: A 12-month entrance pass for $50 that is accepted by all parks.
- ♦ Golden Age Passport: A pass available to U.S. Citizens and permanent residents 62 and older.
- ♦ Golden Access Passport: A pass for persons with disabilities.

Parks do not waive camping and tour fees for people with these passes, but they may offer discounts.

Backcountry Permits

Backcountry permits are usually required. They are often free of charge. Even parks that do not require backcountry permits recommend that backcountry campers check in with the visitor center or ranger station for their own safety.

Accessibility

In most national parks, the visitor center, restrooms and some campsites are handicapped accessible. Check at the main visitor center for other amenities such as accessible trails and exhibits, TDD, captioned films, large print brochures and audio or video tours of the park.

Reservations

Campgrounds at many parks fill up very quickly on a first-come, first-served basis. Most of the larger parks have a range of campsites to accommodate different camping styles, from tents to recreational vehicles.

The National Park Service contracts with DESTINET to handle campsite reservations in many of the national parks. For more information, call DESTINET at 1-800-

388-2733. You may also write DESTINET, 9450 Carroll Park Drive, San Diego, CA 92121-2256.

Pets

Most national parks require pets be kept on a leash. Pets are not allowed on trails, in the backcountry or in public buildings such as the visitor center. Pets should be kept restrained at scenic overlooks. Pet regulations at private campgrounds vary, so call ahead. Some of the larger parks have kennels or pet boarding available.

Wildlife

All animals in the parks are wild. That means they are unpredictable and potentially dangerous. Observe and photograph them from a distance. There are federal laws to protect wild animals from harassment and ensure that breeding and nesting sites are not disturbed.

The National Park Service repeatedly warns visitors against feeding any wildlife. Feeding animals creates serious problems for both animals and visitors.

For More Information about the National Parks

To contact the NPS Office of Public Inquiries, call 202-208-4747 or contact the NPS Internet site at http://www.nps.gov.

PARK QUICK REFERENCE

A Summary of Activities and Amenities in the National Parks

	Programs/Tours	Self-Guided Trails	Guides for Hire	Picnic Areas	Campgrounds	Group Camp Sites	Backcountry Permits	Hiking	Climbing	Horse Trails	Swimming	Boating	Boat Ramp	Fishing	Hunting	Bicycle Trail	Snowmobile Route	Cross-Country Ski Trails	Cabin Rental	Hotel/Motel/Lodge	Restaurant/Snack Bar	Services (Disabled)
Acadia	■	■	□	■	■	■	□	■	□	■	■	■	■	■	□	■	□	■	□	■	■	■
American Samoa	■	■	■	■	□	□	□	■	□	□	■	■	□	■	□	□	□	□	□	□	□	■
Arches	■	■	□	■	■	■	■	■	■	■	□	□	□	□	□	□	□	□	□	□	□	■
Badlands	■	■	□	■	■	■	□	■	□	■	□	□	□	□	□	□	□	□	□	■	■	■
Big Bend	■	■	□	■	■	■	■	■	□	■	□	■	□	■	□	□	□	□	□	■	■	■
Biscayne	■	■	■	■	■	□	■	□	□	□	■	■	■	■	□	□	□	□	□	□	□	■
Bryce Canyon	■	■	■	■	■	■	■	■	□	■	□	□	□	□	□	□	□	■	□	■	■	■
Canyonlands	■	■	□	■	■	■	■	■	■	■	□	■	□	□	□	■	□	□	□	□	□	■
Capitol Reef	■	■	□	■	■	■	■	■	■	■	□	□	□	■	□	□	■	□	□	□	□	■
Carlsbad Caverns	■	■	■	■	□	□	■	■	□	□	□	□	□	□	□	□	□	□	□	□	■	■
Channel Islands	■	■	■	■	■	■	■	■	□	□	□	■	□	■	□	□	□	□	□	□	□	■
Crater Lake	■	■	□	■	■	■	■	■	□	□	□	■	□	■	□	■	□	■	□	■	■	■
Death Valley	■	■	□	■	■	□	■	■	□	□	■	□	□	□	□	■	□	□	□	■	■	■
Denali	■	■	□	■	■	■	■	■	■	□	□	□	□	■	□	■	□	□	□	■	■	■
Dry Tortugas	■	■	□	■	■	■	■	■	□	□	■	■	□	■	□	□	□	□	□	□	□	■
Everglades	■	■	□	■	■	■	■	■	□	□	□	■	■	■	□	■	□	□	□	■	■	■
Gates of the Arctic	□	□	■	□	□	□	□	■	■	□	□	■	□	■	■	□	□	□	□	□	□	□
Glacier Bay	■	□	■	□	■	□	□	■	■	□	□	■	□	■	□	□	□	□	□	■	■	■
Grand Canyon	■	■	■	■	■	■	■	■	□	■	□	■	□	■	□	□	□	■	■	■	■	■
Grand Teton	■	■	■	■	■	■	■	■	■	■	■	■	■	■	□	■	■	■	■	■	■	■

	Programs/Tours	Self-Guided Trails	Guides for Hire	Picnic Areas	Campgrounds	Group Camp Sites	Backcountry Permits	Hiking	Climbing	Horse Trails	Swimming	Boating	Boat Ramp	Fishing	Hunting	Bicycle Trail	Snowmobile Route	Cross-Country Ski Trails	Cabin Rental	Hotel/Motel/Lodge	Restaurant/Snack Bar	Services (Disabled)
Great Basin	■	■	□	■	■	□	■	■	■	■	□	□	□	■	□	□	□	■	□	□	■	■
Great Smoky Mountains	■	■	□	■	■	■	■	■	□	■	□	□	□	■	□	□	□	■	□	■	■	■
Guadalupe Mountains	■	■	□	■	■	■	■	■	■	■	□	□	□	□	□	□	□	□	□	□	□	■
Haleakalā	■	■	□	■	■	■	■	■	□	□	□	□	□	□	□	□	□	□	■	■	■	■
Hawaii Volcanoes	■	□	□	■	■	■	■	■	□	□	□	□	□	□	□	□	□	□	□	■	■	■
Hot Springs	■	■	■	■	■	■	□	■	□	□	□	□	□	□	□	□	□	□	■	■	■	■
Isle Royale	■	■	□	■	■	■	■	■	□	□	■	■	■	■	□	□	□	□	■	■	□	■
Joshua Tree	■	■	□	■	■	■	■	■	■	■	□	□	□	□	□	■	□	□	□	■	■	■
Katmai	■	■	■	■	■	□	■	■	□	□	□	■	□	■	□	□	□	□	■	■	■	■
Kenai Fjords	■	■	■	■	■	□	■	■	■	□	□	■	□	■	□	□	□	■	■	□	□	■
Kobuk Valley	■	□	■	■	□	□	■	■	□	□	■	■	□	■	■	□	□	□	□	□	□	■
Lake Clark	■	□	■	□	□	□	■	■	■	□	■	■	□	■	■	□	□	□	■	■	■	□
Lassen Volcanic	■	■	□	■	■	■	■	■	□	■	■	■	□	■	□	□	□	■	□	■	■	■
Mammoth Cave	■	■	□	■	■	■	■	■	□	■	□	■	□	■	□	□	□	□	■	■	■	■
Mesa Verde	■	■	■	■	■	■	□	■	□	□	□	□	□	□	□	□	□	■	■	■	■	■
Mount Rainier	■	■	■	■	■	■	■	■	■	□	□	□	□	■	□	□	□	■	■	■	■	■
North Cascades	■	□	□	■	■	■	■	■	■	■	□	■	□	■	□	□	□	□	■	□	□	■
Olympic	■	■	■	■	■	■	■	■	■	■	■	■	■	■	□	□	□	■	■	■	■	■
Petrified Forest	■	□	□	■	□	□	■	■	□	□	□	□	□	□	□	□	□	□	□	□	■	■
Redwood	■	■	■	■	■	□	■	■	□	■	■	□	□	■	□	■	□	■	□	□	□	■
Rocky Mountains	■	■	■	■	■	■	■	■	■	■	□	□	□	■	□	□	□	■	□	■	■	■
Saguaro	■	■	■	■	□	■	■	■	□	■	□	□	□	□	□	■	□	□	□	□	□	■
Sequoia & Kings Canyon	■	■	■	■	■	■	■	■	■	■	□	□	□	■	□	□	□	■	■	■	■	■
Shenandoah	■	■	□	■	■	■	■	■	■	■	□	□	□	■	□	■	□	□	□	■	■	□
Theodore Roosevelt	■	■	□	■	■	■	■	■	□	■	□	■	□	■	□	□	■	■	□	■	■	■
Virgin Islands	■	■	■	■	■	□	■	■	□	□	■	■	□	■	□	□	□	□	□	■	■	■
Voyageurs	■	■	■	■	■	■	□	■	□	□	■	■	■	■	□	□	■	■	■	■	■	■
Waterton-Glacier	■	■	■	■	■	■	■	■	■	■	■	■	■	■	□	■	□	■	■	■	■	■
Wind Cave	■	□	□	■	■	■	■	■	□	■	□	□	□	□	□	□	□	□	□	□	■	■
Wrangell-St. Elias	■	■	□	□	□	□	■	■	■	□	■	■	□	■	■	□	■	□	■	■	■	■
Yellowstone	■	■	■	■	■	■	■	■	■	■	□	■	■	■	□	□	■	■	■	■	■	■
Yosemite	■	■	■	■	■	■	■	■	■	■	■	□	□	■	□	■	□	■	■	■	■	■
Zion	■	■	□	■	■	■	■	■	■	■	□	□	□	□	□	□	□	□	■	□	■	■

A Few Tips

* *The waters around Acadia are calm, but the coastline is jagged and its cluster of islands calls for navigational skill. Don't venture too far offshore.*
* *Visit the ranger station for navigational charts and tide tables. Let them know your itinerary.*
* *Summer is busy season at Acadia and there are only two campgrounds in the park. Make your reservations well in advance. Expect traffic jams in July and August.*

New England's only national park, Acadia is renowned for its unspoiled, austere beauty. In most coastal areas, the sea stubbornly gives way to a buffer zone of sand and marsh before any forested land appears. But at Acadia, dense evergreen forests of spruce, pine, balsam firs and other conifers extend almost to the rugged, pink granite of its Atlantic coastline.

Most of the park is situated on the lobster-claw shaped Mt. Desert Island, a hodgepodge of parkland, private property and seaside resort villages. Mt. Desert Island is topped by 1,530 foot Cadillac Mountain, the tallest peak on the eastern coast of the United States. Sections of Isle au Haut and Schoodic Peninsula have also been incorporated into the park.

Although it is the fifth-smallest national park, Acadia's picturesque beauty and location make it the national park system's second most popular site. Visitors come to hike, swim, fish, birdwatch, paint, or practice their nature photography. Acadia is

ACADIA NATIONAL PARK

Maine ◆ **Established 1919**

very much a water park and amateur marine biologists have long been fascinated by barnacles and other specially adapted organisms that can be studied in Acadia's tidal zone.

Hikers can enjoy Acadia too. The park has 150 miles of trails. Its 44 miles of carriage roads are open only to hikers, cyclists and horses. In winter, the carriage roads are set aside for skiing and showshoeing. There is also a 27-mile scenic drive along lakes, mountains and the seashore.

More than 300 species of birds are indigenous to the park, including oceanic ducks, or common eider, and the herring gulls who live on scraps from commercial fishing boats. Boats are still built on the island, and the waters off Acadia are harvested by lobster fishermen. Other marine life includes Atlantic bottle-nosed dolphin, northern starfish, seals and green sea urchins.

PLANNING YOUR VISIT

Park Open

The park is open year-round. Hulls Cove Visitor Center is open from May 1 to November 1. Peak visitation occurs in July, August and late September.

Seasons

Summer temperatures are usually in the 70s and 80s. Fog is common. Crowds turn out for spectacular foliage changes in late

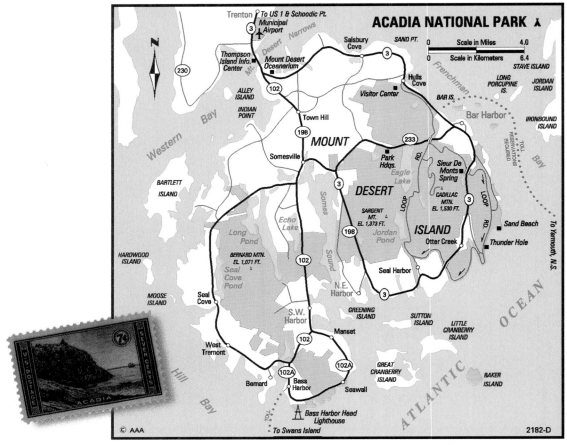

Park size: 41,409 acres

September. Spring and fall highs are usually in the 50s and 60s. Winter lasts from November to April, with highs in the 30s and lows below zero. There is occasional snowfall.

Entrance Fees

Fee per vehicle $5
Fee per individual $2
   Fees are good for seven days

Permits & Licenses

   No license is required for saltwater fishing. A Maine fishing license is required for freshwater fishing. No backcountry camping is permitted.

Access and Transportation

   The park is on the east coast of Maine, southeast of Bangor. From Bangor, take U.S. 1 to Highway 3. Go 48 miles to the Mount Desert Island Entrance. Alternatively, take U.S. 1 to Highway 3, go on to Highway 186 and to the Schoodic Peninsula. Or take Highway 3 to Highway 172 to Highway 15. Go 70 miles to Stonington, then take a passenger ferry to Isle au Haut.

   Greyhound Bus service operates between Bangor and Bar Harbor during the summer months. Downeast Transportation runs a local service connecting Mount Desert Island towns with Ellsworth. Major car rental offices are located at the Bangor and Bar Harbor airports and in Ellsworth. The nearest airport is in Bangor. Vehicles are restricted to designated roads and are not allowed on the carriage roads.

Special Needs

Accessibility guides are available at the visitor center. Some restrooms and carriage paths are wheelchair accessible.

Amenities

Nature walks ♦ Photography workshops ♦ Stargazing ♦ Naturalist-led activities ♦ Gift shop ♦ Bus tours ♦ Bay and island cruises ♦ Carriage rides ♦ Auto tape tour ♦ Hiking ♦ Bicycling ♦ Horseback riding ♦ Fishing ♦ Cross-country skiing ♦ Snow-shoeing ♦ Ice-skating ♦ Ice-fishing ♦ Snowmobiling ♦ Canoe and bicycle rental

Travel Advisory

Wear thick-soled hiking shoes. Rocks and ledges are slippery and loose stones can cause you to lose your footing. Watch out for strong storm waves during spring and fall. Mosquitoes and black flies are common in June. There is poison ivy on the trails.

Emergency Information

The nearest hospital is in Bar Harbor. The ranger station can provide first aid. Call 207-288-3369.

Visitor and Information Centers

Park headquarters on Highway 233, three miles west of Bar Harbor, serves as the winter visitor and information center. Hulls Cove Visitor Center, south of Hulls Cove, is open between April and November. The visitor centers offer a 15-minute presentation about the park. A self-guided tape tour of the park is for sale or rent and there is free information about park routes and the cultural/natural history of the area. Pick up free maps and a biking guide at park headquarters.

HISTORIC ACADIA

Native American Abnaki people lived on the mainland but they often came to Mt. Desert Island, then called Pemetic, to fish.

Samuel De Champlain, a French mariner and the first European to arrive, ran aground there in 1604 and surprisingly dubbed the island "L' Isles des Monts Deserts" or the Island of Barren Mountains. Perhaps the fog which caused him to run aground prevented him from seeing the lushly forested slopes.

Between 1716 and 1763, as the French and English battled for supremacy in North America, the area called Frenchman's Bay served as a hiding place for French war ships. With the English victory in 1763, commercial endeavors — farming and lumbering, fishing and boat building — began to flourish.

The inauguration of regular steamship service in the mid-1800s brought the island's first influx of "summer people," predecessors of the wealthy and artistic seasonal residents who visit today.

Campgrounds

There are two major campgrounds in the park. Both have a 14-day limit. There are also private campgrounds in the area.

Blackwoods Campground. This area is off Highway 3, five miles south of Bar Harbor. It has 306 sites, toilets, picnic tables, fire rings and amphitheaters. It is open all year with limited facilities in winter. Costs are $12 per night from mid-June to mid-September, $10 per night from mid-may to mid-June and from mid-September to mid-October. There is no fee from October 10th to mid-May. Reservations are required.

Seawall Campground. On Highway 102A, go four miles South of Southwest Harbor. There are 218 sites, toilets, picnic tables, fire rings and amphitheaters. The site is open late May to late September, first come, first served (no reservations). Costs are $10 per night for drive-up campsights, $7 per night for walk-in campsites. A small store is half a mile away.

Picnic Areas

Meals are served in the park seasonally. Buy food and supplies in Bar Harbor, Northeast Harbor or Ellsworth. There are several great sites with tables for a picnic, including Bear Brook, Fabbri Seawall, Pretty Marsh, Thompson Island and Frazier Point on Schoodic Peninsula.

Cabins, Lodges and Hotels

There are no lodgings inside the park. Lodgings are available in nearby Bar Harbor, Northeast Harbor, Southwest Harbor and Ellsworth, all within 20 miles of the park. The price range is $50–80 a night.

Restaurants

Jordan Pond House. Tea and popovers are served afternoons on the lawn.

Things to Do and See

Kayak through Acadia's waters. Paddle from island to island with equipment from a nearby outfitter, such as Coastal Kayaking, based in Bar Harbor. They offers a range of kayak adventures, from a few hours to three-day camping expeditions. Call 800-526-8615.

Drive to the top of Cadillac Mountain for spectacular scenery. Nearby Somes Sound is the only fjord in the eastern United States. Schoodic Peninsula offers scenery well worth the short drive.

The Abbe Museum. Found at Sieur de Monts Spring, the museum displays artifacts of the aboriginal Abnaki people.

The Isleford Museum. On Little Cranberry Island, this museum is reachable by ferryboat. It displays ship models, tools and photos of island life over the last two centuries.

Five lighthouses operated by the U.S. Coast Guard. These are Bear Island, Baker Island, Bass Harbor, Head and Egg Rock.

Other Scenic Drives. The 20-mile Park Loop Road connects Mount Desert Island's mountains and seashore. Enjoy the panoramic views. There are parking areas and restrooms along all the roads.

Hiking. There are more than 120 miles of trails ranging from short, level, surf walks and easy lowland paths to the rugged mountain routes such as the Precipice Trail. Hiking the carriage roads takes you over 16 stone bridges with stunning views of Somes Sound and Frenchman's Bay. (Overnight backpacking is not allowed.)

Bicycling. The carriage roads are open to bicyclists. There is a bike path loop

around Eagle Lake. Bicycles may be rented in Bar Harbor, Northeast Harbor and Southwest Harbor.

Boating. Boat rentals, charters, cruises and ferry service are available in the villages. Courtesy mooring at Valley Cove on Mount Desert Island and Frazier Point on Schoodic Peninsula is available.

Fishing. Maine state laws govern fishing. Licensed freshwater fishing is allowed in all the ponds.

Swimming. Summer lifeguards are on duty at freshwater Echo Lake and at saltwater Sand Beach. Be forewarned: the water is cold.

Horseback Riding. Carriage roads are open for horseback riding. Carriage rides are available starting in mid-June.

Winter Activities. Cross-country skiing, snowmobiling, ice fishing and winter hiking are permitted in the park.

Sightseeing. Local firms operate scenic boat trips and bus trips in the park.

Near Acadia National Park

Saint Croix Island International Historic Site, Red Beach. This island is about 120 miles north of Bar Harbor and is accessible by boat only. There is no ferry service to the island. You may take a boat to the island for picnics and hiking, but there are no visitor facilities except for a pit toilet. There is also a small display that explains the history of the island's original French settlement in 1604.

For More Information

Superintendent
Acadia National Park
PO Box 177
Bar Harbor, ME 04609
Tel. 207-288-3338

NATIONAL PARK OF AMERICAN SAMOA

American Samoa ♦ Established 1993

American Samoa is a unincorporated U.S. territory that is 2,400 miles south of Hawaii. The National Park of American Samoa has the distinction of being the only national park south of the equator. It spreads across several South Pacific islands.

This island culture is 3,000 years old.

Present day Samoans are descended from Polynesians who migrated from Southeast Asia. There are several archaeological sites on the Manu'a Islands (Ta'u, Ofu and Tutuila). Ta'u is the home of the original Samoans. This park was created to protect the

only U.S. rain forest. The park also extends to a coral reef and white sand beaches on the island of Ofu. Volcanic peaks that rise from the coastline give American Samoa a dramatic beauty.

This is the only national park where the land is leased from its traditional owners. Hiking and camping on private land requires the permission of the landowners. The National Park of American Samoa is undeveloped and has no federal facilities. In fact, tourism is in its infancy in all of American Samoa. (The good news: Tipping is not a local custom.) The Samoan way of life, *Fa'a Samoa*, is a relaxed approach.

A FEW TIPS

♦ *Pack a hat, rain gear, mosquito repellent and sunscreen.*
♦ *Consider a "flightseeing" tour of the islands.*
♦ *Respect local customs. Samoa has a 3,000-year-old culture.*

Visitors can snorkel and swim, go boating or fishing, or just relax on pristine beaches while basking in the year-round warmth. Hiking through the rain forest is an unforgettable experience, filled with strange and beautiful birds and plants.

There are no poisonous snakes or plants to worry about. Ta'u, Tutuila and Ofu are home to two species of flying foxes. These large, soaring, fruit bats pollinate plants in the rain forest. They may look frightening, but they are harmless to humans.

The most park acreage is on Ta'u. The terrain is untamed. Rain forest covers most of the park land. Spectacular sea cliffs along the south coast drop from the top of a mountain to a rugged coast. The mountain, Lata, is American Samoa's highest peak at 3,100 feet.

Tutuila is the largest of the five main islands. The park land on this island encompasses rain forest, as well as a seabird nesting site. The north shore includes sheer cliffs, dramatic ridges and sheltered coves. Two scenic waterfalls to look for are Leone Falls and Virgin Falls. Rainmaker Mountain rises behind the city. Ride the tram from Solo Hill to Mount Alava, a mile across the harbor, for a beautiful view of the city.

The Ofu unit of the park is known for some of the loveliest beaches in the South Pacific as well as a healthy coral reef.

PLANNING YOUR VISIT

Park Open
The park is open year-round.

Seasons
Weather is warm year-round. During winter in the Southern Hemisphere — April through September — it is slightly cooler and drier than the summer months of October through March. Heavy rains occur throughout the year. In fact, American Samoa gets twice as much rain as Western Samoa.

Entrance Fees

There is no entrance fee. However, you must present a passport or other proof of citizenship.

Permits and Licenses

None are needed. However, remember to get permission from local landowners before you hike or camp.

Access and Transportation

There are several flights each week from Honolulu to Pago Pago National Airport on Tutuila. The flight is just under six hours. Flights from Pago Pago to Ofu and Ta'u are about 35 minutes. There are regularly scheduled island-hopping flights.

Emergency Information

The closest hospital is LBJ Tropical Medical Center on Tutuila. There are no medical facilities on Ofu or Ta'u.

Picnic Areas

There are picnic areas on the islands.

Cabins, Lodges and Hotels

There are accommodations on the islands, but none within the park itself.

Restaurants

Food and supplies are available in nearby villages.

THINGS TO DO AND SEE

Hiking in Ta'u. An easy one-hour walk takes you to the south side of Ta'u. Day hikes farther into the park are possible but are more difficult. The trail deteriorates and you must hike cross-country. There are no trails on the uplands.

Hiking in Tutuila. The hiking trail starts at Fagasa Pass. A moderately strenuous trail passes through craters, along cliffs, through gullies and along the ridge to the top of Mount Alava. The views are spectacular.

Hiking in Ofu. Ofu is easily accessible from the airport. From Va'oto Lodge by the coastal road walking time is about 10 minutes.

For More Information

Superintendent
The National Park of American Samoa
Pago Pago, AS 96799
Tel. 011-684-633-7082

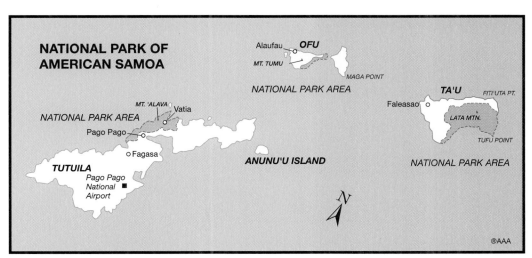

NATIONAL PARK OF AMERICAN SAMOA

Park size: 8,870 acres

ARCHES NATIONAL PARK

Utah ♦ **Established 1971**

True to its name, there are more natural arches in this park than anywhere in the world — more than 2,000. These sandstone formations were created by water, extreme temperatures and underground salt movement. Fantastic shapes are a rainbow in rock, in shades of pink, red, lavender, cream, gold and orange.

Many of the arches and pedestals can be seen from the road, but a mere mile-long walk past the end of the park road will reward hikers with magnificent examples of nature's sculpture. This breathtaking scenery has made Arches one of the country's most popular parks.

The most famous landmark is Delicate Arch. The La Sal Mountains form a beautiful backdrop for this 32-foot, free-standing arch.

This dry land was once a sea. When it evaporated, it left a salt bed that was covered with residue for millions of years. Eventually, the residue was compressed into rock which exerted pressure on the salt bed. Since salt is

unstable under pressure, the bed buckled and moved, thrusting earth upward into domes. This earth cracked and eroded into narrow sandstone walls or "fins."

Frost, snow and rain soaked into the sandstone, dissolving it and causing it to erode at different rates. The strange shapes we see today resulted. This slow chiseling continues. Ten years from now, the arches in the park may not look the same.

Historically, the most significant pathway through Arches is the Old Spanish Trail. Trappers and traders en route to California crossed the Colorado River and continued through the park. Another vestige of the 1800s is the home of a disabled Civil War veteran. John Wesley Wolfe settled on the bank of Salt Wash below Delicate Arch. You can see evidence of his cabin, root cellar and corral.

The desert is a challenging environment, but this park teems with wildlife. The for-

A FEW TIPS

♦ *Arches National Park is one of the most popular parks in the country. Definitely visit off-season — in early spring or late fall — if you can.*

♦ *Allow at least half a day for the scenic drive. Before setting off, check at the visitor center for road conditions and weather forecasts.*

est and desert scrub are home to squirrels, coyotes, foxes, deer and more than 100 species of birds. Adapting to the extreme heat of the area, many of these animals are nocturnal. You may spot mule deer or kit foxes as well as small rodents and reptiles during the day. Coyotes, bobcats and foxes come out at dusk. Mountain bluebirds and migratory golden eagles, red-tailed hawks and flocks of blue pinon jays dot the skies over Arches.

PLANNING YOUR VISIT

Park Open

The park is open year-round. Peak visitation is in August. A visit in early spring or late fall is highly recommended — you'll beat the crowds and the heat.

Seasons

From June through September, temperatures often exceed 100°. In December through February, temperatures drop below 32°. Although temperatures can vary as much as 50 degrees in a 24-hour period, there is one constant: this is dry country.

Entrance Fees

Per vehicle $10
Per individual...$5
Fees are valid for 7 days.

Permits and Licenses

Backcountry hikers must obtain a free permit from the visitor center. Fees are also charged for Fiery Furnace permits and guided walks.

Access and Transportation

The park is in eastern Utah, five miles northwest of Moab off U.S. 191. From I-70, take U.S. 191 south for 27 miles to the park entrance. Alpine Air flies from Salt Lake City to Canyonlands Airport. There is no scheduled taxi service from the airport to Moab. Greyhound stops 50 miles north of the park in Green River, Utah. Amtrak stops 40 miles northeast of the park in Thompson Springs, Utah. Rental cars are available in Moab.

Special Needs

Restrooms at the visitor center and toilets in the campground are accessible. So, too, are facilities at Devils Garden picnic area and Windows Trailhead. A short trail at

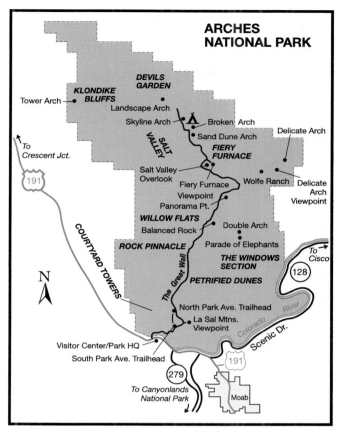

ARCHES NATIONAL PARK

Park size: 73,379 acres

Park Avenue is accessible. There is one accessible campsite available on a first-come, first-served basis. The site is adjacent to accessible restrooms. A new Delicate Arch Viewpoint and trail area are accessible.

Amenities

Interpretive exhibits ♦ Self-guided nature trails ♦ Walking and auto tours ♦ Junior ranger program ♦ Campfire programs

Travel Advisory

Hikers must carry water. Temperatures can top 100°. Climbing or hiking on sandstone is hazardous.

Emergency Information

First aid is available in the park. The closest hospital is in Moab.

Visitor and Information Centers

The visitor center is five miles northwest of Moab on U.S. 191. A short orientation program is presented in the auditorium on the hour and half-hour. A bookstore run by the Canyonlands Natural History Association sells books and educational materials about the area.

Campgrounds

Individual campsites are reserved at Arches Visitor Center between 7:30 and 8:00 a.m. or at the entrance station after 8:00 a.m. To reserve group sites call 801-259-4351. There is a $10 reservation fee for group sites.

Devils Garden Campground. This area is 18 miles from the park entrance. It has 50 tent and trailer sites and two group sites for ten or more people camping in tents. There are toilets and running water in the summer. The campground is often filled by mid-morning from March through October.

Picnic Areas

There are three designated picnic areas in the park. Food and supplies are available in Moab. No food is available in the park.

Cabins, Lodges and Hotels

There is no lodging in the park.

Restaurants

There are no restaurants in the park.

THINGS TO DO AND SEE

Nature Walks. There are regularly scheduled walks led by rangers from mid-March through October. The popular Fiery Furnace guided hike requires reservations 48 hours in advance. Check the schedule at the visitor center. There is a fee for the Fiery Furnace tour.

Scenic Drives. A 48-mile, paved, round trip leads to major park features. Allow half a day for this scenic drive.

Hiking. There are a number of trails of varying difficulty. Most lead to the arches; some to the heart of the park. A must-see hike is Devils Garden Trail. It starts at the end of the paved road and continues for six miles past five arches, including Landscape Arch, the world's longest, natural, stone arch. A shorter hike is Park Avenue, a one-mile trail starting at Courthouse Towers.

Near Arches National Park

Canyonlands National Park. This national park in Moab is nearby. Please see the entry for Canyonlands for more information.

Dead Horse Point State Park. This nearby park offers viewpoints, hiking trails, a campground and a visitor center.

For More Information

Superintendent
Arches National Park
PO Box 907
Moab, UT 84532
Tel. 801-259-8161

BADLANDS NATIONAL PARK

South Dakota ✦ **Established 1978**

Eighteenth century French-Canadian trappers dubbed this stark and forbidding region of present day South Dakota *les mauvaises terres à traveser*, or "bad lands" to travel across. The trappers, slogging tortuously along on foot and horseback, assumed this new country was far too rugged to settle.

To the first white men in the region, the Badlands were fit to be colonized only by jackrabbits, coyotes, rattlesnakes, buffalo and prairie dogs. The trappers would have been astonished to learn that this same region had already continuously supported human life for nearly 12,000 years. Ironically, the Lakota Native American people had also given the area a name in their own tongue: *mako sica*. Bad land.

Passing over a seemingly endless, mixed-grass prairie, the explorers from both cultures encountered a mysterious terrain of varicolored cliffs, gorges, mesas, soaring spires, keen-edged ridges and canyons. There was ample reason for the region's ghostly atmosphere. Hints of past lives were everywhere, embedded in dried up stream beds, the faces of cliffs and in the very ground underfoot.

The park is famed as one of the richest fossil beds of the Eocene-Oligocene epoch, dating back as far as 34 million years. The fossils are studied by scientists, unlocking the evolution of species such as the horse, sheep and pig. The soft rock still yields new secrets.

The Arikara people had inhabited the area since the 1700s. They were displaced by the Lakota, or Sioux people. The Lakota were formidable hunters and horsemen. To them, the Badlands became a sacred trust from the Great Spirit. Seventy-seven different species of grass supported seemingly unlimited numbers of buffalo and of pronghorn antelope, the fastest mammals on the continent. Food was plentiful and the new land revealed a desolate beauty to those who were tough enough to survive there. Then as now, in the spring the prairies come alive with cottonwood, wild roses and blankets of wildflowers.

It all started to go wrong for the Lakota when gold was discovered in the nearby Black Hills. The Stronghold area of the park became a battleground. The Massacre at Wounded Knee took place in 1890, only 25 miles from the park.

With the Lakota defeat, treaty promises were forgotten and homesteaders and ranchers settled in the region. Very few of them made good. In 1939, when the federal government decided to preserve the parklands most of the settlers were content to leave.

Today, the buffalo once again graze in the sage creek basin, fully protected and multiplying in number. Bighorn sheep, which had vanished from the Badlands, have been reintroduced and are flourishing. The protected wilderness of the park is also the new home to the black-footed ferret, the most endangered North American land mammal. The skies overhead are full of swifts, swallows, rock wrens and the seldom-seen golden eagle.

The Lakota people are still here, too. The Pine Ridge Reservation, administered by the National Park Service in agreement with the Oglala Sioux tribe, has become a part of the Badlands National Park.

PLANNING YOUR VISIT

Park Open
The park is open all day, every day. Peak visitation is in August.

Seasons
Between Memorial Day and Labor Day, when most people visit the park, the day-time temperatures are in the 90s. In autumn, the weather is sunny and warm, with temperatures usually in the 60s and 70s. By November, the thermometer can fall to below zero and the first snowfall is seen. Spring is typically wet, cold and unpredictable. Surprise snowstorms as late as April are not uncommon.

Entrance Fees
Per vehicle..$10
Per individual $5
Fees are valid for seven days.

Permits and Licenses
There is a $10 a night camping fee. Special fees apply to buses and commercial vehicles. Off-road driving is prohibited.

Access and Transportation
Take I-90 east from Rapid City to Highway 240. This road makes a 30-mile scenic loop through the park. Take exit 131 (Cactus Flat) or exit 110 (Wall) and follow signs to the park.

From the North. Take I-90 50 miles east of Rapid City to exit 110. Go eight miles south on Highway 240 to Pinnacles Entrance.

A FEW TIPS

♦ *When afoot, stay well clear of wildlife, especially buffalo.*
♦ *Don't go hiking without a topographical map and plenty of water.*
♦ *Expect extremely high winds. You'll need hats and sunglasses.*

From the Northeast. Take I-90 71 miles west of Rapid City to exit 131. Go four miles south on Highway 240.

From the South. Take Highway 377. Go two miles east of Interior.

The closest airport is in Rapid City, South Dakota, 75 miles from the park.

Jackrabbit Bus lines serves Wall, which is approximately seven miles from the park entrance. There is no train service to the park. Rental cars are available at the airport in Rapid City.

Special Needs

Both Fossil Exhibit Trail and Windows Trail are wheelchair accessible. So are both visitor centers, including displays and restrooms. The park orientation video is captioned. Two restrooms in the Cedar Pass Campground are wheelchair accessible. Fossils, bones, rocks and plants may be handled in the Touch Room. An accessibility guide is available at the visitor centers. Access to Stronghold Unit is limited.

Amenities

Scenic drives ♦ Hiking ♦ Naturalist programs

Travel Advisory

Be alert for rattlesnakes and wildlife. Drink water from approved sources. Winds can be quite strong throughout the year.

Emergency Information

First aid is available inside the park. There are doctors in Wall, Philip and Rapid City. The nearest hospital is in Philip, 35 miles northeast of Cedar Pass.

Visitor and Information Centers

The Ben Reifel Visitor Center is two miles northeast of Interior on Highway 240. It is open except on Thanksgiving, Christmas Day and New Year's Day. The White River Visitor Center is in the Stronghold Unit on Highway 27. It is open daily in the summer.

Campgrounds

Campsites are available year-round with a 14-day limit. Only group reservations will be accepted. Write ahead or check in at visitor centers for backcountry camping information.

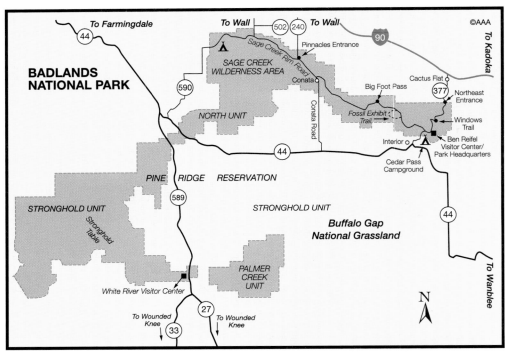

Park size: 243,244 acres

Cedar Pass Campground. There are 100 sites available. In summer, sites are available on a first-come, first-served basis. The campground has water, restrooms, tables and dump stations. In winter there are pit toilets and no water, but the camping fee drops to $8 a night.

Sage Creek Primitive Campground. Sites are available on a first-come, first-served basis. There are tables and pit toilets and there is no camping fee.

Picnic Areas

There are tables and pit toilets available at Sage Creek and Conata. No open fires are permitted at the picnic areas or campgrounds. Cooking stoves and charcoal grills are allowed in campgrounds. Food and supplies are available in Interior, Wall and Kadoka.

Cabins, Lodges and Hotels

Cedar Pass Lodge. The lodge has 23 rustic cabins and is open from May to October. It is on Highway 240. For reservations call 605-433-5460.

Restaurants

Meals are available at the Cedar Pass Lodge from March to late October. There are restaurants in Interior, Wall and Kadoka.

THINGS TO DO AND SEE

Tours. The major attraction of the park is the fantastically colored and eroded cliffs, ridges and hills that stretch across the park in a 200-foot high band. The surrounding prairie grassland is a fine place to view wildlife, especially in the Wilderness Area, where you may see grazing herds of buffalo.

Park naturalists and rangers give guided nature walks and nightly programs in the Cedar Pass Campground. Don't miss the Fossil Exhibit Trail or the Oglala Sioux cultural exhibits and video at the White River Visitor Center.

Scenic Drive. A loop road runs through the park. Highway 240 will take you past

many overlooks and exhibits which will give you a good introduction to the Badlands.

Hiking. Hiking is unrestricted in the Badlands and the best way to appreciate what the park has to offer is on foot. There are eight trails in the Cedar Pass area, some self-guided, ranging from easy to difficult.

You can also go backcountry hiking in the Sage Creek Wilderness Area, but you'll want to purchase a topographic map and inform a ranger of your trip. Highly-recommended, easy trails are the Fossil Exhibit Trail, Cliff Shelf Nature Trail and Door Trail.

Near Badlands National Park

Mount Rushmore. You won't want to leave South Dakota without a visit to Mount Rushmore National Memorial in Keystone. Artist Gutzon Borglum intended his heroic sculpture of Mount Rushmore's granite face to represent Presidents Washington, Jefferson, Lincoln and Roosevelt. The monument symbolizes independence, representation in government, leadership in world affairs, equality and a strong union. The Mount Rushmore visitor center is two miles southwest of Keystone on Highway 244 and 25 miles south of Rapid City on U.S. 16. There is a $5 parking fee. Meals are served during the summer. For more information, call 605-574-2523.

For More Information
Superintendent
Badlands National Park
PO Box 6
Interior, SD 57750
Tel. 605-433-5361

BIG BEND NATIONAL PARK

Texas ♦ **Established 1944**

As the Rio Grande meanders south, separating Texas and Mexico, the river abruptly doubles back on itself in an enormous horseshoe shaped curve. The rugged Chihuahuan desert inside the horseshoe is the Big Bend country of Texas. The Big Bend National Park covers 118 miles on the southern tip of the river's curve. It is the largest wilderness area in Texas.

Big Bend is among the most inaccessible of America's national parks. Its hot and arid trails take their toll even on the most intrepid birdwatcher or naturalist. The U.S. Army once used this terrain as a field laboratory to test the feasibility of using camels as pack animals.

Still, the park is all the more rewarding in its remoteness, demonstrating the pure and delicate interdependence of river, mountain and desert. In fact, the flora and fauna here are so varied that Big Bend seems to be three parks doing business under a single name.

Desert vegetation blankets most of the park, but the land is far from barren. The infrequent, heavy rainfall replenishes the desert, swelling baked, dry creekbeds with rushing, green-brown water and bringing the wildflowers into bloom. There are over 60 kinds of cactus and prickly pear flourishing in Big Bend's desert areas. The lechuguilla, native only to this area, grows in dense thickets all over the park. Its needle-sharp spines pose a hazard to unwary hikers.

The Big Bend bluebonnets, creosote bushes, yucca, bunchgrasses and sotols growing there share a common trait. Each species has developed strategies for withstanding the relentless sun and for finding and conserving the water it must have to survive.

The animals of Big Bend are equally well adapted. Evolution has equipped the local jackrabbits with

A Few Tips

♦ *As a minimum, carry one gallon of water, per person, per day.*
♦ *Advise rangers of your hiking and river float plans.*
♦ *Wear sturdy shoes, a hat, tough clothing and sunscreen.*
♦ *Watch out for rattlesnakes.*

extra large ears that function as radiators, keeping the big jacks cool by channeling heat away from their body. Other mammals living in the park include beavers, bobcat, gray foxes, coyotes, pronghorns, kangaroo rats, mule deer and mountain lions. The roadrunners, ground foraging cousins to the cuckoo, rely on fleetness of foot as a survival mechanism, outpacing the wily coyotes as they race over the desert floor. More than 450 species of birds have been spotted in Big Bend,

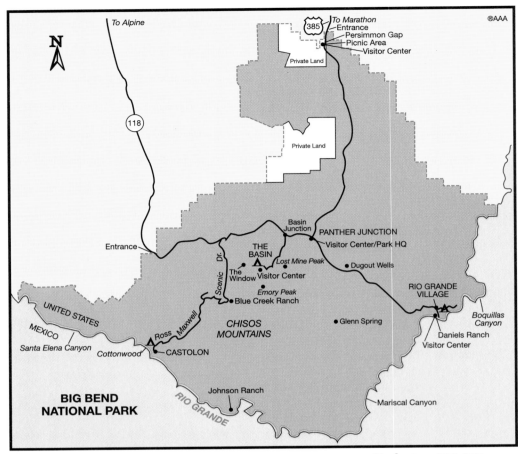

To Alpine

®AAA

N

To Marathon
Entrance
Persimmon Gap
Picnic Area
Visitor Center

385

Private Land

118

Private Land

Basin
Junction

PANTHER JUNCTION
Visitor Center/Park HQ

Entrance

THE
BASIN

Lost Mine Peak

Dugout Wells

Scenic Dr.

The
Window

Visitor Center

Emory Peak

RIO GRANDE
VILLAGE

Blue Creek Ranch

UNITED STATES

CHISOS
MOUNTAINS

Glenn Spring

Boquillas
Canyon

MEXICO

Ross

Maxwell

Daniels Ranch
Visitor Center

Santa Elena Canyon

Cottonwood

CASTOLON

BIG BEND
NATIONAL PARK

RIO GRANDE

Johnson Ranch

Mariscal Canyon

Park size: 802,163 acres

more than in any other U.S. national park. Ducks and other water birds are at home near the river, and so are cardinals, white winged doves, vermilion flycatchers and blue grosbeaks.

Just beyond the desert are the lush floodplains of the Rio Grande, full of narrow, steep canyons. Hundreds of millions of years ago, two seas flowed into this region in quick succession. They left behind thick deposits of shale and limestone as well as an abundance of fossils. Here, in 1971, paleontologists uncovered the remains of the largest winged creature the earth has ever known, a pterodactyl with a wingspan measuring 38 feet. These great flying reptiles became extinct 60 million years ago.

All of today's mountains, except the Chisos, came thrusting up from the earth when the Rockies made their appearance,

roughly 75 million years ago. The magnitude of that upheaval caused a 40-mile trough to sink along fault lines. The collapsed terrain comprises most of the present day parklands. The aftermath left the cliffs of Santa Elena Canyon to the west and Sierra del Carmen to the east towering 1,500 feet above the desert floor. Thirty-five million years later, volcanic activity in the center caused molten rock to ooze out of the ground, forming the Chisos.

The higher and cooler mountain elevations are home to a completely different order of plant life than you'll see in the desert. Masses of juniper grow in the high country, as do ponderosa pines, maple, piñons, small oak trees, Douglas firs, aspens and madrones.

Prehistoric Native Americans traversed the desert more than 10,000 years ago, leaving their pictographs etched into rocks.

Over the centuries, Apaches, Spanish Conquistadors, Comanches, U.S. Cavalry troopers, Mexican revolutionaries and outlaws followed in their footsteps. In 1836, the Big Bend country became part of the Lone Star Republic of Texas. Real exploration of the river had to wait until 1852, when U.S. Army engineers conducted a boundary survey.

PLANNING YOUR VISIT

Park Open

The park is open year-round. Peak visitation is in March. If you can avoid visits during holiday weekends, especially spring break, you can enjoy one of the least-crowded national parks. Visitation is lowest in August and September.

Seasons

Fall and winter are probably the best time to visit. In autumn the deciduous trees in the mountains turn color. Winters are mild. Summer temperatures in the desert can soar above 110°, but expect temperatures five to ten degrees higher along the river. The temperature is always five to ten degrees cooler in the Chisos Mountains.

When there has been enough rainfall, the desert is fully and beautifully in bloom from March through May, and once again from August through September. Birdwatching is good throughout the year, but is at its peak from March through May.

Entrance Fees

Per vehicle $10
Per individual $5
Fees are valid for 7 days.

Permits and Licenses

A permit is required for Rio Grande float trips. You can pick up a free backcountry camping permit at any of the four visitor centers. A Texas license is required for fishing.

Access and Transportation

The park is in Southwest Texas on the border of Mexico.

North Entrance. Take U.S. 385 for 69 miles south of Marathon.

West Entrance. Take Highway 118 for 108 miles south of Alpine. From San Antonio, a 410-mile trip, go to Panther Junction via U.S. 90 to Marathon and south via U.S. 385. From El Paso, a 323-mile trip, take the I-10 to Van Horn, then take U.S. 90 to Alpine and south via Texas 118.

There is no public transportation within the park. The nearest airport is Midland-Odessa Airport, 230 miles northeast. Rental cars are available at Midland and El Paso.

Special Needs

Window View trail, a quarter-mile loop in the Chisos Mountains, is wheelchair accessible.

Amenities

Scenic drives ♦ Hiking ♦ River running ♦ Fishing ♦ Naturalist programs ♦ Showers ♦ Service stations ♦ Telephones ♦ Post office ♦ Laundry facilities ♦ Bookstores ♦ Many rangers are bi-lingual and speak Spanish and English.

Travel Advisory

The spines and thorns of park cacti and other plants can be a serious hazard. Be careful if you hike off trails. Carry tweezers to remove spines too small to be removed by hand. Swimmers and waders should be aware of the Rio Grande's swift currents, sudden dropoffs and submerged snags. In the case of flooded water crossings, wait out the high water. Otherwise your vehicle may be washed downstream.

Emergency Information

First aid is available at headquarters and ranger stations. The nearest hospital is in Alpine, 100 miles away.

Visitor and Information Centers

There are four visitor centers: Panther Junction, Chisos Basin, Persimmon Gap and Rio Grande Village. There is a visitor contact station at Castolon. Panther Junction and Chisos Basin Visitor Centers are open daily all year. Rio Grande Village visitor center is open November through April. There is also an information station at Persimmon Gap. All visitor centers provide backcountry permits and park information.

Campgrounds

There are four campgrounds, each with a 14-day limit. The sites are open all year and available on a first-come, first-served basis. Wood and ground fires are prohibited. Carry out all refuse. Campsite occupancy is limited to eight people and two vehicles or one RV plus one vehicle.

Chisos Basin Campground. This area has 63 sites and eight group sites, toilets, water, tables, grills, overhead shelters and a dump station. The fee is $7 a night.

Rio Grande Village RV Park. This is the only campground in the park with RV hookups.

Rio Grande Village. This campground has 100 sites, toilets, water, tables, grills, overhead shelters and a dump station. The fee is $7 a night.

Cottonwood Campground. This area has 35 sites and one group site, pit toilets, tables, grills and water. The fee is $7 a night.

Backcountry camping is allowed throughout the park but a permit is required. To reach many backcountry sites requires a four-wheel drive vehicle. Some roadside campsites are available throughout the park but have no services or facilities.

Picnic Areas

There are five picnic areas with tables just off the paved road. There are tables and grills at the campsites. There are limited supplies available at campgrounds, Panther Junction, park headquarters, Rio Grande Village and Castolon.

Restaurants

There is a dining room in the Chisos Mountains Lodge.

Cabins, Lodges and Hotels

Chisos Mountain Lodge This lodge has 72 motel rooms and six stone and frame cottages. Rooms are priced from $48.50 to $60.50 a night. Cottages start at $65.60. It is air conditioned and has a restaurant. For reservations and information call 915-477-2291. The proprietors recommend reservations one year in advance.

There are hotels and motels outside the park in Terlingua and Marathon.

THINGS TO DO AND SEE

Rio Grande Float Trips. You can take float trips on open stretches of the Rio Grande or through beautiful canyons, such as Mariscal Canyon. The Rio Grande Wild and Scenic River, a specially designated stretch of the river, is managed by the National Park Service. The river is slow and quiet, but the canyon walls are sheer and steep. White water in certain locations is potentially dangerous to novices. A permit is required. A river guide is available at park headquarters. River rafting trips are offered by several outfitters but there are no equipment rentals in the park. Contact headquarters for a list of river outfitters.

Scenic Drive. The Ross Maxwell Drive to Castolon and the Chisos Mountain Basin Drive are scenic drives. The Chisos Mountain Basin Road is not recommended for trailers more than 20 feet or RVs more than 24 feet.

Hiking. There are more than 150 miles of trails. The Chisos Mountains are the park's main attraction. A hiking trail leads to the spectacular view from the summit of Emory Peak, the highest point in the park. For an easier walk, choose Lost Mine Trail, a five-mile round trip from Panther Pass.

Historic Sites. For a glimpse of Historic Texas, visit the Rio Grande Village, the Castolon Settlement, the Johnson, Daniels and Blue Creek ranches and the Glenn Spring Ruins.

Near Big Bend National Park

Big Bend Ranch State Park. This 287,000-acre preserve is adjacent to the park on the west. Like Big Bend, it features noteworthy geology, plants and animals. For more information call 915-229-3416.

Mexico. Adjacent to the park are Santa Elena, Chihuahua and Boquillas, Coahuila. The visitor centers have more information about sidetrips to these Mexican border towns.

For More Information

Superintendent
Big Bend National Park
PO Box 129
Big Bend National Park, TX 79834
Tel. 915-477-2251

BISCAYNE NATIONAL PARK

Florida ♦ **Established 1968**

The mangroves, bays, keys and coral reef of Florida's southeastern peninsula form Biscayne National Park located on the Atlantic south coast of Miami. Biscayne's coral reef is the only one in the continental United States. The Florida Keys are barrier islands, protecting the brightly colored fish, plants and coral of the bay from ocean waves. The park was redesignated a national park and enlarged in 1980. Its islands, called keys, are accessible only by boat.

Biscayne is a water park, with lots of opportunities for boating, water skiing, snorkeling, diving and canoeing. Snorkeling and scuba trips may be reserved at the visitor center. Canoes are also available for rental. You can also rent snorkels and qualified divers can rent dive gear. A glass-bottom boat offers daily tours of the living coral reef.

Rangers narrate the glass-bottom boat trips. Reservations for these activities are required, but you may grab a last-minute seat. (Under-booked cruises can be canceled in the off-season.)

Landlubbers can walk along the board-walk, listening to cormorants and herons and watching pelicans dive head long into the water for dinner. You can also go lobstering.

Hurricane Andrew hit nearby Homestead in 1992, but the park has recovered and all facilities are open.

PLANNING YOUR VISIT

Park Open

The park is open year-round. Peak visitation is in February.

Seasons

Florida's dry season is mid-December to mid-April. If you visit during the summer, expect an afternoon downpour and non-stop mosquito attacks.

Entrance Fees

There are no entrance fees or camping fees. There is a $15 per night overnight docking fee at Elliott Key and Boca Chita Key harbors. Boat tours and rental of canoes, snorkels and diving gear are available for a fee.

Permits and Licenses

Permits are not required to hike in Biscayne National Park. There is no back-country camping allowed.

A FEW TIPS

♦ One of the rules of eco-tourism — traveling with respect for the environment — is "leave only footprints, take only photographs." That's a good rule to follow in Biscayne National Park.

♦ Coral, which is a living thing, is protected. Removing coral from the reef is prohibited by law. Handling coral is also prohibited since, in addition to coming away with cuts and serious infections, just touching can injure the coral.

♦ You also must leave any pirate treasure you find. There are 50 shipwrecks off the keys in the park waters but federal law protects these sites from souvenir hunters.

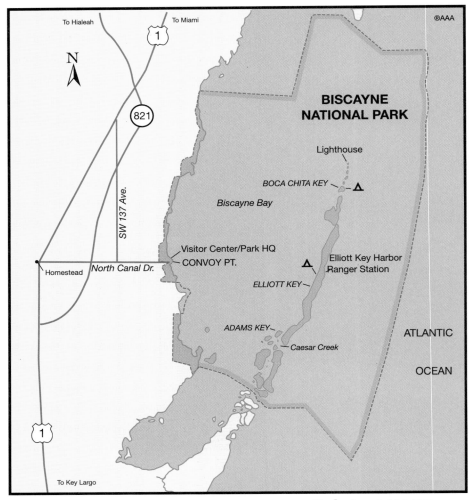

To Hialeah

To Miami

N

821

SW 137 Ave.

BISCAYNE
NATIONAL PARK

Lighthouse

BOCA CHITA KEY

Biscayne Bay

Homestead   North Canal Dr.

Visitor Center/Park HQ
CONVOY PT.

Elliott Key Harbor
Ranger Station

ELLIOTT KEY

ADAMS KEY

Caesar Creek

ATLANTIC

OCEAN

1

To Key Largo

®AAA

Park size: 2,221,766 acres

Access and Transportation

The park is 45 minutes south of Miami by car. From Miami, take the Florida Turnpike south to exit 2 (Campbell Drive). Following the signs, the park is 7 miles east on SW 328th Street (North Canal Drive). The park entrance is on your left.

From the north or south on U.S. 1, turn east on SW 328th Street (North Canal Drive or Lucy Street). The park entrance is 9 miles east on the left.

You can enter the park by boat via the Intercoastal Waterway. The closest airport is Miami International, 35 miles from the park.

Special Needs

The Convoy Point Visitor Center and all park restrooms are handicapped accessible. Tour providers assist people boarding the glass-bottom boat.

Amenities

Free boat docks ♦ Canoe rental ♦ Snorkel and dive gear rental (to qualified divers) ♦ Boats for hire ♦ Tent camping at Elliott Key and Boca Chita Key.

Travel Advisory

Wear sunscreen and insect repellent, especially if you visit between April and December. Know the signs of heat exhaustion and limit your time in the intense sunlight.

Emergency Information

First aid is available at Convoy Point Visitor Center and from rangers in the park. The nearest hospital is in Homestead.

Visitor and Information Centers

Convoy Point Visitor Center is open daily (except Christmas Day), year-round. This center offers exhibits, video presentations, book sales and information. The concessioner's office at Convoy Point offers canoe rentals and reservations for glass-bottom boat tours, snorkel and SCUBA trips.

Campgrounds

There are tent campsites on Elliott Key and Boca Chita Key. There are restrooms on both islands and drinking water and showers on Elliott Key. There is no fresh drinking water on Boca Chita Key. The islands are across the bay from the Convoy Point Visitor Center and are only accessible by boat. Campers must have boat transportation to the island or arrange transportation with the park concessionaire. Call 305-230-1100 to arrange a boat trip.

Picnic Areas

Bring food with you from nearby Homestead or Florida City. Picnic tables and grills are available on the mainland and islands for your use. You must pack out trash for disposal on the mainland. Raccoons are a problem, so secure trash and food in hard-sided containers.

Cabins, Lodges and Hotels

There are no lodges or hotels in the park. You can find hotels and motels in nearby Homestead and Florida City. Rates for hotels and motels in South Florida are highest from December through mid-April. Prices given are for two people in a double room. All of these accommodations have air-conditioning and a pool.

Coral Roc Motel. 1100 N. Krome Avenue, has 16 units, some with kitchenettes, for $58. Call 305-247-4010.

Knights Inn. 401 U.S. Highway 1, has 108 units, some with kitchenettes, $53–$65. Call 305-245-2800.

MANATEES, UNLIKELY MERMAIDS

Did lonely sailors too long at sea mistake manatees for mermaids? Some folklorists think so. Dwindling numbers make manatees nearly as scarce as mermaids, but Biscayne National Park and Everglades National Park are prime viewing areas.

The manatee looks like a seal, but it is heavier and slower moving. Adults can grow to 15 feet. The manatee is nearly hairless, with thick skin, a strong, broad tail and weak front flippers. It uses these flippers to push water plants into its mouth.

In shallow waters, you may notice prop scars on the bodies of these gentle mammals. They are often injured by pleasure boats. Many Florida license plates, sold to raise money to protect endangered species, feature the manatee.

Seaglaze Motel. 1223 N.E. First Avenue, has 49 units, some with kitchenette, for $58. Call 305-247-6621.

Days Inn. 51 S. Homestead Blvd., has 100 units, and a restaurant. $78 per night. Call 305-245-1260.

Everglades Motel 605 S. Krome Avenue, has 19 units, 6 with kitchenettes for $52. Call 305-247-4117.

There are also lodgings in **Hampton Inn, Best Western, Econo Lodge, Holiday Inn Express** and **Howard Johnson** in Homestead and Florida City.

Restaurants

There are no restaurants in the park. Buy food and supplies in Homestead or Florida City.

Things to Do and See

Biscayne National Underwater Park, Inc. offers daily three-hour glass-bottom boat tours (10:00 a.m.), four-hour snorkel trips (1:30 p.m.), SCUBA trips (mornings) and occasional transportation to the islands for campers. Canoe rentals are also available. Call 305-230-1100.

Glass-Bottom Boat Reef Tour. There is a daily tour of the reef in a glass-bottom boat that lasts three hours. The glass bottom of the boat allows passengers to appreciate the park's unique features and get a good look at sea life in brilliant color: fish, shrimp, lobsters, sponges, crab, sea turtles, and brain and star coral.

Near Biscayne National Park

Most visitors to Biscayne National Park also visit nearby Everglades National Park. Divers may want to make a side trip to Key Largo and animal lovers can visit three wildlife refuges in Big Pine Key.

John Pennekamp Coral Reef State Park. Divers visit this 55,000-acre undersea park to see a living coral reef. (Non-divers can view it through glass-bottom sightseeing boats). The park is handicapped accessible and has a visitor center and campsites. Visitors can enjoy hiking, boating and water sports, fishing and picnic areas. It is open year-round during daylight. The park is in Key Largo, about 40 miles from Biscayne National Park (about 35 miles from Everglades National Park). For more information call 305-872-2239.

Wildlife Refuges. There are three wildlife refuges at Big Pine Key about 100 miles from Biscayne National Park. They are the National Key Deer Range, the Great White Heron National Wildlife Range and Key West National Wildlife Refuge. Florida's endangered white-tailed deer is losing its habitat. Please do not feed deer in the park, but do enjoy hiking, boating, fishing and scenic drives. The park is open year-round during daylight. The 7,600-acre white heron preserve is accessible by boat only. During your visit to this series of

mangrove islands, you may also spot a roseate spoonbill. The park has no facilities. It is open all year during daylight hours. The islands west of Key West are also a refuge for ospreys, ibis, egret, falcons, herons and other birds. For more information about all three wildlife refuges, call 305-872-2239.

For More Information

Superintendent
Biscayne National Park
PO Box 1369
Homestead, FL 33090-1369
Tel. 305-230-7275

BRYCE CANYON NATIONAL PARK

Utah ✦ **Established 1928**

Bryce Canyon is not really a canyon. It is actually the eroded edge of the Paunsaugunt Plateau that forms a series of natural amphitheaters. It is also a kaleidoscopic geology lesson. The rock formations you see at every turn are millions of years old and still changing. The formations known as "hoodos" are fancifully named — Thor's Hammer, Queen's Garden, Chinese Wall and Wall of Windows.

The colors are as improbable as the shapes. Stone spires below Paunsaugunt Plateau gleam gold, pink, orange and yellow, with traces of lavender and blue. The colors come from the iron and manganese oxides in the rocks.

As you enjoy the panoramic view from the plateau, you'll also be sharing some of the cleanest air in the nation with owls and hawks.

Geology is upstaged only by astronomy. Stargazers have as much to delight them as rock hounds, thanks to clear nights with virtually no man-made light to dim the brilliance of the stars.

Atop the plateau, mule deer live in the cool forests of ponderosa pines, manzanita and bitter brush. Other wildlife in Bryce Canyon includes gray foxes, bobcats, porcupines, skunks and marmots. You may not feed wildlife. There is also no hunting in the park.

The best way to see Bryce Canyon is to drive the 18 miles to the southern end of the park. When you reach Rainbow Point, enjoy the majestic views. Head back to the park entrance, stopping at the 14 major viewpoints along the way. The most popular are Sunrise, Sunset, Inspiration, Bryce and Paria. Overlook areas are paved and spur roads offer opportunities for viewing and trailhead parking. The best time to enjoy the views during the summer and avoid the crowds is to visit them before 10 a.m. and after 5 p.m.

A FEW TIPS

✦ *Protect your skin with hats, long sleeves and sunscreen year round.*
✦ *Pace yourself as altitudes range from 8,000 to 9,000 feet.*
✦ *Take shelter during summer storms. Lightning strikes are common.*
✦ *Wear hiking boots with good tread and ankle support. Stay on designated trails.*

There are 65 miles of trails varying in difficulty. Most trails lead down over the edge of the plateau and allow you to walk among the limestone hoodos. Peekaboo Trail is both a horse trail and hiking trail that loops through the canyon's bottom.

Biking is permitted on paved roads only. Bikes are not allowed on park trails and there are no bike lanes.

PLANNING YOUR VISIT

Park Open
The park is open year-round. Winter storms bring some temporary road closures but roads are soon plowed.

Seasons
Summer days are pleasant and nights are cool, but expect afternoon thunderstorms. Winter days are cold, but the temperature is offset by the high-altitude sun and dry climate. Winter nights are sub-freezing. When cold fronts from Alaska hit, temperatures plummet well below zero. Snow is a possibility from October through April. The park's peak visitation is in July, lowest visitation is in December and January.

Entrance Fees
Fee per vehicle
    (per person)...............................$10
Fee per individual
    (per person)................................$5
    Fees are good for seven days

Permits and Licenses
You must get a $5 permit for back-country camping.

Access and Transportation
From Southwest Utah. Take U.S. 89 to the junction seven miles south of Panguitch with Utah State Highway 12. Take Highway 12 east for 17 miles to the junction of Highway 63. Take

Highway 63 south three miles to the park entrance.

Trailers are not permitted past Sunset Campground.

Bryce Canyon Airport. This airport is four miles from the park. Air Nevada offers flights from Las Vegas from April to mid-November. For information call 800-634-6377. Private planes also are permitted to land at this airport. Other commercial airports are in Cedar City, 78 miles away, and Salt Lake City, 260 miles away.

Rental car agencies are in Cedar City and Salt Lake City airports.

Special Needs

Facilities at this park are older than most. Much of the terrain is not wheelchair accessible. Handicapped parking is marked and accessible sites are available at Sunset Campground. Stop at the visitor center for an accessibility guide.

Amenities

Ranger-led hikes and rim walks ♦ Geology programs ♦ Bus tours ♦ Snowshoe and ski rental ♦ Horseback trails ♦ Campfire programs ♦ Picnic areas ♦ Gift shop ♦ Sightseeing buses and shuttle service

Travel Advisory

If you have heart or respiratory problems, keep in mind that popular overlooks range from 8,000 to 9,000 feet in elevation. Don't overexert. Everyone should protect their skin from the sun, regardless of the season.

Emergency Information

First aid is available at the visitor center and at the lodge during summer. The nearest hospital is in Panguitch, 26 miles away.

Visitor and Information Center

Bryce Canyon's visitor center is open year-round, except Thanksgiving, Christmas and New Year's Day. Hours are typically 8 a.m. to 4:30 p.m., with longer hours in the summer months. Visit the center for slide shows, exhibits and publications. You can also pick up your backcountry permit here.

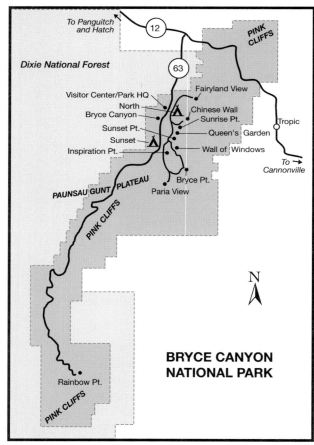

Park size: 35,835 acres

You will also meet VIPs who can help you. VIPs are Volunteers in the Park who staff information desks, present naturalist programs, patrol trails and serve as campground hosts.

Campgrounds

There are two campgrounds, North and Sunset, with a total of 218 sites. The camping fee is $10 per night and sites are available on a first-come, first-served basis. Coin-operated showers are located at the general store at Sunrise Point. There is a limit of six people, two tents and two vehicles at each site. One group site is available by reservation only. Make reservations through DESTINET by calling 800-328-CAMP

The U.S. Forest Service and State parks also operate campgrounds throughout the area. The 22-Mile Trail area has eight primitive camp sites. Riggs Spring Loop has four primitive sites. A $5 permit is required for overnight backcountry camping.

Picnic Areas

There are picnic areas in the park. From April through October, TW Recreational Services runs a general store at Sunrise Point, with groceries, souvenirs, supplies and quick meals. Private stores are located

throughout the area. There is a snack bar at the general store at Sunrise Point.

Cabins, Lodges and Hotels

TW Recreational Services operates Bryce Canyon Lodge, which has 114 rooms including suites, motel rooms and renovated western cabins. The lodge is open late April through mid-October. For reservations, call 801-586-7686.

There is a 70-unit motel in the park and several near the entrance that fill up during peak season.

Restaurants

There is a dining room at Bryce Canyon Lodge and a snack bar at the general store at Sunrise Point.

Things to Do and See

Bus Tours. Sightseeing bus tours of Bryce Canyon leave from St. George, Cedar City and Kanab in spring and summer. They stop at the 14 major scenic overlooks.

Hiking. Mostly day hikes are in Main Bryce Amphitheater, with trailheads just a few miles from the visitor center. Take the five-and-one-half mile long Rim Trail from Fairyland Point to Bryce Point. More difficult trails are Fairyland Canyon, Queen's Garden and Navajo Loop. Off the beaten path, but worth it, is Under-the-Rim Trail, a 23-mile hike past Bryce Point to Rainbow Point. Overnight stays require a $5 backcountry permit.

Trail Rides. Tackle the trails on four feet. In spring, summer and fall, wranglers lead horseback rides into the Bryce Amphitheater via the horse trail and Peekaboo Loop. They depart from the corral near the lodge. Call 801-679-8665 for more information.

Winter Sports. In winter, Fairyland and Paria roads are unplowed and designated as trails for snowshoeing and cross-country skiing. You can rent ski equipment at Ruby's Inn, just outside the park. Snowshoes are available on loan with a deposit, on a first-come, first-served basis.

For More Information
Superintendent
Bryce Canyon National Park
PO Box 170001
Bryce Canyon, Utah 84717-0001
Tel. 801-834-5322

HOODOOS, THE LIVING SCULPTURE OF BRYCE CANYON

Sixty million years ago, lakes and rivers deposited layers of sand, silt and lime that were compacted into rock. About 16 million years ago, this rock was slowly lifted to elevations more than a mile above sea level. Faulting separated the rock layers into the huge blocks that ultimately became the plateaus of southwest Utah.

As time wore on, so did the rock. Rain, frost and thaw, thunderstorms, snow melts and plant roots widened gaps and fractures in the plateau. Water trickled through the Pink Cliffs, sculpting the shapes we see today. Erosion creates the colorful rock formations collectively called hoodoos.

Although the hoodoos of Bryce Canyon look timeless, they are in the process of changing. The hard layers that cap Thor's Hammer at Sunset Point make it resistant to erosion, but the head of the hammer rests on a slim handle that time and the elements are eating away.

CANYONLANDS NATIONAL PARK

Utah ◆ **Established 1964**

This is primarily a backcountry destination, but don't be scared off by the forbidding terrain. Canyonlands is one of the most visually dazzling parks in the southwest. Determined visitors who accept the challenge of this arid landscape on its own terms will be rewarded by a lasting memory of its surreal beauty. Canyonlands is full of steep walled canyons, flat topped mesas, Technicolor buttes and the Colorado and Green Rivers.

Much of what Canyonlands has to offer can only be seen on foot, horseback or in four-wheel drive vehicles. There are 200 miles of four-wheel drive roads that take explorers into the heart of the wildest and least traveled land in North America.

One of the most singular geological sites in the park is Upheaval Dome.

Measuring 1,500 feet deep, it looks more like a crater than a dome. There are conflicting theories about how the dome came to be.

The winding Colorado and Green Rivers separate the park into four zones. There are three areas to explore. They are so widely separated you must exit the park and drive for miles to reach them.

The Maze district is the most remote area in the park. Here, eroded buttes and stone towers stand sentinel over a labyrinth of canyons that crazily twist and turn in all directions.

Islands in the Sky is an area consisting of flat topped mesas of mostly bare rock. This northern section of the park overlooks the canyon floors.

The Needles district in the southeastern part of the park got its name from thousands of pillars, spires and colorful rock formations.

The confluence of the Colorado and Green Rivers is at the heart of Canyonlands. Where the two mighty rivers meet, their combined power rockets through Cataract Canyon, creating 14 miles of white water. Raft trips down the rivers enable you to see remote sections of the park that are not accessible on foot.

Like any seemingly barren desert, the park is actually an open air museum of evolution and adaptability. Gnarled piñon pine and junipers, the expert water conservationists of the plant world, put down their roots in the rimlands wherever enough soil collects. Deer, coyote, bighorn sheep, mountain lions and foxes live in the park. Most of these species are nocturnal, having learned to shun the intense heat of the daytime.

The park features some of the finest Native American rock art in the country. Ancient Native Americans left their traces in the park not only in their pictographs and petroglyphs, but also in the form

A FEW TIPS

♦ *Never camp in a dry wash or attempt to drive across a wash during a storm. Sudden thunderstorms turn bone-dry washes into deep, fast-moving waters.*
♦ *Use care near cliff edges and dry rock surfaces. Falls here are often fatal.*
♦ *Always carry plenty of water when hiking. One gallon per person per day minimum.*

of ruined stone and mud dwellings and storehouses.

PLANNING YOUR VISIT

Park Open
The park is open year-round. Flash floods from July to September often close dirt and gravel roads. Call headquarters for information on road conditions.

Seasons
Summer is very hot, with daytime temperatures between 80° and 100°. Nighttime temperatures range between 50° to 60°. Spring and fall bring daytime temperatures ranging between 60° to 80° and nighttime temperatures between 20° to 50°. High winds and blowing sand are common. Winter is short but cold, and has light snowfall. Peak visitation to the park is in May.

Entrance Fees
Per vehicle...$10
Per individual $3
Fees are valid for 7 days.

Permits and Licenses
Permits are required for backcountry camping, rafting and boating, technical rock climbing and horseback riding. Fees are subject to change, but expect to pay $5 or more for a day's backcountry camping, $10 or more for backpacking or for flat water use and $25 or more for four-wheel drive campsites and Cataract Canyon white water rafting. Permits are required for entry into Salt, Horse and Lavender Canyons in the Needles district. For more information, call 801-259-4351.

Access and Transportation
The park is in east-central Utah. There are three entrances to the park.

Island in the Sky Entrance. Take U.S. 191. Go nine miles north of Moab to Highway 313, then go 26 miles southwest.

The Needles Entrance. Take U.S. 191 and go 14 miles north of Monticello to Highway 211. Then go 35 miles west or 41

miles south of Moab to Highway 211 and go 34 miles west.

The Maze Entrance. Take I-70 west of Green River to Highway 24 and go 24 miles south to a two-wheel drive dirt road. Continue for 46 miles east to Hans Flat Ranger Station. This road is not passable at certain times during the year.

Redtail Aviation is a commuter airport which is 15 miles north of Moab. Alpine Air provides service from Salt Lake City. The closest major airport is at Grand Junction, Colorado, 115 miles east. Greyhound serves Green River, Utah, 55 miles from Moab.

Amtrak serves Thompson, Utah, 40 miles from Moab.

Rental cars are available at the airport in Grand Junction, Colorado.

Special Needs
The Islands In the Sky and Needles visitor centers are wheelchair accessible and both campgrounds have wheelchair accessible bathrooms. Grandview Point and Buck Canyon overlooks are paved with

curb cuts and designated parking, but assistance may be needed. The lodge, general store, laundry and showers are accessible. The Sunset to Sunrise Point Trail is accessible with assistance.

Amenities

Scenic drives ♦ Hiking ♦ Boating ♦ Bicycling ♦ Driving tours ♦ Horseback riding ♦ Rock climbing ♦ Ranger-led programs

Travel Advisory

Stay on trails. Avoid climbing on sandstone, it is slippery and crumbles easily and without warning.

Emergency Information

There are no accessible phones within the park. Contact a park ranger. First aid is available in the park. The nearest hospitals are in Moab and Monticello.

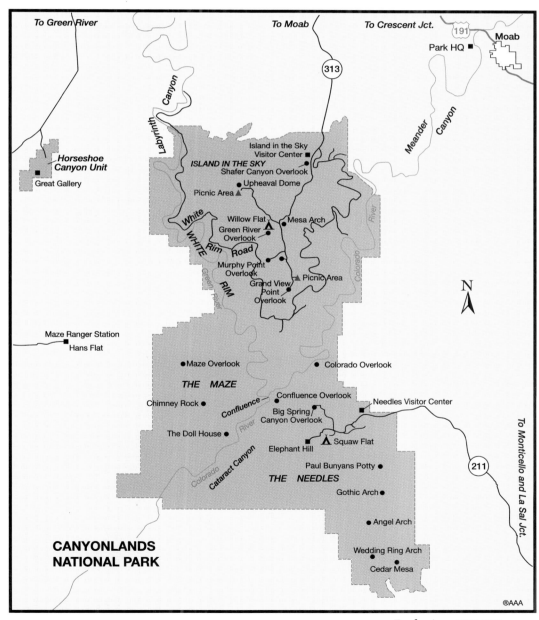

Park size: 337,570 acres

Visitor and Information Centers

There are visitor centers at Island in the Sky and Needles districts. There is an information center in the Maze district at Hans Flat Ranger Station, 46 miles on a dirt road east of Highway 24. Park headquarters is in Moab. All centers offer information, publications, exhibits and maps.

Campgrounds

Island in the Sky district. Willow Creek Campground has 12 sites with tables, fireplaces and pit toilets. Camping is free.

Maze district. Primitive campsites accessible to 4-wheel drive vehicles are available. Camping is free.

Needles district. Squaw's Flat Campground has water, tables, fireplaces and pit toilets. Camping is $6 a night.

Group Sites. Group campsites for 11 or more people can be reserved in the Needles district. There is a $10 reservation fee plus $2 per person, per night. Call 801-259-4351 for more information.

Backcountry Camping. Primitive campsites accessible by 4-wheel drive vehicles are off White Rim Road. Reservations are recommended. Call park headquarters at 801-259-7164.

Picnic Areas

There are picnic areas with tables, fireplaces and pit toilets at Grandview, Upheaval Dome and at the campgrounds.

Supplies are available in Moab, Monticello and Green River. There is a small grocery and gas station near the Needles entrance at Needles Outpost. It is open spring through fall.

Cabins, Lodges and Hotels

There are none in the park.

Restaurants

There are none in the park.

THINGS TO DO AND SEE

Canyonlands Field Institute. The institute offers photo workshops, guided tours and seminars. Write to Canyonlands Field Institute, Box 68, Moab, UT 84532.

Guided Raft Tours. Concessionaires in nearby Moab offer guided raft trips of the Colorado River and Green River. For a complete list of tours, ask at headquarters or any visitor center. For river trips, call Adrift Adventures at 800-824-0150, Sheri Griffith River Expeditions at 800-332-2439 or Dvorak's Expeditions at 800-824-3759.

Other Tours. Mountain bike tours and rental bikes are also available from concessionaires in nearby Moab. Four-wheel drive tours and horseback tours are also available from concessionaires in nearby Moab.

Horseshoe Canyon. Pictographs on the walls of Horseshoe Canyon, a detached unit of the park reachable by dirt road, are considered the finest prehistoric rock drawings in the country. The Great Gallery is the most spectacular and best known series of panels.

Hiking. Short hikes of less than a mile lead to major scenic overlooks. Pick up a map at the visitor centers. Trails are primitive with only rock cairn markings. Trails penetrating into the park are rugged.

Boating. River access is at Green River for the Green River and Moab for the Colorado River. Several river outfitters operate in the park.

Trail Tours. Horseback trail rides and horses for hire are available from outside concessionaires. Contact with park headquarters before arriving on horse. There are designated areas for riding.

Scenic Overlooks. The major attractions of the park most easily reached by road are overlooks at Shafer Canyon and Buck's Canyon, as well as Elephant Hill in Needles. Many worthwhile views, including Upheaval Dome, the White Rim, Mesa Arch, Angel Arch and the Doll House can only be reached by four-wheel drive vehicle.

Climbing. Climbing is restricted to designated areas. The Salt Creek Archaeological District in Needles is closed to all technical climbing. Chalk and webbing left at permanent anchor points must closely match the color of the rock.

Near Canyonlands National Park

Westwater Canyon, Utah. About 80 miles northeast of the park, this 17-mile stretch of white water rapids is for experienced rafters only. The names of the rapids hint at what you can expect: Funnel Falls, Sock It To Me, Skull and Last Chance. Sights include an abandoned mine, a desperado's hide-out and natural arches. There is primitive hiking, fishing, swimming and picnicking in the area. For more information call 801-259-8193.

For More Information
Superintendent
Canyonlands National Park
125 West, 200 South
Moab, UT 84532
Tel. 801-259-7164

CAPITOL REEF NATIONAL PARK

Utah ♦ **Established 1971**

Millions of years ago, the continental plate deep under North America collided with the plate beneath the Pacific Ocean. The terrific pressures generated by that event caused the earth's crust to buckle. The result is the astonishing Waterpocket Fold, a brilliantly colored 100-mile long wrinkle of parallel ridges that spring abruptly from the desert like stone waves, frozen in the act of rolling toward shore.

Exposed to eons of wind and water, the edges of the uplift have eroded into slickrock cliffs, enormous domes, pinnacles hundreds of feet tall and a maze of twisting canyons. Geologists proclaim the Waterpocket Fold to be one of the largest and most impressive monoclines in North America.

Seventy-two miles of the Waterpocket Fold are within the Capitol Reef National Park. "Capitol" refers to the white dome shaped formations at the top of the reef, thought by many to resemble the U.S. Capitol building. The second part of the park's name is a legacy of early pioneers in the region, where sheer cliffs near the Fremont River formed a barrier which reminded them of an ocean reef. Hence, Capitol Reef.

Although a highway now crosses the reef, visitors wishing to see some of the park's more remote regions will need a little pioneer spirit of their own. The park's 378 square miles are full of dramatic beauty, but it is so remote that the nearest traffic light is 78 miles away. The area around the park has been unexplored until quite recently and many of the park roads are still unpaved. A four-wheel drive vehicle is necessary to travel to many points of scenic interest. The fold itself can only be crossed at three points. Even so, Capitol Reef is still visited by more than 680,000 people a year.

The park is full of harsh, arid, desert land. Although summer thunderstorms flood the area, plants and animals have to scramble to find water in streams and dry washes. Cottonwoods, box elders, junipers, sego lilies, piñons and willows grow here. The exotic tamarisk is seen in some of the open areas in great numbers, and fragrant sagebrush flourishes on the desert flats.

A FEW TIPS

♦ *Check the visitor center for up-to-date weather and road conditions before you explore the backcountry. Capitol Reef is subject to flash floods from summer through early fall. These floods can leave you stranded in backcountry or in a canyon.*

♦ *Hikers must carry water. The water at Capitol Reef is not safe to drink.*

Canyon wrens, swallows, swifts and golden eagles inhabit the park, as do salamanders, canyon tree frogs, snakes, badgers and coyotes. There is a large deer population near Fruita.

The southern end of the fold offers excellent wilderness backpacking in Halls Creek Narrows and Muley Twist Canyon. Cathedral Valley lies to the north, with its many jagged monoliths rising 400 to 700 feet high. Other interesting formations in the park include Twin Rocks and Chimney Rock near the west entrance on the paved road, and Hickman Natural Bridge, 72 feet high and spanning 133 feet.

It is believed legendary outlaw Butch Cassidy sometimes used the region as a hiding place. Cassidy Arch is named after him.

The 19th century Mormon village of Fruita is a green oasis along the Fremont River in the middle region of the park. The irrigation ditches the Mormon pioneers dug still replenish fruit bearing trees in fields cultivated 700 years ago by Fremont Indians. Mule deer now graze in the orchard grasslands. Park visitors help themselves to apricots, apples and peaches from the trees.

The Fremont people left behind baskets, pottery, and a splendid collection of rock art. Figures on many petroglyph panels represent bighorn sheep. The last known sighting of the native desert bighorn, a species indigenous to the park, was reported in 1948. Their disappearance has been blamed on hunters and diseases caught from domestic sheep. However, the National Park Service reintroduced desert bighorn to Capitol Reef in 1984 and the transplanted herd has survived.

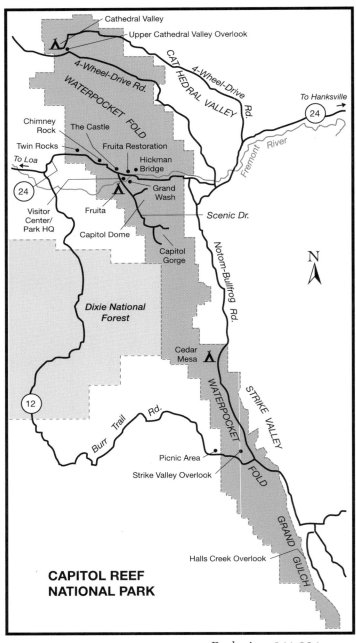

CAPITOL REEF NATIONAL PARK

Park size: 241,904 acres

PLANNING YOUR VISIT

Park Open

The park is open year-round. Peak visitation is in September.

Seasons

Flash floods are common. Summer daytime temperatures reach the 90s, with 100° temperatures in June and July. Nights are cool, with temperatures in the 50s and 60s. Cold weather predominates from mid-December through February, with temperatures below 50°, and sometimes subzero temperatures at night. Snowfall is usually light.

Entrance Fees

Per vehicle on scenic drive.......................$4

Permits and Licenses

Permits are required for backcountry camping. Pick up free permits at the visitor center. Vehicles and mountain bikes are restricted to established roads.

Access and Transportation

The park is in south-central Utah.

From the West. Take U.S. 89 south of Salina to Highway 24. Then go southeast for 69 miles.

From the East. Take I-70 west of Green River to Highway 24. Go southwest for 70 miles.

There is no regularly scheduled public transportation to the park. The nearest airports are at Grand Junction and Salt

Lake City, Utah. Rental cars are available at the airports.

Special Needs

The visitor center and campgrounds have wheelchair accessible restrooms. There are also accessible restrooms on Loops B and C and one accessible camp site on Loop B of the Fruita Campground.

Amenities

Scenic drive ♦ Hiking ♦ Horseback riding ♦ Bicycling ♦ Ranger-led programs

Travel Advisory

With the exception of the scenic drive, most roads are unpaved and may be closed during winter or rainy weather. Most dirt roads will require high clearance/four-wheel drive vehicles. For latest road and weather conditions, call park headquarters.

Emergency Information

First aid is available in the park. The nearest clinic is in Bicknell, 19 miles west of the visitor center. The nearest hospital is in Richvield, 72 miles away.

Visitor and Information Centers

The park headquarters and visitor center is 11 miles east of Torrey on Highway 24, or 37 miles west of Hanksville via Highway 24. The center offers an orientation program and exhibits displays on early Native American and Mormon settlers.

Campgrounds

The three park campgrounds are open all year with a 14-day limit. Reservations are made on a first-come, first served basis.

Fruita Campground. This area is one mile south of the visitor center and has 71 sites with water, restrooms, tables and grills. These sites can accommodate RVs. Camping fee is $7 a night.

Cathedral Valley Mesa Campground and **Cedar Mesa Campground.** Each has five primitive sites with pit toilets, tables and grills. Camping is free. Both of these sites are accessible to 4-wheel drive vehicles. Group sites can be reserved in advance by contacting the park. Additional campgrounds are at Dixie National Forest and Fishlake National Forest.

Backcountry camping is allowed throughout the park with permit, but open fires and wood fires are prohibited.

Picnic Areas

There is no food available in the park. Buy food and supplies in nearby Torrey, Bicknell and Loa, east of the visitor center on Utah Highway 24. There are picnic areas with tables, grills, water and restrooms near the Visitor Center. There are tables on Burr Trail.

Cabins, Lodges and Hotels

There are no accommodations in the park.

THINGS TO DO AND SEE

Sites. The Fruita Restoration has the Mormon's old one-room schoolhouse, part of the original orchards, a pioneer dwelling, barn, blacksmith shop and smokehouse. Fruit may be picked for free in the orchards.

Scenic Drives. The major attraction of the park is the multicolored rock layers of Waterpocket Fold. Beautiful views can be seen on the main road. Also, many of the best known rock formations in the park, including Twin Rocks, Chimney Rock, the Castle and Hickman Natural Bridge can be seen on the main road. If you have a four-wheel drive vehicle and don't mind rough, unpaved roads, check out Capitol Gorge, Grand Wash, Strike Valley and Cathedral Valley.

Hiking. There are 30 miles of marked trail and 50 miles of trails with cairn markers. Grand Wash is a two-mile trek along the flats in the shadow of steep canyon walls. More demanding trails lead to Cassidy Arch and Golden Throne. Off the Burr Trail, the Strike Valley Overlook yields a spectacular view of Waterpocket Fold. Many trails wind past the Fremont River and take you up close to rock formations such a the Hickman Bridge.

Riding. Horses are permitted on some of the trails. Before arriving on horseback, contact the park for a copy of regulations regarding horses in the park.

Bicycling. Bicycling is allowed on established roads. Suggested routes include Scenic Drive, Cathedral Valley Loop, South Draw and the Norton-Burr Trail-Boulder Mountain Loop.

Harvest Homecoming. This celebration is held the last Friday and Saturday in September. The two-day festival features American Indian dancing, draft horse and farm implement demonstrations, crafts and a host of cultural events highlighting the legacy of Capitol Reef's pioneers.

For More Information
Superintendent
Capitol Reef National Park
HC 70, Box 15
Torrey, UT 84775
Tel. 801-425-3791

CARLSBAD CAVERNS NATIONAL PARK

New Mexico ♦ Established 1930

When comedian Will Rogers visited Carlsbad Caverns, he described them as "the Grand Canyon with a roof on it." New Mexico ranchers of the 1880s had little idea of what the barren Chihuahuan desert beneath their feet concealed.

Two hundred fifty million years ago, an inland sea evaporated, leaving behind a reef covered with salt deposits. A few million years ago, erosion and a buckling of the earth's surface uncovered this reef of rock. Slightly acidic rainwater seeped into cracks in the reef, dissolving the limestone and forming massive underground chambers. When the water table lowered, these chambers filled with air. New rainwater seeped in from the surface absorbing calcite from the limestone. Calcite is the basic building block of most rock formations found in the caverns. When the drip was slow enough, the water evaporated leaving a crystal of calcite behind.

Trillions of drops later, stalactites, or icicle shaped deposits hanging down from the roof of the cave, were formed by dripping limewater. Stalagmites, the cone shaped lime deposits rising from the floor of the cave, are often found underneath stalactites.

Pictographs near the cave entrance prove that Native Americans knew about the Caverns a thousand years ago. Anthropologists speculate that the Indians never penetrated too far into the interior.

If local ranchers were aware of the caverns at all, they knew them as the "bat caves." Every evening the skies around the cave entrance would darken as millions of Mexican free-tailed bats, on the hunt for insects, poured forth at a rate of 300 per second. The bats had been tenants of the caverns for at least 17,000 years.

The Caverns started to become famous when James Larkin White, a local boy,

♦ *The caverns get crowded on summer weekends and holidays.*

♦ *Wear sturdy shoes with good traction and a light jacket or sweater for any of the cave tours.*

♦ *Check with a ranger prior to attempting the Natural Entrance walk, which involves walking down 75 stories.*

went exploring underground with a kerosene lantern. When he re-emerged, he told anyone who would listen about the subterranean wonders he had seen. White described huge underground chambers and scores of fantastic rock formations. His stories eventually reached the ears of officials from the General Land Office and the U.S. Geological Survey. Follow-up explorations confirmed that White had been telling the truth.

By the early 1920s, early photographs of the caverns attracted increasing numbers of visitors.

White became the first tour guide and concessionaire at the Caverns. In those pre-elevator days, his clients were obliged to climb into a miner's bucket attached to a windlass (a creaky, harrowing contraption), which lowered them 200 feet to the cavern floor. Then, as now, they discovered that to enter the Carlsbad caverns is to leave the sunlit world behind and experience an eerie new world of strange, silent beauty.

The Carlsbad Caverns consist of a vast series of underground rooms and corridors. More than 30 miles of the caverns have been explored so far, but for safety and conservation reasons, only 12 of the more than 80 caves in the park are open to the public.

The Big Room is the most remarkable of the underground chambers. Seven hundred and fifty feet underground, the cross shaped room is 1,800 feet long and 1,100 feet wide. Its ceiling is 255 feet high. The Big Room could contain fourteen football fields and is tall enough to comfortably accommodate an 18 story building. It is the largest underground room in the world. The Big Room is filled with stalagmites, stalactites, columns, draperies and flowstone formations.

The Giant Dome is Carlsbad's largest single formation. This massive column is 62 feet thick and 62 feet high. Elsewhere in the caverns, the Green Lake Room features thousands of stalactites and an 8-foot deep pool of water.

The Papoose Room is known for its stone draperies. The Queen's Chamber is 829 feet beneath the surface. The Bottomless Pit is a black hole 140 feet deep.

Lechuquilla Cave captured the world's attention during a suspenseful life and death rescue in 1981. Emily Davis Mobley, an expert spelunker, (i.e. cave explorer) broke her leg 1,000 feet underground.

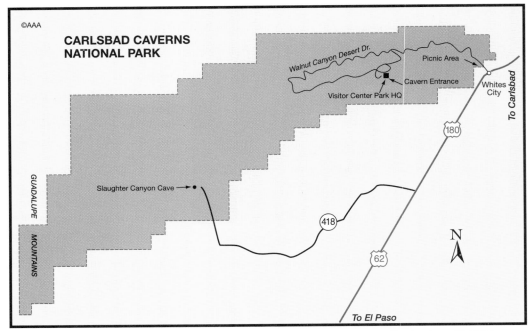

©AAA

**CARLSBAD CAVERNS
NATIONAL PARK**

Walnut Canyon Desert Dr.

Picnic Area

Cavern Entrance

Visitor Center Park HQ

Whites
City

To Carlsbad

180

GUADALUPE

Slaughter Canyon Cave →

MOUNTAINS

418

62

N

To El Paso

Park size: 46,755 acres

Mobley had been mapping the rugged back-country cave when she was hurt. Injured spelunkers often succumb to hypothermia unless they receive prompt assistance. It took an expert rescue team four agonizing days to carry, lift and pull the injured Mobley out of the cave to safety. Don't worry though, unless you're a similarly qualified expert on a specially sanctioned descent, you won't be venturing into any dangerous cave sites. There are more than 80 caverns still being explored today.

PLANNING YOUR VISIT

Park Open

The park is open year-round except Christmas Day. Peak visitation is in July. Summer season hours begin the Saturday before Memorial Day and end the third Sunday in August.

Seasons

The temperature underground remains constant at 56°. The main cavern gets crowded in the summer and on major holiday weekends. The desert is in bloom in

spring and fall. If there has been sufficient rainfall, the scenery will add to your trip. The bats fly from April or early May through October. It is a memorable sight.

Entrance Fees

The basic user fee for the two self-guided trips is $8 for adults, $5 for ages 6 to 15, and no charge for children under six. There are five major cavern tours and prices vary.

The Kings Palace tours cost an additional $5 for adults and $2.50 for ages 6 to 15. Slaughter Canyon tours cost $10 for adults and $5 for ages 6 to 15. Children under six are not permitted. Caving trips are available on a limited basis in small numbers, with fees ranging from $5 to $15. Inquire at the visitor center or call 505-785-2232, ext. 429 for further information. Reservations are required for all tours led by rangers.

Permits and Licenses

Overnight backcountry trips require a permit. Permits are available at the visitor center.

Access and Transportation

The park is 20 miles from Carlsbad, New Mexico, and 150 miles from El Paso, Texas. The park entrance is on U.S. 62-180, southwest of Carlsbad at Highway 7.

Greyhound and TNM&O buses travel to Carlsbad from Whites City and El Paso, Texas. A shuttle bus runs from Whites City to the visitor center. Trains serve El Paso, Texas, 150 miles from the visitor center. Mesa Airlines offers passenger service from Carlsbad to Albuquerque. The closest airport is in Carlsbad, 27 miles from the visitor center. Rental cars are available in Carlsbad and El Paso, Texas.

Special Needs

The visitor center and its restrooms are wheelchair accessible, as is the picnic area. Most of the Big Room route is accessible, but the Natural Entrance route descends 75 stories and is not wheelchair accessible. An access guide to the park is available at the visitors center.

Amenities

Cave tours ♦ Bat flight program ♦ Scenic drives ♦ Hiking ♦ Ranger talks

Travel Advisory

When in the cave, stay on trails — even for picture taking. There are steep drop-offs and unlighted corridors where you could get lost or injured. Touching cave formations can damage them and is prohibited. No smoking, eating, or drinking is permitted in the cave. Nothing may be thrown into the cave pools. Photography is not permitted when you join a ranger-guided tour.

Emergency Information

First aid is available in the park. The nearest hospital is in Carlsbad, 27 miles from the visitor center.

Visitor and Information Centers

The park headquarters and visitor center is on Highway 7. Tours of Carlsbad Caverns begin here. There is an *Official Cavern Guide* book and a three-dimensional model of the cavern available here. There is also a nursery and a kennel. The Carlsbad Caverns-Guadalupe Mountains Association operates a bookstore in the visitor center.

Campgrounds

There are no lodgings or campgrounds inside the park. Several campgrounds and other overnight accommodations are available in

Who You Guano Call? Bat Miners

In the middle 1880s mining entrepreneurs began digging out the cavern's rich deposits of bat waste. They sold thousands of tons of the nitrate-rich guano (bat dung) as fertilizer to Southern California citrus farmers. The excavations decimated the bat population from its estimated peak of nine million to present day levels of approximately 500,000. Guano mining never became economically viable. By 1923, the guano mining came to an end, as all good things must.

nearby Carlsbad and Whites City. The Carlsbad Chamber of Commerce can recommend a list of lodgings. Call 800-221-1224 (in New Mexico call 505-887-6516).

Picnic Areas

Picnic tables are available near the visitor center and at Rattlesnake Springs. The Cavern Supply Company provides food service, kennels and a gift shop at the visitor center. Call 505-785-2281 for more information. Restaurants and supplies are available in Whites City and Carlsbad.

Restaurants

There is a restaurant in the visitor center. Underground, there is a lunchroom that serves sandwiches, box lunches and drinks. There are many restaurants in nearby Carlsbad and Whites City.

Things to Do and See

Self-Guided Routes. There are self-guided routes of the Big Room and the Natural Entrance. Both follow paved, well-lit trails. Exhibits are located along the trails and park rangers are there to answer questions and offer assistance. The tours run continuously and may be started at any time during the posted hours. *The Official Cavern Guide* is an audio guide electronically triggered as you move through the tour. It features commentary, music and sound effects.

The Big Room route is one-and-a-quarter miles long and lasts about one-and-a-half hours. The tour explores the Big Room, which is reached by elevator. Most of the route is fairly level.

The Natural Entrance route is one-and-a-quarter miles and approximately two hours long. The route is strenuous and not recommended for those who have walking, respiratory or heart problems.

Slaughter Canyon Cave Tour. This two-hour ranger-guided tour explores Slaughter Canyon Cave. This cave is 23 miles from the visitor center so allow an hour to drive there. This flashlight tour is given daily in the summer and on weekends the rest of the year. Reservations are required. The number of visitors in a party is limited. Flashlights and water are required.

Bat Flight Program. From May through October (approximately) you can witness the Mexican free-tailed bats leaving the cave from an outdoor amphitheater at the cave's natural entrance. The bats fly in front of the seating area, but away from visitors. Check at the visitor center for the anticipated time. Flash photography is not permitted.

Cave Tours. Try to take in the Big Room route and the Kings Palace tour, where you will see the beautiful Green Lake Room, Papoose Room and Queens Chamber. The Giant Dome in the Big Room is the largest stalagmite in the cavern. The flight of the bats is unforgettable.

Scenic Drives. There is a nearly 10-mile drive that loops through beautiful desert country. Walnut Canyon Desert Drive is one-way, gravel-covered and not recommended for trailers or motor homes.

Hiking. Although Carlsbad Caverns itself is the major attraction of the park, the surrounding desert is beautiful when in bloom. The terrain has much to offer hikers: rocky canyons, ridges, cliffs and forests. The park's trail system includes short nature walks and more than 50 miles of primitive, backcountry trails. Trailheads are located along each of the park roads. The

flatlands offer excellent views of the Delaware Basin. Take plenty of water. Maps are available at the bookstore.

Near Carlsbad Caverns National Park

Guadalupe Mountains National Park. This Texas national park is 55 miles southwest of Carlsbad. Please see the entry on Guadalupe Mountains National Park for more information.

Lincoln National Forest. The Lincoln National Forest adjoins Carlsbad National Park on the west, and is about 20 miles from the park's visitor center. In 1950 a Lincoln game warden made history by rescuing a badly burned bear cub and naming him Smokey. Smokey the Bear became the forsest service's anti-fire mascot. Lincoln's life zones range from desert to sub-alpine forest. The 1,103,441-acre forest has unexplored limestone caves of its own. There are 368 campsites and visitors can hunt, fish, climb, ride and picnic here. The forest is open year-round. Campsites are open May to September.

For More Information

Superintendent
Carlsbad Caverns National Park
3225 National Parks Highway
Carlsbad, NM 88220
Tel. 505-785-2232

CHANNEL ISLANDS NATIONAL PARK

California ◆ **Established 1980**

The Channel Islands are eight small islands in two groups, directly off the coast of Southern California between Point Conception and the Mexican border. Five of the islands, Anacapa, Santa Cruz, Santa Rosa, San Miguel and Santa Barbara and the nautical mile of ocean surrounding them, comprise the national park. The Channel Islands Marine Sanctuary, also established in 1980, extends for six nautical miles around each island.

The park and the marine sanctuary work hand in hand to preserve a giant kelp forest and to protect nearly a thousand different species of fish, animals and marine plants. They also safeguard the environment by detecting and measuring the wastes of man-made islands; the seagoing oil rigs of the Santa Barbara Channel. The park manages a long-term ecological research project that is considered one of the finest in the National Park Service.

A Few Tips

♦ *When hiking on the islands, stay on the trails and well clear of the cliffs.*
♦ *All the birds, animals, tide pools, shells, fish and plants on the island are protected. No souvenir hunting. Take nothing but photos.*
♦ *Screeching and diving birds indicate you are near breeding activity. Stay away from nests.*

The islands are between 10 and 70 miles from the mainland, near enough to the coastline so that some of them can be plainly seen on a clear day. As near as they are, they couldn't be further in spirit from the crowding and over-development of the mainland. These windblown little islands and islets have remained a wild environment. Here in the fusion of sea, land and intertidal zone, a microcosm of life flourishes. The price for witnessing this delicate balance of nature is crossing the rough waters of the Santa Barbara Channel. Most visitors will testify the trip was worth their effort.

The islands' mountains, valleys and meadows support more than 600 species of plants. In spring, wildflowers bring vivid color to the islands, including a sunburst of coreopsis, a giant yellow sunflower. Hikers will find challenging cliffs, beaches, canyons and mountains to explore. Visitors can enjoy diving, kayaking, snorkeling and sailing around the islands, though they may face rough waters in late afternoon.

In prehistoric times, the northern Channel Islands were a part of the Santa Monica Mountains which had broken off to form a greater island geologists have named Santarosae. Before the continental ice sheets melted, the sea level was much lower. When the water rose, the islands were isolated. Thousands of years of wind, sea and rain have eroded them to their present diminutive size.

An unusual variety of animal species have made their homes here. Sea lions, seabirds and harbor seals use the islands as a resting place. Both gray whales and blue whales frequent the nearby waters on their migratory routes.

Many of the animals native to the island have evolved with slight differences from their mainland cousins over the years. The largest land mammal on the islands, the native island fox, is closely related to foxes on the mainland, but is a much smaller animal. The islands offer shelter to the only breeding colony of northern fur seals south of Alaska.

You will also see hawks, owls, snowy plover, cormorants and the California brown pelican, an endangered species protected by federal law.

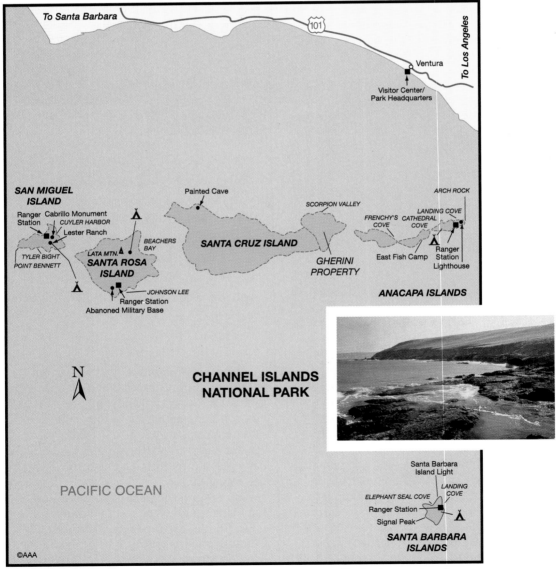

Park size: 248,515 acres
(125,000 acres underwater)

To protect animals indigenous to the island, park managers have had to "deport" many non-native species, including burros, rabbits and even abandoned house cats, who had reverted to the wild. An ongoing campaign to eradicate black rats — descendants of ship jumping ancestors — has so far proved less successful.

Anacapa island is about 14 miles from Ventura, making it the closest island to the mainland. Anacapa is really three small islets. From January through March, migrating whales are seen in the waters nearby. West Anacapa is closed to the public because it is the primary nesting sight for the West Coast pelican.

Santa Cruz is the largest of the Channel Islands and has the most diverse habitats. There are more than 600 plant species, 140 land bird species and an island-specific collection of land animals. Santa Cruz has been privately owned since the early 1800s and access is limited.

About 85% of Santa Rosa is grassland. Its sandy beaches are a breeding ground for harbor seals and the island is encircled by large kelpbeds.

San Miguel consists of a plateau, 400 to 500 feet in elevation, with two rounded hills. San Miguel is famous for a chemical reaction that hardens the wind-blown sand covering many of the island's plants. When the plants entombed within the hardened sand decay, what remains is caliche, a kind of hollow sand sculpture.

Santa Barbara, at 640 acres the smallest of the islands, is a rookery of sea lions. During World War Two, the U.S. Navy used Santa Barbara as an early warning outpost.

Juan Rodriguez Cabrillo, a Portuguese navigator sailing with the Spanish, is believed to have been the first European to visit the Channel Islands in 1542. Native Americans of the seagoing Chumash tribe lived on the islands, but were removed to missions on the mainland in the early 1800s. Russian and American fur traders attempted to trade in Channel Island sealskins for a time, but by the middle 19th century ranchers took over, raising sheep and cattle.

During the 1900s the islands were the linchpin in California's coastal defenses.

Santa Rosa and San Miguel have proven archaeologically significant in recent years. Many Chumash village sites have been uncovered. Charred remains of a dwarf mammoth discovered on Santa Rosa have been tentatively identified as being about 40,000 years old. If correct, this indicates that the Chumash sites represent one of the earliest evidences of people living in North America.

PLANNING YOUR VISIT

Park Open
The park is open year-round. The visitor center is closed on Thanksgiving and on Christmas Day. Peak visitation is in July.

Seasons
This can be a harsh environment. The wind often blows for several days at a time at 30 mph even in the summer. Long spells of wet fog are frequent. Winter and spring rains turn campgrounds and trails into sticky mud. Late afternoon can bring choppy waters. Spring is the best season for hikers to visit. Divers will find the best visibility in winter if they are willing to brave a water temperature in the 50s.

Entrance Fees
None.

WHALE WATCHING AND SEAL SPOTTING

From late December through March, gray whales make their way to and from Mexico. The Channel Islands are along their migratory route. Island Packers offers 3-hour whale-watching cruises to Anacapa Island and Santa Cruz Island with commentary. To view blue and humpback whales, plan a trip for June through October. For information about cruises, call Island Packers Information Line, 805-642-7688.

Channel Islands National Park also attracts people hoping to see seals and sea lions at play. On Anacapa Island, you may watch sea lions frolicking in the coves and resting along the rocky shore. On Santa Barbara Island, there is an even larger population of sea lions. On San Miguel Island, your chances of seal spotting are best of all. San Miguel is home to five species of seals, sea lions and elephant seals. Because the breeding grounds at Point Bennett are off-limits to hikers, you will probably get the best view from the water. Island Packers offers seal-spotting voyages from March through October. Call 805-642-1393 for more information.

Permits and Licenses

Between June 1 and September 1, you may camp along the southeast side of Santa Rosa Island from East Point to South Point. Between September 1 and December 1, the entire island is open to beach camping with the exception of Carrington on East Point, Cluster Point, Arlington Canyon, Ford Point, Jolla Vieja, Officers Beach and China Camp. The Water Canyon Campground is the only camping area along the northeast section of the island from Carrington Point to East Point. This campground is one-quarter mile from the beach. You may hike no more than 1000 yards inland from mean high tide. Skunk Point on Santa Rosa Island is closed to visitors from March 1 through September 15 because it is an important nesting area.

Access and Transportation

The easiest debarkation point to the islands is from Ventura, 70 miles north of Los Angeles and 30 miles south of Santa Barbara. From U.S. Highway 101 northbound, take the Victoria exit, left onto Victoria, then right onto Olivas Park Drive through Harbor Boulevard. Olivia Park Drive runs straight into Spinnaker Drive.

The visitor center is located at the very end of Spinnaker Drive in the Ventura Harbor.

The islands can only be reached by a boat, or more rarely, a plane. A park concessionaire offers regular boat trips throughout the year to all the islands. Reservations are recommended. Call 805-642-1393. Channel Islands Aviation flies visitors to Santa Rosa island for camping or day trips. Call 805-937-1301. Island Packers Company also arranges transportation to the islands. Call 805-642-1393.

There is no public transportation on the islands themselves. Bus service is available to Ventura. Amtrak serves Santa Barbara and Oxnard. The nearest airports are Los Angeles International, Burbank, Oxnard and Santa Barbara. Oxnard Airport has regular commuter service. Rental cars are widely available in Ventura and at all airports.

Special Needs

The visitor center is wheelchair accessible. Because of difficult landing conditions, islands are not wheelchair accessible. Assistance from the park staff is available upon request. Efforts are underway to provide some wheelchair accessible areas on Santa Rosa Island.

Amenities

Hiking ♦ Boating ♦ Scuba diving ♦ Swimming ♦ Fishing ♦ Authorized trips to Santa Cruz Island ♦ Whale watching and seal spotting ♦ Ranger-led programs

Travel Advisory

Smoking is prohibited except at the dock/landing and picnic areas. Dress in layers to adjust to rapid changes in weather. Stay away from cliffs. Stay away from the lighthouse on East Anacapa Island, its high-intensity foghorn could permanently damage your hearing.

Emergency Information

First aid is available in the park. The nearest hospital is in Ventura, four miles from headquarters and 18 miles from Anacapa Island. In an emergency, contact park rangers or U.S. Coast Guard on Channel 16 of a marine band radio.

Visitor and Information Centers

The visitor center on the mainland is on Spinnaker Drive in Ventura. The center offers a 25-minute film, photo displays, an exhibit of Chumash Native American artifacts and a native plant display.

Campgrounds

Camping is free in the park's four campgrounds but reservations are required. Bring a stove for cooking and pack your trash out when you depart. You must pack in and pack out all supplies, including water. No open fires are permitted.

East Anacapa Campground. This area has seven sites for a maximum of 30 campers. It has fire pits, tables and latrines. You must climb 154 steps from the landing cover to the island top and walk a quarter mile to the campground. There is a seven-day limit per stay, 14 days per year.

Santa Barbara Campground. This area has eight sites and a limit of 30 campers. There are picnic tables and latrines.

San Miguel Campground. This area has nine sites and a limit of 30 campers. There are pit toilets.

Santa Rosa Campground. This area has 15 sites and a 50 camper limit. The area has tables and latrines. There is a seven-day limit per stay.

East Santa Cruz. This area has 35 campsites for four to six people per site.

The Nature Conservancy allows some camping on the western side of Santa Cruz, with advance permits.

Picnic Area

There is no food available on the island. On East Anacapa, there are picnic sites with tables and latrines.

Cabins, Lodges and Hotels

There are no accommodations on the islands.

Restaurants

There are no restaurants on the islands.

THINGS TO DO AND SEE

Nature Conservancy. The conservancy conducts day trips to Santa Cruz Island for both organized groups and the general public. For information contact: Nature Conservancy's Santa Cruz Island Project, 213 Stearn's Wharf, Santa Barbara, CA 93101. Call 805-962-9111.

Island Packers, Inc. This concessionaire provides guided trips to Scorpion Valley on the east side of Santa Cruz island. Call 805-642-1393.

Each island has its own special features.

Anacapa. Cathedral Cove is a popular area for diving. On the west side of the island Frenchy's Cove and the beach are scenic. Arch Rock is on the tip of the island. Watch for sea lions and migrating whales. A recommended hike is the Anacapa Loop Trail, a two-mile figure-eight loop that covers most of the terrain at easy elevations. Anacapa is also a good spot for scuba diving, snorkeling, fishing and bird watching.

Santa Cruz. The island is known for its nesting seabirds. There is also an 1850s era ranch here. The National Park Service owns the eastern 10 percent of the island, the rest of the island is owned by the Nature Conservancy.

Santa Rosa Bechers Bay is the scenic high point. Look for harbor seals and large kelp beds off shore. There are over 180 active archaeological sites on Santa Rosa, including Chumash villages and fur hunter camps and also an 1850s cattle ranch, still in operation. A recommended hike is Lobo Canyon Trail. Rangers lead explorations of canyons and beaches.

San Miguel. The island is best known for its caliche forest of fossilized trees. It is the wildest and most fragile of the park's islands. A 14-mile hike takes you from Cuyler Harbor to Point Bennett, at the island's scenic western tip. There are more than 500 archaeological sites on the island. Hike the Lester Point Tail and discover the Lester Ranch, which belonged to island caretakers of the 1930s and 1940s. Also on the island, the Cabrillo Monument honors the explorer.

Santa Barbara. Hike Canyon View Trail for ocean views, a close look at rookeries and perhaps a glimpse of seals and sea lions. Five miles of trail cross the island. Moderately difficult treks include Arch Point Loop Trail, Elephant Seal Cove Trail and Signal Peak Loop Trail. There is a primitive campground on the island and opportunities for diving, snorkeling and fishing. There is a sea lion rookery offshore. Elephant Seal Cove is scenic. Signal Peak is the highest point on the small island.

Near Channel Islands National Park

Santa Monica Mountains National Recreation Area. This 150,000-acre recreation area is about 30 miles from the visitor center in Ventura. The area has 100 campsites and is open all year. Visitors can hike, fish, boat, ride horses and enjoy water sports. The area's varied habitats range from oak woodlands, to chaparral, to rocky canyons, marshes and sandy beaches. Natural and cultural resources include Paramount Ranch, a working movie set, Mulholland Drive, Malibu Beach, the Cold Creek Canyon Preserve and the Will Rogers State Historic Park. For information about the Santa Monica Mountains National Recreation Area call 818-888-3770.

For More Information

Superintendent
Channel Islands National Park
1901 Spinnaker Drive
Ventura, CA 93001
Tel. 805-658-5700

CRATER LAKE NATIONAL PARK

Oregon ♦ **Established 1902**

Crater Lake, high in the Cascade Mountains of southern Oregon, is 1,932 feet deep, the deepest lake in the country.

Ringed by 2,200-foot mountains, forests and volcanic peaks, the lake lies inside the rim of a dormant volcano, Mt. Mazama. Visitors approach by a road that clings to the rim of the mountain, finally getting their first sight of Crater Lake from a scenic overlook that looks down from steep 1,000-foot slopes.

Their first impression will probably be of the lake's inky, intense blue. Native American stories say the mountain bluebird was a dull gray before he dipped into Crater Lake's waters. A more mundane explanation is that the lake reflects the color of the sky. The suns rays are absorbed on the lake's surface one ray at a time as they pass through clear water. Some of the blue light returns to the surface, imbuing Crater Lake with its stunning color.

The lake was born after Mt. Mazama collapsed. About 7,700 years ago, Mazama experienced a colossal eruption so violent that the top of the mountain collapsed. Only the base of the mountain was left, forming a huge caldera, or basin-shaped depression. Rain and snow accumulated in the caldera, gradually swelling the lake to its present size 26 miles in circumference and six miles wide at its widest point.

Water flowing into the lake is offset by evaporation and seepage, so its depth remains remarkably constant, seldom varying by more than three feet. In 1988 and 1989, a manned submarine expedition discovered evidence of hydro-thermal venting on the lake bottom. There are no private boats allowed on the lake, but there are guided boat tours daily and scientific vessels.

Various species of fish were introduced into Crater Lake's waters. Today, only rainbow trout and kokanee salmon remain. To stabilize the lake's ecosystem, no restocking has taken place since 1941.

The land surrounding the lake is heavily forested and patches of wildflowers flourish briefly in July. The winters are long and rigorous at the lake, often bringing more than 45 feet of snow.

A FEW TIPS

♦ *Hiking inside the caldera rim is permitted only on Cleetwood Trail. Volcanic rock and soil are unstable and dangerous to climb on.*

♦ *Keep your distance from wildlife and do not feed the animals.*

There is abundant animal life in the vicinity of Crater Lake. Ravens, jays, squirrel, deer and chipmunks are often spotted by visitors. Elk, black bears, foxes, porcupines, bald and golden eagles, chickadees and mule deer are more elusive.

Crater Lake is a magnificent setting for day hikes. Thanks to some of the cleanest air in the United States, you can see for more than 100 miles at some points along the park's 70 miles of trails.

PLANNING YOUR VISIT

Park Open
Rim Village and Highway 62, from the south and west, are open all year. The North entrance and Rim Drive close with the first snowfall, usually in late September to mid-October. They open again in mid-June or early July. Visitor facilities are closed on Christmas Day. Peak visitation is in August.

Seasons
Summer is clear, with cool evenings and daytime temperatures between 70° and 90°. Snow usually covers the higher elevations from October to July. Stored heat from the summer sun keeps the lake from freezing.

Entrance Fees
Fee per vehicle $5
Collected May through October, or later if the weather permits.

Permits and Licenses
Backcountry permits are required for overnight stays. Permits are free and may be obtained at Steel Center, the visitor center and on the Pacific Crest Trail at the park boundary. No fishing license is required. All vehicles are restricted to designated roads. Descent to the lake is permitted only on Cleetwood Cove Trail.

Access and Transportation
From the West. Take I-5 to Highway 62 at Medford. Then go northeast to Annie Spring entrance.

From the South. Take U.S. 97 to Highway 62, northwest to Annie Spring entrance.

From the North. Take I-5 to Highway 138 at Roseburg, east and south to north entrance.

There are airports at Klamath Falls (60 miles away) and Medford (80 miles away).

There is train service from Klamath Falls.

Rental cars are available at Klamath Falls and Medford.

Special Needs

Most viewpoints are wheelchair accessible, as are the visitor center, Rim Center, Mazama Campground and the cafeteria and giftshop at Rim Village.

Amenities

Scenic drives ◆ Boat tours ◆ Fishing ◆ Cross-country skiing ◆ Snowmobiling

Travel Advisory

Accessibility is sometimes hindered by snow and ice. For weather and road reports in the Crater Lake area, turn your car radio to 1610 AM.

Emergency Information

First aid is available inside the park.

An ambulance service is available in Chiloquin, Oregon. The nearest hospitals are in Medford and Klamath Falls.

Visitor and Information Centers

Rim Village Visitor Center overlooks the lake. It is seven miles off Highway 62. The center is open daily from June through mid-September only. Steel Center, located at the park headquarters, is open all year except Christmas Day.

Campgrounds

There are two campgrounds. Both have 14-day limits and reservations are on a first-come, first-served basis at $10 to $15 a night. Lost Creek, on Pinnacles Road, is open from mid-July to mid-September. It has 16 tent sites with water and flush toilets. Mazama Campground, seven miles south of Rim Village, has 198 sites, and is open from late June to mid-October. Mazama offers tent and RV sites but no hookups and has restrooms and dump sites.

Picnic Areas

There are 12 areas with tables throughout the park.

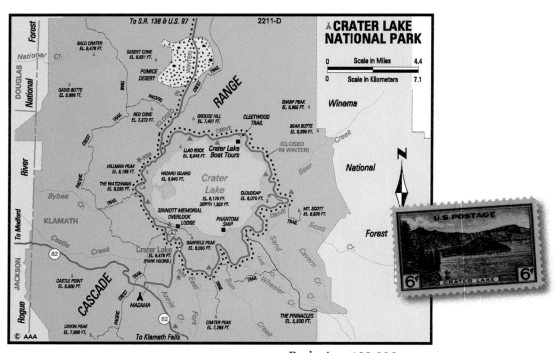

Park size: 183,226 acres

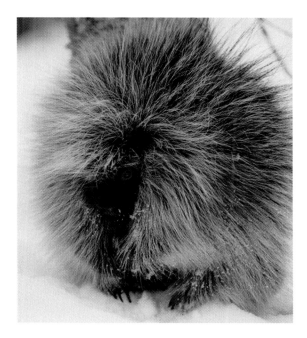

Cabins, Lodges and Hotels

Mazama Motor Inn. The inn's 40 rooms are open late spring, summer and early fall at $80 per night. They have a restaurant. Call Crater Lake Lodge Company at 541-830-8700. Reservations are suggested.

The Crater Lake Lodge. The lodge has 71 rooms which were renovated in 1995. It is closed from mid-October to mid-May. Write to Rim Village, Crater Lake, OR 97604, or call 541-830-8700. Reservations are recommended.

Restaurants

Food service is available inside the park. There is a dining room at the Crater Lake Lodge. There is a cafeteria in Rim Village and dining rooms located in Prospect, Diamond Lake and Chiloquin, approximately 35 miles from the park.

THINGS TO DO AND SEE

Guided Boat Tour. Guided boat tours of the lake are offered by concessionaires. The boats carry 60 passengers on a one and three-quarter hour circuit of the lake narrated by a ranger. Tours usually begin by the first of July and run through mid-September. There are nine tours a day beginning at 10 a.m. The last tour leaves the dock at 4:30 p.m. The cost is $12.50 for adults and $6 for children 11 years old and under. Children under two ride free.

Wizard Island. Wizard Island is the small conical island in the west side of the lake. You can visit the island briefly if you take the boat tour. You can hike climb, fish and picnic on the island, but be aware that the water is very cold, just 45° to 55°. Remember, the last boat leaves at 4:30 p.m., so don't miss it.

Scenic Drives. Weather and road conditions permitting, you can drive entirely around Crater Lake's rim, a 33-mile circuit which affords many breathtaking views. A seven-mile spur road off Rim Drive leads to the Pinnacles, eerie spires of volcanic pumice. The surrounding area features spectacular canyon country.

Hiking. There are more than 70 miles of trails in the park but most are closed until July. A paved footpath near the Rim Village visitor center leads to the Sinnott Memorial, an outdoor natural history display with a great view of the lake. The lake itself is accessible only via the steep Cleetwood Trail, a two-mile round trip that is easy enough to descend, but a tough climb on the return leg.

Fishing. Fishing is permitted from Cleetwood Cove and Wizard Island.

Winter Sports. Cross-country skiing is permitted on roads that are not plowed during winter, such as Rim Drive. However, skiing is never permitted on the three-mile stretch of road between park headquarters and Rim Village. Skiers must watch for ice and avalanche areas. You must rent skis before entering the park. Snowmobiling is permitted on the North entrance road only.

For More Information

Headquarters
Crater Lake National Park
PO Box 7
Crater Lake, OR 97604
Tel. 541-594-2211, ext. 402

DEATH VALLEY NATIONAL PARK

California ◆ **Established 1994**

At just under 3.4 million acres, Death Valley National Park is the largest national park outside of Alaska. Bounded on the west by 11,049-foot Telescope Peak and on the east by 5,475-foot Dante's View, the park also encompasses the lowest point in the Western hemisphere: Badwater, 282 feet below sea level.

Death Valley is a desolate place, yet it appeals to some untamed part of us and figures in our national history. Some are drawn by the desert scenery and complex geology, while others are attracted to the rare and singular wildlife. Some come with a determination to experience the hottest day of the year in the hottest place in North America.

In 1849, would-be California gold miners, dreading the snowstorms of the nearby Sierra Nevada, chose this region as an alternative route to the goldfields. Drinking water quickly proved to be far more precious than gold. It's no wonder they named such punishing territory Death Valley. Place names used by the original inhabitants, the Timbisha Shoshone people, were replaced by names drawn from the bitter memories of surviving pioneers. Many topographical features are known by these evocative names to this day: the Devil's Golf Course. Furnace Peak. Coffin Peak. The Funeral Mountains.

In 1881, near Furnace Creek, prospectors discovered borax, the so-called white gold of the desert. Rowdy mining encampments like Rhyolite and Skidoo sprang up.

The warm water springs at Furnace Creek are the closest thing Death Valley has to an oasis. Because the park receives less than two inches of precipitation a year, most plant and mineral life is found near this limited source of water.

A FEW TIPS

♦ *It may be difficult to find a campsite during the 49er Encampment Days, held the first two weekends in November.*
♦ *Be prepared for serious driving. With more than three million acres, there is quite a distance between points of interest. Be sure your vehicle is in good mechanical condition, fueled up at all times. Carry plenty of water.*
♦ *Most Death Valley stores and attractions won't accept checks or credit cards.*

There are cottonwoods and palms, magnolias and for a very few days a year, scattered wildflowers.

The salt water pupfish, a species native only to this area, lives in the pool at Salt Creek, burying itself in the mud during the winter months and coming to life again in the summer. There are also bobcats, coyotes and rabbits, and at the higher elevations, kit foxes and elusive bighorn sheep. Between 60 and 100 feral burros, direct descendants of miner's livestock, still wander the park.

These wild burros were overgrazing vegetation the bighorn sheep needed to survive, so they have been culled in recent years.

Park Open

The park is open year-round. Peak visitation is in April.

Seasons

Death Valley is the hottest place in North America, and the air is almost always hot and dry. From May through September, daytime highs typically range from 99.5° to 116°. Summer temperatures, even at night, can remain above 100° for a week. In 1972, the National Park Service recorded a ground temperature of just over 200°. Between December and February, daytime highs are between 65° and 75°, and nighttime lows are between 40° to 50°.

Entrance Fees

Per vehicle...$10
Per individual $3
Fees are valid for 7 days.

Permits and Licenses

Vehicles of all kinds are limited to designated roads.

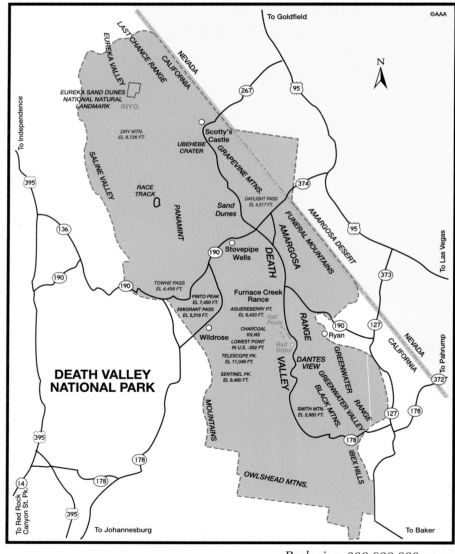

Park size: 336,000,000 acres

Access and Transportation

It is between 140 and 155 miles to Death Valley from Las Vegas, about a three hour drive. It is between 260 and 315 miles from Los Angeles, a six-and-one-half hour drive.

From Las Vegas. Follow U.S. 95 north for 86 miles to Amargosa Valley and the town of Lathrop Wells. Turn south to take Nevada Highway 373. This Highway turns into Highway 127 and takes you to Death Valley Junction. From Death Valley Junction, take California Highway 190 west for 29 miles to Furnace Creek. There are several other routes. The shortest is via Highway 160 to the north end of Pahrump, Nevada. There, turn left on Bella Vista Road which leads left to Death Valley Junction.

From Los Angeles. Take I-5 to San Fernando and then travel east on Highway 14 for 129 miles to U.S. 395. You can take I-15 to reach U.S. 395, which leads to Red Mountain. Pick up Highway 178, heading east into the park at Towne Pass. For a more scenic trip, take the southeastern route through the Mojave Desert. Take I-15 through Barstow and Baker. At Baker, head north on Highway 127 to Shoshone. At Shoshone, either turn west on Highway 178 and drive to the park via Furnace Creek or continue north on Highway 127 to Death Valley Junction, where you can connect with Highway 190 into the park.

Warning: Fill your gas tank. There are no service stations for 69 miles between Shoshone and Furnace Creek.

The closest major airport is in Las Vegas, 120 miles away. There is a small airport at the Furnace Creek Ranch. There is no train or bus service to the park. Rental cars are available in Lone Pine, California, and in Pahrump, and Beatty, Nevada.

Special Needs

Furnace Creek has the most accessible services and facilities. Access is limited in other areas due to the severe desert environment and the age of the facilities.

Amenities

Scenic drives ◆ Hiking ◆ Camping ◆ Biking ◆ Interpretive exhibit ◆ Nature photography ◆ Horseback riding ◆ Picnicking ◆ Guided tours

Travel Advisory

The dry desert air can leech the moisture out of your body without perceptible perspiration. Drink and carry plenty of water to avoid heat exhaustion. Bring a hat, a long sleeved shirt, sturdy walking shoes and plenty of sun protection.

Emergency Information

Ranger medics and ambulance provides emergency first aid only within the park. Air and ground transport service is available to area hospitals in Las Vegas and Tonopah, Nevada, or Lone Pine, California.

Visitor and Information Centers

The Furnace Creek Visitor Center is located in the center of the park and houses exhibits, an information desk and the Death Valley Natural History Association Book

Store. There is a contract station at Stovepipe Wells Village, and a museum, ticket office and book sales outlet at Scotty's Castle.

Campgrounds

Backcountry camping is allowed. Information and voluntary registration is free at the visitor center. There are 1,500 sites at nine campgrounds, although not all of them are open year-round. Furnace Creek, Mesquite Spring and Wildrose Campgrounds are open all year. Texas Spring, Sunset and Stovepipe Wells are open from November to April. Thorndike and Mahogany Flat are open March to early November. Fires are allowed in grates, but wood gathering is prohibited.

Although most sites are available on a first-come, first-served basis, reservations are accepted for Furnace Creek Campground and for group sites at Texas Spring Campground from October through April. Call DESTINET at 800-365-2267.

Picnic Areas

There are picnic areas at Furnace Creek, Scotty's Castle and the Salt Creek Trailhead.

Cabins, Lodges and Hotels

There is a great variety of accomodations at Death Valley, including a lovely inn that is a U.S. Historical Landmark. The Furnace Creek Inn dates back to 1927. It is closed from mid-May to mid-October and reservations should be made at least a month in advance. The Furnace Creek Ranch is convenient and affordable. Stovepipe Wells Village Motel has rooms and 14 RV hookups. All properties are under the same management. Call 619-786-2154 for reservations.

Restaurants

The Furnace Creek Inn has a dining room and L'Ottimo's, an Italian restaurant. Furnace Creek Ranch as two family-style restaurants. The Stovepipe Wells Village Motel has a family restaurant with an Old West atmosphere. There is an open-air lunch spot at Furnace Creek Golf Club.

THINGS TO DO AND SEE

Van Tours. Guided tours in passenger vans are offered by the Fred Harvey Company between October and May. Call 619-786-2345, ext. 222. All tours depart from Furnace Creek: The cost is between $20 and $30 for adults, with a four-passenger minimum.

Lower Valley Tour. This tour stops at Mushroom Rock, the Devil's Golf Course, Badwater, Mustard Canyon and the Harmony Borax works. It also offers a drive to 5,745-foot-high Dante's View, the highest point in the east valley, and concludes with a visit to Death Valley Junction's Amargosa Opera for a dance-mime performance by the famous desert diva Marta Beckett.

Scotty's Castle. The National Park Service runs 50-minute walking tours of Scotty's Castle. Tours are limited to 19 people, year-round. Call the visitor center at 619-786-2331 or Scotty's Castle at 619-786-2392 for tour times. Tickets are sold the day of the tour on a first-come, first-served

basis. The tours are conducted by rangers in 1930s costumes. Prices: $8 for adults, $4 for adults over 62, $4 for children. Children under the age of five are free.

Zabriskie Point. This is a favorite vantage for nature photographers because it offers a magnificent view of Golden Canyon. Another stunning vista in the black mountains is 5,745-foot Dante's View. From here you can see the Funeral Mountains, Greenwater Valley and Death Valley itself, backed by the Panamint Mountains.

Mosaic Canyon. At nearby Mosaic Canyon you will see a natural art gallery of water-polished mosaics of black, gray and white rock. It was created when the canyon's stream gravels were cemented into dazzling patterns, set off by the canyon's long, white marble walls.

Scotty's Castle. This is the premier tourist attraction in Death Valley. Constructed at a cost of $2.3 million dollars in 1924, the Castle was the winter retreat of eccentric Chicago insurance tycoon Albert Johnson. Johnson formed an unlikely bond with a desert rat named Walter Scott, a.k.a. Death Valley Scotty. Scott, a prospector, cowboy and incorrigible yarn spinner, pretended to be a gold miner who had struck pay dirt somewhere in the valley. He hinted at the existence of a huge treasure trove concealed somewhere within the castle. Johnson played along with the gag and paid the bills.

The Mediterranean Hacienda Johnson. Built in remote Grapevine Canyon, the hacienda is full of hand-painted tiles and hand-crafted furniture, and even includes innovations like solar water-heating panels. Park rangers dressed in 30's garb explain how the decor reflects the owner's eccentricities. Tours fill up quickly, so arrive early for the available spots.

For More Information
Superintendent
Death Valley National Park
PO Box 579
Death Valley, CA 92328
Tel. 619-786-2331

DENALI NATIONAL PARK

Alaska ♦ **Established 1917**

Denali, or "the high one," is the native Athabascan name for 20,320-foot high Mt. McKinley, the tallest peak in North America. The surrounding national park takes its name from the mountain and its rugged character from Alaska, the last great untamed American frontier.

Denali is a pristine, subarctic wilderness of forests, tundra, glaciers and free roaming animals. The mountain slopes of the Alaska range, of which Mt. McKinley is the anchor, are a 600-mile long crescent of summits dividing south-central Alaska from the vast interior. These mountains are covered in snow and ice year-round. The frigid temperatures at their peaks prevent the vast glaciers from melting. More than half of Mt. McKinley wears a permanent mantle of snow and ice. Permafrost, earth that has frozen solid, underlies most of the park's flatlands, starting a few feet beneath the surface and extending as deeply as several hundred feet.

A thin layer of topsoil thaws out during the summer months, but only plants and animals well-adapted to an unforgiving environment with long, bitterly cold winters can hope to survive here.

Denali's plant life is divided between taiga and tundra. Taiga is a Russian term for boreal forest. Taiga in the park extends to elevations up to 2,700 feet. Trees in the taiga are often gnarled and stunted, victims of the fierce winter winds. White and black spruce are the most numerous of these stubborn survivors, but there are also many shrubs in the taiga, as well as balsam, larch poplar, quaking aspen and paper birch.

The tundra begins above the tree line. Tundra, another Russian term, means a vast, frozen, treeless plain. Denali's tundra is a fascinating miniature forest full of dwarfed shrubs, moist, swampy fields of tussocks and in the summer, multi-colored miniature wildflowers. Crowberries, blueberries and cranberries grow profusely on the tundra and are prized by both people and animals.

Mt. McKinley's granite core is sheathed in glacial ice. In some places it is hundreds of feet thick. Glaciers, which left their stamp everywhere on Denali's topography, are abundant in the Alaska range, and many are visible within the park. Muldrow Glacier is only half a mile from the main park road.

As spectacular as Denali's landscape is, many of the hundreds of thousands of annual visitors to the park come just to see its abundant animal life. Visitation to the park has increased nearly thirty-fold in the last 20 years. Bring your camera. Denali is one of the world's premiere spots for nature and wildlife photography.

A FEW TIPS

♦ *Some areas may be closed because of bear or other wildlife activity. Avoid bears and learn what to do if you encounter a bear.*

♦ *Be aware that crossing glacial rivers is dangerous.*

Denali draws more visitors than Alaska's seven other national parks combined. Other than the looming presence of Mt. McKinley, the park's incredible wealth of wildlife is it's greatest distinction. There are grizzly bears, caribou, wolves, moose and Dall sheep. Smaller mammals found in the park include beavers, red fox, arctic ground squirrels, lynx, wolverines, marten, mink and weasels.

Golden eagles soar overhead, along with ravens and 157 other species of birds, including the willow ptarmigan, Alaska's state bird, a kind of brown and white speckled grouse.

Denali is a marvel when it comes to accommodating hordes of visitors while guarding the environment. A bus system which promotes maximum wildlife viewing while minimizing traffic is in place. The enormous six-million acre park has been apportioned into separate management units, each with strict visitation ceilings calculated to prevent damage to flora and fauna and provide opportunities for solitude. The park's campgrounds have been designed to be unobtrusive and modest. Be prepared to wait for campground and bus reservations when you get to Denali. (Call or fax ahead.) Be reassured, you will Alaskan landscape enthralling and inspirational.

PLANNING YOUR VISIT

Park Open

The park is open year-round. Peak visitation is in July. The park road is open from Memorial Day to mid-September if weather allows. Car travel is restricted beyond Savage River, 14 miles into the park. Animal activity may close back-country areas.

Seasons

The optimum time to visit is between May and September. Mt. McKinley may be

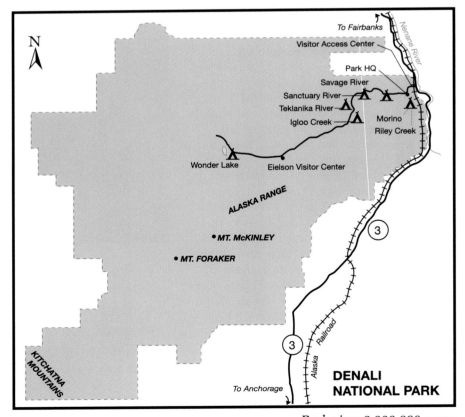

Park size: 6,028,090 acres

Airports. The nearest major airports are at Fairbanks and Anchorage. There's a smaller airport at Talkeetna.

Bus Service. Several companies provide service to the park in summer. Contact Denali Express, 800-327-7651; Alaska Sightseeing Tours, 907-276-1305 or Grey Line of Alaska/Westours; 907-277-5581.

Train Service. The Alaska Railroad provides daily summer passenger service to the park from Fairbanks and Anchorage. Passenger service is limited in winter. Call Alaska Railroad Corp. at 800-544-0552.

Rental Cars. Vehicles are available at Fairbanks, Anchorage and Wasilla.

Special Needs

The shuttle bus, five of the seven campgrounds and most buildings are wheelchair accessible. A pamphlet on services and facilities is available at the visitor centers or from headquarters.

Amenities

Scenic bus rides ◆ Hiking ◆ Mountaineering ◆ Air tours ◆ Fishing ◆ Bicycling ◆ Ranger-led tours ◆ Dogsled exhibitions

Travel Advisory

Cars are prohibited within the park beyond the 14.8 mile point.

Emergency Information

A clinic staffed by a physician's assistant is in Healy. The closest hospitals and doctors are in Fairbanks.

hidden with cloud cover in summer and even in summer temperatures at the summit are severe. Summer is cool and wet and snow may fall. Temperatures range from 30 to 90 degrees. The winter is long and cold with heavy snow from October into May. The park road is not snowplowed beyond headquarters (at mile 3.5) during the snow season. This limits access to skiers and dogsledders.

Entrance Fees

Fees are $5 per person and $10 per family.

Permits and Licenses

Alaska licenses for hunting and fishing are required and are available in Anchorage and Fairbanks. Permits are also required for campground and backcountry camping. They are available for $10 at the visitor centers.

Access and Transportation

Park Entrance. On Highway 3, go 24 miles north of Anchorage or 120 miles south of Fairbanks.

Visitor and Information Centers

The Visitor Access Center is at the east border of the park. It is open daily from late May to late September. Eielson Visitor Center is open from early June to mid-September. Off-season information is available at park headquarters, open daily all year. Call 907-683-2686 for a recorded message.

Campgrounds

Register for all campgrounds in person at the Visitor Access Center. There is a 14-day maximum at $12 a night. Campfires are allowed only in certain campgrounds. Trash must be packed out. Food must be stored in the bear-resistant food lockers or locked in vehicles at night. Campgrounds are open May through September, except for Riley Creek Campground, which is open year-round. Call ahead for reservations.

Riley Creek Campground. This area is accessible by private vehicle. It is half a mile west of Highway 3, has 102 sites, toilets, water in summer and is open all year.

Morino Campground. This area is accessible without vehicle. It is at mile 1.5 and has 15 sites (four persons/site), toilets and water.

Savage River Campground. This area is accessible by private vehicle. It is located at mile 12 and has 34 sites, toilets and water.

Sanctuary River Campground. This campsite is accessible by bus. It is at mile 22 and has seven sites for tents only. There are pit toilets and water.

Teklanika River Campground. This area is accessible by private vehicle. It is at mile 29, and has 50 sites, pit toilets and water.

Igloo Creek Campground. This area is accessible by bus. It is at mile 34 and has seven sites for tents only. There are pit toilets and water.

Wonder Lake Campground. Wonder Lake is accessible by bus. It is at mile 85 and has 28 sites for tents only. There are pit toilets and water.

Picnic Areas

Near Riley Creek Campground there are picnic tables.

Cabins, Lodges and Hotels

The Denali National Park Hotel. The hotel has 100 units for $119 a night, double occupancy. It is near the park entrance and open late spring to early autumn. For reservations call 907-683-2215 (summer) or 907-276-7234 (winter).

The North Face Lodge. The lodge has 15 rooms for $210–$235 per person, all inclusive. It is a mile west of Wonder Lake. Call 907-683-2290 (summer) or 603-675-2248 (winter).

Denali Backcountry Lodge. The lodge is open mid-May to October. It has 200 units at $150 a night, double occupancy, including two meals. It is near Kantishna. Call 907-683-2643 for reservations.

Restaurants

The Denali National Park Hotel has a dining room. Limited food supplies are available at a small store near the hotel or in Healy, 12 miles north of the park.

THINGS TO DO AND SEE

Bus Tours. National Park Service shuttle buses travel from the visitor center to Eileson Visitor Center to Wonder Lake between 5:00 a.m. and 3:00 p.m. Trips are not narrated, but buses stop for wildlife watching. Also, twice daily there is a camper's bus. Shuttle bus pass reservations are available for between $12 and $36 a person. Call 907-272-7275 or 800-622-7275. It may take a day or two's wait to be issued a bus pass.

Guided private bus tours depart from the Denali National Park Hotel. More comfortable than the park service bus, the private tours are narrated and serve a lunch. The tour lasts six or seven hours and costs $51 for an adult and $22 for children age 11 and under. A shorter natural history tour is available for $25 per adult and $14 for children age 11 and under.

Flightseeing. Concessionaires offer small airplane and helicopter tours of the park for prices ranging from $70 to $170 per person. Information is available at either visitor center. Air tours of the park may be chartered from Denali Air as well as other commercial operators. For more information call Denali Air, 907-683-2261.

Rafting Tours. White-water rafting tours are also available from local commercial operators. Ask for list of guide services at headquarters.

Sightseeing. The 85-mile shuttle bus trip along the park road to Wonder Lake takes 11 hours, round trip. You'll see wildlife and scenery you'll never forget including Mt. McKinley, the Alaska Range, the white mountain sheep of Cathedral Mountain, grizzly bears and caribou around Sable Pass, the Muldrow Glacier and Wonder Lake. Take a lunch and binoculars and don't hesitate to get off the bus. National Park Service buses stop when you flag them down if you have a pass.

For More Information
Denali National Park
PO Box 9
Denali National Park, AK 99755
Tel. 907-683-2294

In 1513, Ponce de Leon discovered and named this cluster of coral islands in the Gulf of Mexico for its many sea turtles. (Tortuga is Spanish for turtle. The "dry" was added to let travelers know there was no fresh water on the islands.) Today these seven islands and 100 square miles of coral reef and seagrass are the Dry Tortugas National Park.

As befits a place that was once a pirate hideaway, the keys that make up this isolated park are only accessible by boat or seaplane. However, turtles still make their homes here. The endangered hawksbill, Atlantic Ridley, green, and leatherback sea turtles live on the islands.

This area is a favorite with bird watchers as 300 species can be seen here in early spring to late fall.

Sixteen-acre Garden Key is dominated by a sprawling brick and masonry fortification.

Fort Jefferson was a prison for Army deserters during the Civil War. Its most famous prisoner was Dr. Samuel Mudd, accused (but later pardoned) conspirator in the Lincoln assassination.

The fort was proclaimed a national monument in 1935. In 1994, the Dry Tortugas became a national park.

PLANNING YOUR VISIT

Park Open

The park is open year-round. However, you may only visit designated keys during the day, with the exception of some limited camping permitted on Garden Key. Bush Key closes during tern nesting season. Peak visitation is in April.

Seasons

The best time to visit is November through April. The Lower Keys are hot and humid during the wet summer season and biting insects swarm. Wear a sunscreen whenever you visit. Seas are rough from October through January.

Entrance Fees

There is no entrance fee.

Permits and Licenses

Fishermen must have a Florida license. Group camping requires a permit.

Access and Transportation

The park is accessible only by boat and seaplane. Boat and taxi services depart from Key West, the Lower Keys, Naples

DRY TORTUGAS NATIONAL PARK

Florida ◆ **Established 1994**

A FEW TIPS

and Fort Myers in southwest Florida. A ferry boat ride is about three hours. A seaplane ride is about 45 minutes. The Yankee Freedom ferry offers day trips to the park from Key West. For rates and schedule information call 800-634-0939. The closest airport is Key West International.

Special Needs

The restrooms, picnic area and first floor of Fort Jefferson, all on Garden Key, are accessible.

Amenities

Self-guided tours ◆ Fishing ◆ SCUBA ◆ Snorkeling ◆ Swimming ◆ Wildlife observation

◆ *Never swim alone. The current can be quite strong.*

◆ *Contact with coral and sea urchins can cause painful cuts that are slow to heal.*

◆ *High season in the Keys is mid-December through mid-April.*

Travel Advisory

The park is only accessible by boat or seaplane. Rough landings are common. You can arrange for half-day or full-day visits by seaplane. Jet skis are prohibited in the park.

Emergency Information

First aid is available in the park. The closest hospital is in Key West. There is no public phone on the islands.

Visitor and Information Centers

The visitor center on Garden Key features exhibits and a slide program about the islands. Rangers lead nature walks in the winter. The center provides a list of birds found on the islands. You can also borrow snorkel equipment. (Divers must bring their own gear.)

Campgrounds

There are primitive campsites on Garden Key, available on a first-come, first-served basis. Camping fees are $3.00 per person, per night. Groups of 10 or more must secure a permit. For group camping permits, call 305-242-7700 (Everglades National Park).

Picnic Areas

There is a picnic area with toilets on Garden Key. No fresh water is available. All food, water and supplies must be brought from the mainland. You must pack out your trash.

Cabins, Lodges and Hotels

No lodging is available in the park. Hotels and motels in a wide price range are available in Key West, about 70 miles from the park. Accommodations are less expensive in the Lower Keys than in Key West.

Restaurants

There are no restaurants or snack bars in the park.

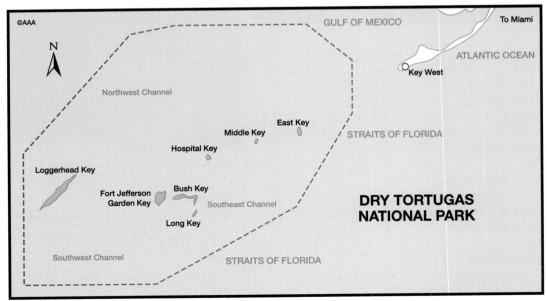

Park size: 64,700 acres

experience with field surveys. For more information call REEF at 305-451-0312

Diving and Snorkeling. Off Garden Key, the shallow, clear water affords a good look at conchs, lobster, crab, shrimp and moray eels. Also watch for loggerheads and other sea turtles feeding on the sea grasses.

Fishing. Fishermen interested in marlin, sailfish, kingfish, yellowtail and grouper will not be disappointed in the Lower Keys. A Florida saltwater fishing license is required.

For More Information

Dry Tortugas National Park
4001 State Road 9336
Homestead, FL 33034-6733
Tel. 305-242-7700

Things to Do and See

Fort Jefferson. Allow the better part of an hour to take the self-guided tour in and around the fort. Be sure to visit the cell of the unfortunate Dr. Mudd. The fort is surrounded by a brick sea wall that affords a great view of the water and sea life. Climb up the stairs to the roof for a beautiful view across the water.

Bird Watching Tour. The Florida Audobon Society sponsors a guided birding trip in April or early May. Bird watchers can witness spring migration and tern nesting at remarkably close range.

Fish Surveys. The Reef Environmental Education Foundation (REEF) teaches volunteers to identify and count fish in the Dry Tortugas. The Dry Tortugas surveys are for people with some

EVERGLADES NATIONAL PARK

Florida ◆ Established 1947

A Few Tips

◆ *Don't wear perfume, cologne or strongly scented shampoo or after-shave, Sweet or citrus scents draw mosquitoes and other biting insects. Wear insect repellent and use it at your campsite.*

◆ *Wear a strong sunscreen and replenish coverage throughout the day. The sunlight is intense.*

◆ *Remember that very young children get overheated easily. Pace yourself and spend some time in the shade to guard against heat exhaustion. On a spring day, the temperature can climb to the 80s.*

Everglades National Park is just the southern tip of the Everglades, from Lake Okeechobee to Florida Bay. This 1.5 million acres of marsh, hammocks, grasses, mangrove islands and coasts are home to 14 of Florida's endangered species, such as the Florida panther and the manatee.

Visitors to the Everglades can go crabbing or shrimping, but must follow state fishing regulations. Visitors can also picnic, photograph wildlife and birds, fish, hike, canoe and enjoy open-air tram and sightseeing boat rides. You should make an effort to see the Everglades on foot and from the water. The Wilderness Waterway runs from Everglades City to Flamingo, covering nearly 100 miles of the western half of the park. Many nature trails provide

boardwalks over the swampland and afford an opportunity to see wildlife up close.

PLANNING YOUR VISIT

Park Open

The park is open year-round. Off-season is May–October. Park services are restricted during this period.

Seasons

The best time to visit is November through April. Peak visitation is in March. The glades are hot and humid during the wet summer season and biting insects swarm.

Entrance Fees

Fee per vehicle (main entrance)............$10
Fee per person (main entrance) $5
Fee per vehicle (Shark Valley, Chekika)..$8
Fee per person (Shark Valley, Chekika)...$4
Fees are good for seven days.

Permits and Licenses

Backcountry permits are available from ranger stations and are $10 for groups of one to six campers. Permits may be picked up one day in advance from the Gulf Coast Ranger Station. Call 941-695-3311. A Florida fishing license is required for fresh water and saltwater fishing. The ideal time for backcountry camping is February and March.

Access and Transportation

From Homestead. Take State Route 9336 for 12 miles southwest to the main park entrance. Other visitor centers are in Royal Palm, Shark Valley, Flamingo and Everglades City. The nearest major airport is Miami International.

No off-road vehicles are permitted in the park. All vehicles are restricted to designated roads. Airboats are banned in the park because they disturb wildlife and destroy saw grass.

Special Needs

Most walking tours and boat tours are handicapped accessible. The Main Visitor Center, Shark Valley Information Center and tram tours are wheelchair accessible. An access guide is available at the visitor centers.

Amenities

Bookstores ♦ Parking ♦ Restrooms (with saltwater toilets only) ♦ Telephones ♦ Boat rentals and ramps ♦ Nature trails with boardwalks ♦ Self-guided walking tours ♦ Picnic areas ♦ Houseboat rental ♦ Canoe rental ♦ Boat tours ♦ Bike rental ♦ Lodge ♦ Marina

Travel Advisory

Wear insect repellent at any time during the year. Wear long pants and a long-sleeved shirt. (It's healthier than lathering on bug spray.) Don't plan to swim unless you're willing to share the water with alligators, snakes, barracuda and sharks.

Emergency Information

First aid is available at ranger stations. The nearest hospital is in Homestead.

Visitor and Information Centers

There are five visitor centers. The Ernest F. Coe Visitor Center is near the

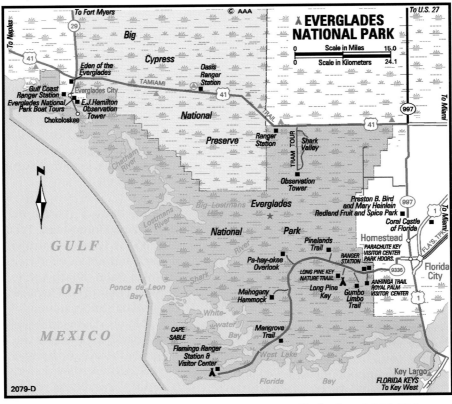

Park size: 2,221,766 acres

$14 per night from September to June. Campsites may be reserved through DESTINET at 1-800-365-CAMP. Group sites can be reserved in advance by calling the park. Backcountry campsites are accessible by boat only.

park entrance, the others are Royal Palm (off the main park road), Shark Valley (at the north end of the park), Flamingo (at Florida Bay) and a ranger station at Everglades City (in the northwest corner of the park). The main visitor center is open daily all year. During off-season, the other centers may close. The Flamingo Lodge and Marina rents boats.

Campgrounds

There are three campgrounds with tent and RV sites but no hook-ups: Flamingo, Lone Pine Key and Chekika. Showers are available at Flamingo and Chekika. From November through May there is a 14-day limit to your stay. The rest of the year the limit is 30 days. Campsites are reserved on a first-come, first-served basis. Fees are

Picnic Areas

Food and supplies are available at Flamingo Marina, as well as nearby Homestead and Florida City.

Cabins, Lodges and Hotels

Flamingo Lodge, Marina & Outpost. This lodge is in the park. Call 1-800-600-3813 to make reservations — well in advance.

There are several hotels and motels in Homestead and Florida City, both about 12 miles from Everglades National Park. Rates are higher in South Florida during the winter season (December through mid-April). These rates are for two persons in a double room during the high season:

Coral Roc Motel. 1100 N. Krome Avenue, has 16 units, some with a kitchenette, for $58 per night. Call 305-247-4010.

The Everglades is Endangered.

The Everglades is irreplaceable. In addition to being part of the national park system, Everglades National Park is a Biosphere Reserve and a World Heritage Site — making it a protected ecosystem — meaning that the park has international resources.

Ironically, the home to so many of Florida's endangered species faces a continuing threat to its own survival. The Everglades is not getting enough water in the right amounts at the right time. Depletion of water habitats has inspired a crusade to purchase privately owned wetlands east of the park.

Knights Inn. 401 U.S. Highway 1, has 108 units, some with kitchenette, for $53–65 per night. Call 305-245-2800.

Seaglaze Motel. 1223 N.E. First Avenue, has 49 units, some with kitchenette, for $58 per night. Call 305-247-6621.

Days Inn. 51 S. Homestead Blvd., has 100 units for $78 per night. There is also a restaurant. Call 305-245-1260.

Everglades Motel. 605 S. Krome Avenue, has 19 units, six with kitchenettes, for $52 per night. Call 305-247-4117.

Restaurants

Flamingo Lodge has a mid-price restaurant open August to the first of June.

Tours

Rangers lead free nature walks and talks as well as evening programs. Canoe and kayak tours are offered by independent guides. Call North American Canoe Tours at 813-695-4666 or Bardy Jones Ibis Tour at 800-525-9411.

THINGS TO DO AND SEE

Tram Tours & Sight-Seeing Boats. Explore the Everglades from a sight-seeing boat or tram, or take a midnight tram tour. However, some tours may not be available off-season. A narrated boat tour explores the mangrove islands along the Gulf of Mexico and you will probably see dolphins, manatees and ibis. Daily cruises depart from Flamingo. Get your ticket at the marina office near the visitor center. For boat tours of the Florida Bay and backcountry areas call 941-695-3101. For boat tours of the gulf coast area call 941-695-2591.

Shark Valley Tram Tour. Tram tours depart from the Shark Valley Information Center. During this two-hour tour in an open-air tram, you will spot alligators and anhinga, a long-beaked water bird.

Mahogany Hammock. Hikers can view the largest living mahogany tree in the United States. You will also notice remnants of pines. Southeastern Florida was covered with pines before Miami was developed.

Near Everglades National Park

Biscayne National Park. The park is near Everglades National Park but there are even fewer campsites at Biscayne. Big Cypress National Preserve is an alternative that offers excellent hiking and backcountry camping.

Big Cypress National Preserve. This 570,000-acre grassy swamp adjoins the Everglades National Park. There are 75 campsites and fishing, hunting, canoeing and hiking trails. However, keep an eye out for alligators, bears and the endangered Florida panther. Take U.S. 41 (also called Tamiami Trail) to reach the preserve in Ochopee. Call 813-695-4111.

For More Information

Everglades National Park
40001 State Road 9336
Homestead, FL 33034-6733
Tel. 305-242-7700

GATES OF THE ARCTIC NATIONAL PARK

Alaska ♦ **Established 1980**

Far above the Arctic Circle, Gates of the Arctic has the distinction of being the northernmost national park. It is also one of the most remote and undeveloped sites in the national park system. There are no roads, trails or services, just eight-and-a-half-million acres of immense valleys and seven wild rivers. Many of the park's landmarks are unnamed. To explore this park you must be self-sufficient and a skilled survivalist.

The park was named by explorer Robert Marshall, who also named Alaska's Frigid Crags and Boreal Mountain on either side of the North Fork Koyukuk River. Marshall considered these two mountains "gates" from the Brooks Range into the Arctic.

Wide valleys add contrast to the high, ragged peaks of the range. The tallest is Mount Igikpak at more than 8,500 feet. The southern slopes of the park are taiga, made up of sparse forests of black spruce. Above the tree line, (2,000 feet) are shrub-sized birch, alder and poplar. The higher areas are alpine tundra with alder thickets and tussocks and dwarf flowers. North of the Brooks Range is the treeless Arctic tundra, resting on a bed or permafrost 2,000 feet thick.

Seasons in this land north of the Arctic Circle are dramatic. Winters are long, dark and at subzero temperatures.

Wildlife in the park includes lynx, moose, Dall mountain goats, whales, seals, eagles, sheep, wolves and snowshoe hares. The park is also a preserve for huge herds of western arctic caribou. Some areas of the park are closed to protect nesting bird colonies, feeding humpback whales or to restrict access to grizzly and black bears.

Nunamiut Eskimos in the small village of Anaktuvuk Pass live as their ancestors before them, fishing and trapping. Athabaskan peoples live in the foothills and taiga. Both small and large tracts of land throughout the park are privately owned. These are not open for public use or travel without the owner's permission. There are free public-access hiking routes across private land. Ask a ranger for directions.

A Few Tips

♦ *Crossing rivers and streams is hazardous. Use caution.*
♦ *Avoid encounters with bears. Get bear safety information from park headquarters.*
♦ *Carry extra food and supplies for emergencies.*
♦ *Dress in layers and invest in good rain gear.*
♦ *Carry insect repellent and mosquito-proof tents.*

PLANNING YOUR VISIT

Park Open

The park is open all year. Peak visitation is in August.

Seasons

Rapid and severe weather changes are common. On southern slopes, midsummer temperatures in the lowlands may rise to 80°, with lows near 50°. The highlands are cool, as are the northern slopes. Freezing temperatures can occur at any time, especially from mid-April to mid-August. There is little snow but what falls stays on the ground. The spring thaw generally occurs in late April through mid-May.

Entrance Fees

There is no entrance fee.

Permits and Licenses

Private motor vessels entering the park between June 1 and August 31 must have a permit. The number of permits is limited, so contact the park well in advance. You must have an Alaskan hunting and fishing license if you plant to hunt and fish. Hunting is allowed only in the preserve adjacent to the park. Campers are also required to obtain a free permit.

Access and Transportation

Scheduled air service is available year-round from Juneau to Gustavus. Bus or taxi service from Gustavus to the park is available. You may also fly from Fairbanks to Bettles, the departure point for many charter flights into the park. Flights are about $100 one-way. Contact park headquarters for a list of air taxis. Reservations are recommended. Many visitors come to Gates of the Arctic by cruise ship.

Special Needs

The Ranger Station at Bettles and its restrooms are wheelchair accessible. The first part of the Forest Loop Trail, which is a boardwalk, is also accessible.

Amenities

General store at Bettles ♦ Guided wildlife viewing ♦ Boating ♦ Kayaking ♦ Ranger programs

Travel Advisory

Visitors staying in the park must be self-sufficient. Even experienced travelers should leave an itinerary with friends and the ranger station. You may carry firearms for protection, but shooting in the park is prohibited except for protection.

Emergency Information

There are no medical services in the park. The nearest hospital is in Fairbanks. There are small clinics in Bettles and Anaktuvuk Pass.

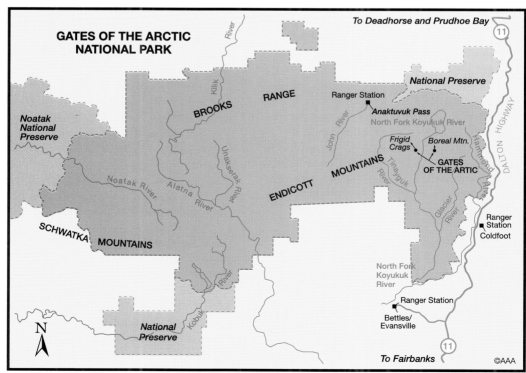

Park size: 7,525,888 acres

Visitor and Information Centers

Park headquarters is in Fairbanks. Ranger stations are at Bettles, Anaktuvuk Pass and Coldfoot. The visitor center is Glacier Bay Lodge at Bartlett Cove.

Campgrounds

There are no developed campgrounds.

There is a primitive campground at Bartlett Cove. You may camp there for free. Camp only on gravel bars or areas of hardy heath or moss. Park headquarters can provide information about low-impact camping requirements and bear safety.

Picnic Areas

There are no developed picnic sites. There is a general store at Bettles and small stores at Anaktuvuk Pass, a Nanumiut Eskimo community inside the park.

Cabins, Lodges and Hotels

There are no accommodations in the park. Limited lodgings (and some bed and breakfast establishments) are available in Bettles, Gustvaus, Anakruvuk Pass and Coldfoot. At Bartlett Cove, Glacier Bay Lodge offers rooms, a restaurant and bar, a gift shop and limited supplies.

Restaurants

The closest restaurant to the park is in Glacier Bay Lodge in Bartlett Cove. There is also a small cafe in Gustavus. You may buy limited food and supplies in Bettles and Anaktuvuk Pass.

Things to Do and See

Guided Tours. Independent outfitters run combination dogsled-ski trips through the Gates of the Arctic in April. The trip starts in Bettles and continues through Kayukuk River Valley. Alaska's Sourdough Outfitters also run summer backpacking, river and cross-country ski trips. For more information, call 907-692-5252. There are also special interest tours for photographers and winter sports enthusiasts.

Boat Tour. Glacier Bay Lodge in Bartlett Cove operates day tour boats during the summer. The trip from the forests of Bartlett Cove to the tidewater glaciers is 65 miles and the scenery is breathtaking. Various cruise lines also bring visitors into Glacier Bay.

Hiking. There are no roads or trails in this park and the going gets tough. Obtain a U.S. Geological Survey topographical map and study it before arrival. Mid-June to September is the best time to hike the park. Remember to bring insect repellent and rain gear. Sturdy, waterproof footgear is a must.

Float Trips. Float trips on Alsec River and guided kayak trips are popular summer attractions. Several independent outfitters offer guided river trips.

Skiing. The best time to ski in the park is March or April. There are guided cross-country ski trips organized by independent outfitters.

Fishing. Lake trout, grayling and char are in the streams and lakes. In the Kobuk and Alatna Rivers you may catch sheefish and chum salmon. Catch-and-release fishing is strongly encouraged. Avoid getting fish odors on clothing and equipment. The smell will attract bears.

Hunting. Sport hunting is prohibited in the park, but it is permitted in the preserve during hunting season.

Guides. Guides can be hired for backpacking and hiking trips, hunting, lake touring and mountaineering.

Near Gates of the Arctic National Park

Arctic National Wildlife Refuge. When it comes to Alaska's national parks, proximity takes on a whole new meaning. Like Gates of the Arctic, the 18-million acre Arctic National Wildlife Refuge is within the Arctic Circle. It is a possible sidetrip by plane or boat for those hoping to spot wildlife. This land is the only protected arctic coast in the U.S. The refuge also encompasses lakes, rivers and the mountains and tundra that make up the northeastern part of the Brooks Range. The wildlife protected here includes grizzlies, polar bears, Dall sheep, wolves and dozens of species of birds. In the heart of the park is the breeding ground for one of the last major caribou herds in the country. For more information about the refuge call the Fairbanks office of the Alaska Public Lands Information Center at 907-456-0527. This office can provide a list of air-taxi services.

For More Information
Superintendent
Gates of the Arctic National Park
PO Box 74680
Fairbanks, AK 99707-4680
Tel. 907-456-0281

GLACIER BAY NATIONAL PARK

Alaska ◆ **Established 1980**

Glacier Bay transports visitors to an ice age where they can watch nature start from scratch. It is one of few places in the world where the retreat of glaciers can be witnessed.

Glaciers here are formed from snow on the peaks of Fairweather Range. Mount Fairweather towers over the mouth of the bay. Layer upon layer of unmelting snow becomes a thick mass of ice that eventually slips down the side of the slopes. When this mass of ice reaches the water, it is called a tidewater glacier. There are 16 such glaciers in the park. Huge blocks of ice break off from the glaciers and crash into the Pacific, causing waves of more than 30 feet. This process is called "calving."

Eventually these blocks form icebergs that melt away, but larger glaciers form icebergs which can last weeks. The glaciers in the park are covering less and less of the land. In geologic time, they are retreating very rapidly.

The bay itself is the result of melting glaciers, which leave behind fjords, islands and inlets.

John Muir, most associated with Yosemite National Park, has a connection to Glacier Bay as well. The naturalist visited the area in the late 1800s. There is a glacier named for him.

Once the glaciers retreat, the land they uncover is barren. First moss forms, building the soil that will support shrubs. Eventually trees grow and form forests. You can see this process at work on a grand scale in the park. The area far inland is bar-

A FEW TIPS

♦ *Attend the camper orientation given at Glacier Bay Lodge.*

♦ *Bear-resistant protection for your supplies is a must.*

♦ *Bring insect repellent to deal with mosquitoes and biting flies.*

ren. Farther out is sparse vegetation. Near Bartlett Cove, at the mouth of the bay, is a lush rain forest.

Glacier Bay is both a national park and a preserve. Animals in the park include coyotes, foxes, moose and mountain goat. Very lucky visitors may spot the rare "glacial" bears, which are nearly blue-black. There are also the more common brown bears and grizzlies in the park. In spring and fall, migratory ducks and geese fill the park. There are also puffins, loons, herons and various shorebirds. In and around the icy waters are otters, porpoises, minke and humpback whales and orca. The park has the highest population of harbor seals along the Pacific Coast.

Glacier Bay can best be appreciated from the water. Many cruise ships offer tours of the bay with commentary from park naturalists on the glaciers, plants and animals in the park. Guided kayak tours

are another great way to explore the beauties of Glacier Bay. There are also charters offering "flightseeing" tours of Glacier Bay.

PLANNING YOUR VISIT

Park Open

The park is open year-round. Visitor services are limited from mid-September to late May. Peak visitation is in July.

Seasons

This area of Alaska is rainy and long periods of overcast, cool weather are typical. In summer, daytime temperatures are 45° to 65°, with slightly warmer temperatures in Bartlett Cove. Nights may cool to near freezing. May through September brings the best weather.

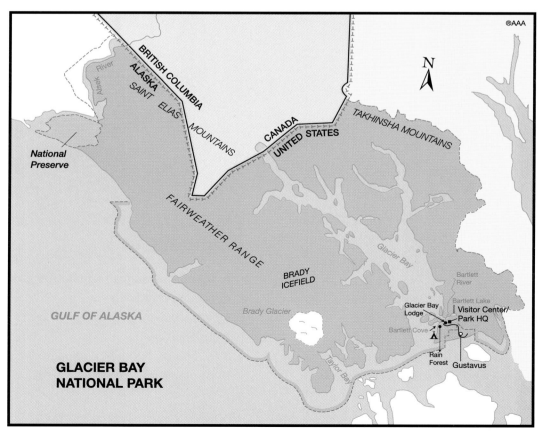

Park size: 3,225,284 acres

Entrance Fees

There is no entrance fee. There is a fee for travel to the tidewater glaciers.

Permits and Licenses

You will need a permit to enter the park from June 1 through August 31. Apply to the park superintendent. Permits are also required for backcountry camping. If you plan to fish, you must have an Alaska fishing license.

Access and Transportation

The park is in southeastern Alaska. It is only accessible by plane or cruise ship. The closest airport is Gustavus, 10 miles from the park. Alaska Airlines flies from Juneau and Anchorage to Gustavus daily during the summer season. Buses and taxis are available at the airport.

Special Needs

The visitor center, restrooms and two cabins at Glacier Bay Lodge are wheelchair accessible. The lodge has ramp and elevator. One section of the forest trail is accessible via a boardwalk. Request an access guide from the visitor center.

Amenities

Naturalist cruises ◆ Seal spotting and whale watching ◆ Guided kayak tours ◆ Flightseeing tours

Travel Advisory

Hats, gloves and good rain gear, including waterproof boots, are a necessity. The peak tourism months in Alaska, July and August, are also the rainiest. If you are camping, you must "bearproof" your supplies.

Emergency Information

First aid is available at park headquarters. The closest hospital is in Juneau, 60 miles from the park by air.

Visitor and Information Centers

The park headquarters and visitor center is upstairs in Glacier Bay Lodge at Bartlett Cove. It is open from May to September. The center provides exhibits, films and slide presentations in the lodge's auditorium. There is a twice-daily camper orientation that is highly recommended.

Campgrounds

Attend one of the camper orientations given twice daily at the lodge.

Bartlett Cove Campground. There are 35 sites available on a first-come, first-served basis from May through September. The campground has fire pits, a warming hut and bear-resistant food caches. There is a 14-day limit. Camping is free and no reservations are needed. Wilderness camping is permitted in the park. Before heading out, get up-to-date information on bear activity and food storage recommendations. Cook-

stoves are needed because wood is scarce and often wet. Tour vessels from Bartlett Cove or Juneau will drop backcountry campers and hikers off at various points. Reservations are needed for this service.

Picnic Areas

There are no picnic areas. The campground has fire pits. There is a small grocery story in Gustavus, 10 miles from the park.

Cabins, Lodges and Hotels

Glacier Bay Lodge. This is the only accommodation inside the park. It is open from May through September. Some of the 55 rustic rooms look out on Bartlett Cove. There are also less expensive dormitory rooms. The lodge has a restaurant and gift shop. A tour boat makes daily expeditions from Glacier Bay Lodge to the glaciers. Call 800-451-5952 for more information.

Glacier Bay Country Inn. They are between the airport and Bartlett Cove. They have 9 rooms with views of the mountains. The lodge has a restaurant and runs charter boat trips to Glacier Bay. Call 800-628-0912 for more information.

Lodging, ranging from inns to bed and breakfasts, are available in Gustavus. For a complete listing, write to Gustavus Visitors Association, PO Box 167, Gustavus, AK 99826.

Restaurants

Restaurants in Glacier Bay Lodge and Glacier Bay Country Inn are open in the summer season. There is a small café in Gustavus.

THINGS TO DO AND SEE

Boat Tours. Glacier Bay's most noteworthy sights are best seen from the water. Day and night cruises to the tidewater glaciers depart from Glacier Bay Lodge. Cruise ships and smaller tour vessels, including charter boats, also tour the bay. Glacier Bay Boats offers boat trips. Call 800-451-5952 for schedule and cost information.

Nature Walks. Park naturalists present evening programs and films in the auditorium and conduct nature hikes that begin at the lodge.

Boating. Private boaters who plan to visit the park from June 1 through August 31 must obtain a permit. The number of permits is limited. Only very experienced sailors should consider entering the bay because navigating near tidewater glaciers and icebergs requires special skill.

Hiking. Rangers lead nature walks from Bartlett Cove. Three miles of maintained trail wind through the rain forest at Bartlett Cove. To reach the backcountry, you must be dropped off by a tour boat or floatplane. There are no backcountry trails, but you can explore beaches, recently deglaciated areas and alpine meadows. Backcountry hikers must be experienced and fully equipped and provisioned.

Guided Kayak Tours. An independent outfitter, Alaska Discovery, guides kayak tours of the bay's icy waters and oversees camping in the wild country. Call 800-586-1911 for more information. There are also outfitters who will provide basic kayak training. Call Glacier Bay Sea Kayaking 907-697-2257.

Fishing. There is good fishing for halibut, salmon, Dolly Varden trout and cutthroat trout. Fishing charters are available at Glacier Bay Lodge.

Flightseeing. See Glacier Bay from the air, courtesy of one of the local "flightseeing" tours. Call Glacier Bay Airways (907-697-2249) or Air Express (907-697-2375).

For More Information
Superintendent
Glacier Bay National Park
PO Box 140
Gustavus, AK 99826-0140
Tel. 907-697-2230

GRAND CANYON NATIONAL PARK

Arizona ◆ Established 1919

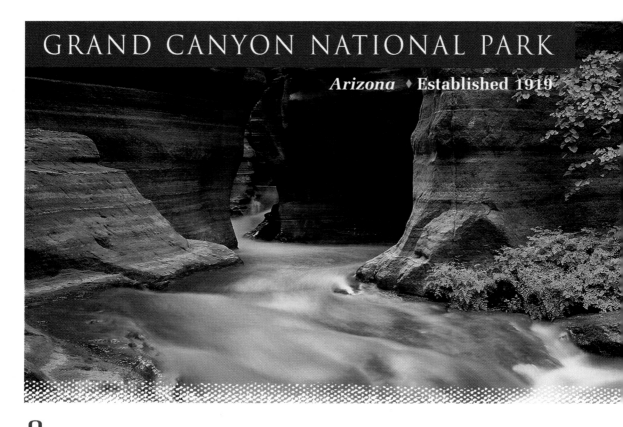

Gazing upon the Grand Canyon always conveys the thrill of the unexpected. Seeing it for the first time over a century ago, naturalist John Muir wrote: "It will seem as novel to you, as unearthly in the color and grandeur and quality of its architecture, as if you had found it after death, on some other star."

If you approach from the south, the terrain gives no hint of the astounding spectacle about to unfold. You cross a plateau that rises slowly and gradually, and suddenly there it is. The solid earth falls away, revealing a massive gorge a mile deep and 18 miles wide.

The panorama of multi-colored canyon cliffs stretches far into the distance, allowing you to see for as far as 200 miles on a clear day. As incompre-

hensibly vast as the scale seems, under the best of circumstances you will still be looking at only a fraction of the canyon's 277 miles.

Sadly, in recent years, air pollution has dimmed views that were once sharp and clear. On a hazy day you might be able to see twenty miles into the distance. There has always been haze in the canyon from natural sources like pollen and forest fires, but lately the scenery has been obscured by industrial pollutants drifting in from copper smelters in Arizona, nearby urban centers, and auto exhaust from California and even Mexico.

If you advance to the rim, where tens of millions of footsteps have polished the rock smooth over the years, you can barely make out the red ribbon of the Colorado River meandering over the canyon floor. The distant and harmless looking river is really an inexorable force

of nature. In some mysterious way, it carved this mighty abyss.

The Colorado River enters the Grand Canyon from the north, coursing between walls of limestone and sandstone. It flows south for 61 miles, sometimes accelerating into short, sharp stretches of rapids. The river water is full of the sand, gravel and rock it has carried away from Colorado, Utah, New Mexico and Arizona. This gritty suspended sediment scores and gouges the sides of the canyon as the river bears it along.

The river has been sculpting the canyon for perhaps as long as 25 million years. The rock here was originally part of a vast level plain. At the base of the cliffs, some of the hard black Precambrian rock is estimated to be 1.7 billion years old, the oldest exposed rock in the world. There are different kinds of rock in the walls of the canyon, and they erode at different rates. Some kinds of rock form slopes, others form cliffs and others are eventually

A FEW TIPS

♦ For recorded information about weather and road conditions, call 520-638-7888.

♦ *Do not climb in the canyon; most of the rock is too crumbly.*

♦ *Avoid overexerting yourself. The heat and high altitudes take a toll. The South Rim averages 7,000 feet. The North Rim averages more than 8,000 feet in elevation.*

washed away. This erosion fashioned the distinctive shapes of the canyon as it appears today. The bands of color visible in the rock are due to trace amounts of iron, sulfur and copper, which announce their presence in subtle tones of red, yellow, and green.

Scientists are still wrangling over several theories explaining the Grand Canyon's creation. At first, geologists believed a general rising of the land caused the Colorado River to flow more swiftly. The slow rise was concurrent with the lifting of the Rocky Mountains, which meant the river had more runoff. That also meant more carrying and cutting power. Therefore, the Canyon's walls grew higher as the river deepened its course.

A more recent theory speculates that the Colorado River once drained eastward, separated by the Kaibab Plateau from another drainage to the west. An upheaval of land along the present Arizona and New Mexico border blocked the river's flow, creating a large lake. The lake was hypothetically tapped when the western drainage eroded towards its source, and thus the period of canyon cutting commenced.

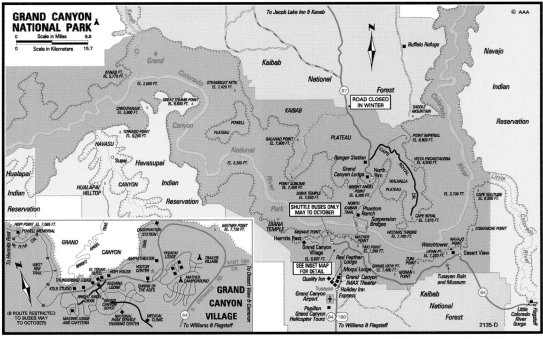

Acreage: 1,218,375 acres

In every theory advanced, the one constant is the Colorado River. It always was, and always will be the catalyst for change in the canyon. The river will continue sculpting the canyon's walls by erosion for as long as it continues to flow.

More than 4 million people visit the park every year. Most of the 1,904 square miles of the Grand Canyon National Park are maintained as a wilderness. There are three distinct sections of the park: the South Rim, the North Rim and the Inner Canyon. Each section has a different climate.

The North Rim is the coldest and wettest. It receives up to 26 inches of precipitation a year, which sustains a lush forest. The South Rim gets only 16 inches. The South Rim is the easiest to reach, and is the most visited section of the park, with more services and amenities. The North Rim offers opportunities for solitary introspection, only a few yards from motels and campgrounds.

The more adventurous visitors to the park arrange to visit the inner canyon. There are two ways to get there, under your own power or perched on the back of a sure-footed concessionaire's mule. The deeper you descend into the canyon, the hotter and drier it gets. The floor of the canyon, approximately a mile beneath the North Rim, is about 35° hotter than the temperature up above. Much of the rain that falls into the canyon evaporates before it hits the ground.

Vegetation in the three sections of the park also varies. There are blue spruce and fir forests on the North Rim, as well as oaks and Ponderosa pine. Deep in the canyon's recesses, the foliage grows sparse and shorter. Piñons and juniper growing along the cliffs give way to dry desert scrub on the canyon floor.

Two of the park's most celebrated inhabitants are the Albert squirrel and the Kaibab squirrel. The Albert squirrel lives on the North Rim. The Kaibab squirrel makes its home only on the South Rim. Both share a common ancestor, the tassel-eared squirrel. Widely separated in the vastness of the canyon habitats, over time the Albert and Kaibab squirrel cousins have evolved into two separate and distinct species.

Native Americans have lived in and around the canyon for 4,000 years or more. The first European visitor was a Spaniard. Don Lopez De Cardenas was led to the great gorge by members of the Hopi tribe in 1540. John Wesley Powell, explorer, geologist and cartographer of the Colorado River, first visited the canyon in the 1869. A large granite monument to his memory stands on West Rim Drive.

This is an extremely popular park. Do your travel planning well in advance and secure reservations as early as you can so you are not disappointed.

PLANNING YOUR VISIT

Park Open

South Rim is open year-round. North Rim is open from mid-May through late October. Peak visitation is in July but the park also gets crowded on winter holiday weekends.

Seasons

Summer temperatures on the South Rim are relatively pleasant, between 50° and 80°. Thunderstorms are frequent. Inner canyon temperatures are extreme, with daytime highs near the river often above 100°. North Rim temperatures are 5° to 10° degrees cooler than on the South Rim. In winter, South Rim has extremely variable weather. Expect snow, icy roads and possible road closures. Canyon views may be temporarily obscured by heavy snow or fog. Storms can strike from September through May, spring and fall. Overall, weather is extremely unpredictable.

Entrance Fees

Fee per vehicle $10
Fee per individual $4
   Valid for 7 days.

Permits and Licenses

Permits are required for stock use, river running and overnight backcountry camping. Fishing licenses and trout stamps are available at Babbitt's Store in Grand Canyon Village and at Marble Canyon Lodge at Lee's Ferry. Vehicles are restricted to established roads.

Access and Transportation

Grand Canyon National Park is in northeastern Arizona, 82 miles from Flagstaff via Highway 180.

South Rim: Take Highway 64 for 60 miles north of Williams or 57 miles west of Cameron.

North Rim: Take Highway 67 for 45 miles south of Jacob's Lake.

Amtrak service is available to Flagstaff, with connecting bus service to the canyon. Grand Canyon Railway offers daily train service from Williams, Arizona to Grand Canyon Village.

Greyhound provides bus service to Flagstaff. Nava-Hopi Bus Lines offers transportation between Flagstaff and the South Rim. Call 602-774-5003.

Commercial airlines serve Phoenix, Flagstaff and Las Vegas. There is limited air service into Grand Canyon airport from Las Vegas and elsewhere. Rental cars are available at all airports.

In-Park Transportation

A van shuttles between South Rim and North Rim. Contact Trans-Canyon Van Service, 602-638-2820. A hiker's shuttle is also available to the South Kaibab Trailhead from the Backcountry Reservations Office and from Bright Angel Lodge.

Special Needs

Accessibility varies from facility to facility. An accessibility guide is available at the visitor center or by writing to headquarters. There is accessible parking. Free wheelchairs may be borrowed from the visitor centers.

Amenities

Scenic drives ♦ Mule trips ♦ Hiking
♦ Colorado River rafting ♦ Bus tours
♦ Air tours ♦ Bicycling ♦ Fishing ♦ Ranger-led programs

Travel Advisory

Use caution near the rims, guardrails are only present at some points. Be prepared for temperature extremes if visiting the inner canyon.

Emergency Information

First aid is available at the information desk in Grand Lodge (North Rim) or at the Grand Canyon Clinic on Center Road, between the South Entrance Station and Grand Canyon Village. The hospital closest to South Rim is 90 miles away in Flagstaff. The hospital closest to North Rim is 81 miles away in Kanab, Utah.

Visitor and Information Centers

Park headquarters is at the South Rim at the east end of Grand Canyon Village. It provides orientation programs, exhibits and books and slides. At North Rim, the visitor center is in the lobby of the Grand Canyon Lodge.

Campgrounds

Camp only in the established campgrounds in developed areas. There is a dump station in summer, adjacent to Mather and Trailer Village.

South Rim:

Mather Campground is open in summer and fall and sites are available on a first-come, first-served basis. For more information call 800-365-2267.

Trailer Village at Grand Canyon Village provides RV sites with hookups. Camping fee is $16 a night. For more information call 800-365-2267.

Desert View Campground is 26 miles east of Grand Canyon Village. It is open mid-May through mid-October and sites are available on a first-come, first-served basis for $10 a night.

North Rim:

North Rim Campground is one half mile from the rim. The campground is open in summer. For more information, call 800-365-2267.

Backcountry camping is allowed, but you can wait a year since the number of permits is limited. Call the Backcountry Reservations Office to make arrangements well in advance.

Cabins, Lodges and Hotels

South Rim:

For reservations at any of the lodges on the South Rim, contact Grand Canyon National Park Lodges, PO Box 699, Grand Canyon, AZ 86023, or call 602-638-2401. All are in the vicinity of Grand Canyon Village, which also contains shops and services.

Bright Angel Lodge. Located on the rim.

El Tovar Hotel. Located on the rim.

Kachina Lodge. Located on the rim.

Thunderbird Lodge. Located on the rim.

Maswik Lodge. Located at the west end of the village.

Yavapai Lodge. Located near Mather Center.

North Rim:

Grand Canyon Lodge. The lodge is open from mid-May through mid-October. For reservations contact TW Recreational Services, Box 400, Cedar City, UT, 84720, or call 801-586-7686.

Canyon Bottom:

Phantom Ranch. The ranch is accessible only on foot or by mule. Overnight dormitory and cabin space is available. Breakfast, lunch and dinner are served. For reservations, contact Grand Canyon National Park Lodges, PO Box 699, Grand Canyon, AZ 86023, or call 602-638-2401.

Restaurants

South Rim:

Babbitt's Delicatessen. Across from the visitor center, it is open from 8 a.m. to 6 p.m.

Bright Angel Restaurant. It is open from 6:30 a.m. to 10 p.m. The lounge is open from 11 a.m. to 12:30 a.m.

Arizona Steakhouse. On the rim near Bright Angel Lodge, it is open from 5 p.m. to 10 p.m.

El Tovar Dining Room. Offering a view of the canyon, this restaurant is open for breakfast, lunch and dinner.

Hermit's Rest Fountain. At the end of the West Rim Drive, this restaurant is open from 9 a.m. to 4:30 p.m.

Maswik Cafeteria. This cafeteria is open from 6 a.m. to 10 p.m. The lounge is open from 11 a.m. to 1 a.m.

Yavapai Cafeteria. Across from the visitor center, this cafeteria is open from 6 a.m. to 10 p.m. with dancing and cocktails from 9:30 p.m. to 12:30 a.m.

North Rim:

Grand Canyon Lodge. Open from mid-May through mid-October, they have a dining room and cafeteria.

Things to Do and See

Mule Trips. Two-day mule trips from the South Rim to the Colorado River at the canyon bottom are available year-round.

Lodge. A one day trip which goes part way to the river is also offered. Call 602-638-2401. Overnight riders stay and eat at the Phantom Ranch. Mule trips are often booked a year in advance. There are size and weight restrictions on prospective riders. Contact the  park superintendent for information. In summer, one day and half day trips from the North Rim are also offered, but they do not go all the way down to the river. Call 602-638-2292 in summer, or 801-679-8665 during the rest of the year.

Whitewater Trips. Commercial whitewater trips through the Grand Canyon begin at Lee's Ferry, six miles from Marble Canyon, Arizona. These trips vary from three to 18 days in length. You must make reservations well in advance. Trips are available March through November. Call 602-638-7888. Your can also contact the River Permits Office, Grand Canyon National Park, PO Box 129, Grand Canyon AZ. 86023.

Scenic Bus Tours. Tours of the South Rim are available through Grand Canyon National Park Lodge. Visitors arriving in the park should proceed to the Bright Angel Lodge transportation desk to make arrangements. A variety of different tours is available throughout the year. Call 602-638-2401 for more information.

Flightseeing. Air Tours depart from Tusayan, Grand Canyon Airport and Las Vegas. For a list of air tour operators, write Grand Canyon Chamber of Commerce, PO Box 3007, Grand Canyon, AZ. 86023

Scenic Drives. Many scenic overlooks are convenient from the paved road along the South Rim. The park shuttle bus replaces private vehicles during the summer months on part of the road.

Museums. The Yavapai Museum is a quarter mile east of the visitors center. It features exhibits illustrating the geological history of the canyon. A splendid panorama of the canyon is visible through the museum's large windows. The Tusayan Museum, three miles west of Desert View, offers a look at Anasazi life at the Grand Canyon almost a thousand years ago. There is a self-guided trail winding through the adjoining Anasazi ruins.

Hiking. The trails range from easy walks to strenuous treks. Summer hiking is discouraged because of the extreme heat. The most popular, but often crowded trail, is Bright Angel Trail, a four-mile hike descending from the South Rim into the canyon. Transept Canyon Trail, is a mile hike along the North Rim.

Near Grand Canyon National Park

Navaho National Monument, Tonalea, Arizona. The monument is located off US 160, about 90 miles northeast of the Grand Canyon. Here Anasazi Native Americans farmed canyon bottomlands and built stone dwellings in the cliffs. Today this land is part of the Navaho Indian Reservation. This 360-acre park has 30 campsites. Visitors can picnic, hike, ride and tour and Keet Seel ruins. The visitor center is open year-round. Campsites are available from mid-April to mid-October. For more information call 520-672-2366.

For More Information

Trip Planner
Grand Canyon National Park
PO Box 129
Grand Canyon, AZ 86023
Tel. 602-638-7888

GRAND TETON NATIONAL PARK

Wyoming ♦ Established 1929

The drama of the Teton Range comes not from its height, but because the sharp walls of the mountains rise directly from the valley floor. There are no foothills. On clear day, the Tetons are twice as dazzling. They shimmer magnificently in the reflection of the park's lakes and the winding Snake River. The waters, wildflowers and clear, blue, Wyoming skies make many swear this is the most beautiful spot in the United States.

Geologically speaking, the Tetons are youngsters. The range is less than nine million years old, making it the newest addition to the Rocky Mountain system. Grand Teton is more than a mile above the valley of Jackson Hole. Twelve other peaks in the range reach 12,000 feet or higher.

The Snake River, once called the Mad River by early trappers and settlers, swells with meltwater. The river supports a variety of waterfowl, woodland birds and other animals. Bald eagles and ospreys nest along its banks, a space they share with otters. Beaver dams create ponds for Canada geese and mallards. Each spring, great blue heron return to a rookery at Oxbow Bend. Trumpeter swans, the largest North American waterfowl, are protected here.

Along the river's banks grow cottonwood, spruce, aspen and the low-growing willow that is part of the moose diet. The largest remaining elk herd in the world a smaller bison herd, live at Grand Teton during the summer. Deer, black bear and grizzlies wander the pine forests and canyons.

Wildflowers bloom on the valley floor in spring through summer. Sagebrush, buttercups, yellowbells and steer's head appear first. As summer deepens so do the colors of the valley, with meadows of scarlet gilia, balsamroot, lupine, larkspur and the alpine forget-me-not that is the official park flower. Autumn visits bring bonuses — fall foliage and a greater chance of seeing and hearing the bull elk.

People have lived on this land for at least 11,000 years, shifting elevation with the seasons. Settlements of Blackfoot,

A Few Tips

♦ *You may encounter grizzly and black bears in the backcountry. Do not feed any animals in the park.*
♦ *Climbers must sign in at the Jenny Lake Ranger Station before and after each climb.*
♦ *In summer, lodging and camping facilities at Grand Teton and Yellowstone fill up by early afternoon. Cars and sports equipment may be impossible to rent. Make reservations for dining to avoid waits of an hour or more.*
♦ *The park's waters are cold and there are no swimming areas with lifeguards. Only experienced floaters should river raft on the Snake River. Swimming in this river is not recommended.*

Crow, Gros Ventre, Shoshone and other Native Americans were scattered throughout the area. Jackson Hole was neutral ground shared by all. After the area's "discovery" by John Colter of the Lewis and Clark expedition, the area became popular with French-Canadian trappers who christened the peaks Les Trois Tetons, or The Three Breasts.

In the late 1800s, ranchers began to settle the valley with irrigation systems that allowed them to stay through the punishing winters. Trappers moved on from the area after the beaver population

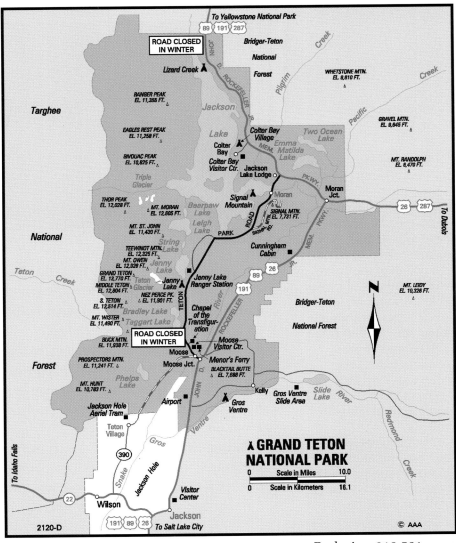

Park size: 310,521 acres

was diminished around 1840. After 1900, settlers started dude ranches; one still operates in the park today.

PLANNING YOUR VISIT

Park Open
The park is open year-round. Visitor centers are closed on Christmas Day. Peak visitation is in August.

Seasons
Winters are long and cold with an average of 16 feet of snowfall that continues as late as March. On average, three to five feet of snow stays on the ground. Blizzards may last for days. Summer days are in the 70s and 80s with cool nights in the 40s. Summer thunderstorms are common but you'll need rain gear throughout the year. Spring and fall are cooler with variable weather.

Entrance Fees
Per vehicle $20
Per individual..$4
Fees are valid for a week's admittance to Grand Teton and Yellowstone National Park.

Permits and Licenses
A Wyoming fishing license is required to fish in the park. Overnight stays in the backcountry require a free permit. You must pay for some permits for motorized and non-motorized watercraft and snowmobiles. Climbers must register with Jenny Lake Ranger Station before and after each ascent.

Access and Transportation
The park is in northwestern Wyoming, south of Yellowstone National Park and north of Jackson, Wyoming.
From Jackson. Take Highway 26/89 north for 12 miles to the park entrance.
From the North. Take Highway 89/287.
From the East. Take Highway 26/287.
The park is a six-hour drive from Salt Lake

City, Utah. Grand Teton Lodge Company runs a bus from the airport to the park from June through September. Call 307-543-2811 or 307-733-2811 for information and reservations. There is no train service into the park. The closest airport is in Jackson Hole. Rental cars are available at the airport and in Jackson.

In-Park Transportation

There is limited shuttle bus service within the park. There is a ferry across the Snake River in the summer. There is also a scenic cruise across Jenny Lake.

Special Needs

There are handicapped access restrooms, picnic areas and campsites. Most trails are rough and rocky. There are asphalt trails in the Jenny Lake area, some of which are initially accessible, but they turn to gravel. The park has a handicapped access handout available at visitor centers.

Amenities

Bus tours ◆ Museum ◆ Ferry service ◆ Equipment rental ◆ Restaurants ◆ Picnic areas ◆ River rafting ◆ Mountaineering ◆ Horseback riding ◆ Boating ◆ Fishing ◆ Snowmobiling ◆ Gas station ◆ Post office ◆ Religious services

Travel Advisory

The main park road is the only one open in winter.

Emergency Information

First aid is available at the visitor centers and ranger stations. The closest hospital is in Jackson.

Visitor and Information Centers

There are five visitor centers: Moose Visitor Center, Jenny Lake Visitor Center, Colter Bay Visitor Center (closed October to mid-May) and Flagg Ranch Information Station. The Moose Visitor Center has wildlife and geology exhibits, relief maps of the area and works by local artists. The Colter Bay Visitor Center gives audio-visual presentations and is home to the Native American Arts Museum. The centers are generally open 8 a.m. to 5 p.m. with extended hours in the summer.

Campgrounds

There are five developed campgrounds in the park. Most are open from early May to mid-September, depending on weather conditions. In summer, campsites fill up as early as 8 a.m. Reservations are required for group campsites from January through mid-May.

Gros Ventre Campground. South of Moose, it has 360 sites and a dump station.

Jenny Lake Campground. North of Moose, it has 49 sites for tents and small campers, with drinking water, flush toilets, fire pits, phones and a ranger station. It fills up early in July and August. It is open from mid-May to late September.

Signal Mountain Campground. North of Jenny Lake, it has 310 sites as well as a dump station.

Colter Bay Tent Village. North of Jackson Lake Junction, it has 310 campsites with showers and laundry facilities. The campground is open June through September. Reservations are suggested.

Lizard Creek Campground. At the north end of the park, there are 60 sites available from mid-June to late September.

There is a campground at **Flagg Ranch** on the John D. Rockefeller, Jr., Memorial Pkwy., south of Yellowstone National Park.

There are trailer villages at **Colter Bay** and **Flagg Ranch** and in **Jackson, Wyoming**. Reservations are suggested. Call 307-543-2811.

Picnic Areas

There are 11 picnic areas off main roads in the park. Camper stores include Dornan's Grocery Store (which also has a gift shop, service station and equipment rental), South Jenny Lake (which also offers a boat shuttle, cruises and a guide service), Signal Mountain, Colter Bay and Flagg Ranch (which offers float trips, snowmobile rental

and snowcoach tours in winter). Go to Jackson for supermarkets and supplies.

Cabins, Lodges and Hotels

Signal Mountain Lodge. There are log cabins (some with fireplaces), motel units and lakefront apartments on Jackson Lake. The lodge is open May through October. For reservations call 307-543-2831.

Colter Bay Cabins. These cabins are on Jackson Lake. They are open May through September. For reservations call 307-543-2811 or 307-543-2855.

Jackson Lake Lodge. The lodge and motel rooms have a swimming pool. The lodge is open June through September. For reservations call 307-543-2811.

Jenny Lake Lodge. Cabins are available in guest-ranch style. The lodge is open June through September. For reservations call 307-543-2811.

Triangle X Dude Ranch. It is 13 miles north of Moose. Guests can participate in ranch activities throughout the year. For reservations call 307-733-2183 or 800-628-9988.

Lodging is also available at Flagg Ranch (800-443-2311) and Dornan's Spur Ranch Cabins (307-733-2415).

In Jackson Hole, consider the **Inn on the Creek** or **Alpine House Bed & Breakfast,** both with double-occupancy rooms available at about $150 a night.

Restaurants

There are several restaurants in the park offering everything from limited buffets to fine dining. Restaurants are located at the Jenny Lake Lodge, Signal Mountain Lodge, Jackson Lake Lodge and Flagg Ranch. There are snack bars at Signal Mountain Lodge, Jackson Lake Lodge, Colter Bay and Flagg Ranch.

Colter Bay Chuckwagon Restaurant. They serve breakfast, lunch and dinner from May through September.

Leek's Restaurant/Marina. They serve light meals and snacks from June through September.

Aspens Dining Room and Coffee Shop. Located in Signal Mountain Lodge, they serve meals and cocktails from May through October.

Colter Bay Grill. They serve meals from June through early September.

John Colter Bar and Colter Bay. They are a cocktail lounge and are open May through September.

Moose Snack Bar. The snack bar is open June through early September.

Mural Room, Pioneer Room and Blue Heron Lodge. Located at Jackson Lake Lodge, they offer meals, cocktails and entertainment from June through September.

Jenny Lake Lodge. This dining room offers meals from June through September. Reservations are suggested. Call 307-733-4647.

Dornan's Chuckwagon. Located at Moose, Dornan's offer meals, sandwiches and barbecue from June through early September.

Dornan's Moose Bar. This cocktail lounge has a view deck that is open all year.

Gross Ventre Slide Inn. This is a snack and gift shop.

Restaurants popular with the locals include **Sugarfoot Café, Snake River Grill** and **Blue Lion** in Jackson Hole.

THINGS TO DO AND SEE

Bus Tours. A bus tour of the park runs from June through mid-September. Call 307-733-2811 for schedules and fees.

Boat Tours. Scenic cruises travel on Jenny Lake and Jackson Lake. Call Teton Boating Company (307-733-2703) for information about the Jenny Lake Cruise and Colter Bay Marina (307-543-2811) for information about the Lake Jackson cruise.

Indian Life Displays and Exhibits. Bay Visitor Center is home to the Native American Arts Museum with displays of 19th century Indian life, especially of the Plains tribe. There are also nature programs and presentations in the amphitheater. During July and August, Native American dances are performed at Jackson Lake Lodge. Check the lodge for schedules and admission price.

Chapel of the Transfiguration. The chapel is a house of worship so please be respectful if you visit. The altar window beautifully frames the Teton peaks.

Teton Science School. The school offers workshops on wilderness craft and lore. For more information write to Teton Science School, Box 68, Kelly, WY 83011.

Ferry Rides. The Menor's Ferry Trail takes you past a pioneer cabin and country store. During a summer visit you can enjoy a ferry ride across Snake River. To reach the ferry, take Teton Park Road one mile north of Moose. A ferry boat also takes you across Jenny Lake to the trailhead at Cascade Canyon.

Scenic Drives. Two main park roads offer excellent views and opportunities for photographers. Teton Park Road skirts the eastern shore of Jackson and Jenny lakes, which reflect the peaks. Rockefeller Memorial Parkway follows Snake River and allows you to view the range as a whole. Signal Mountain Summit Road is a five-mile drive that starts just south of Signal Mountain Lodge and its campground. The road — too narrow for trailers and motor homes — winds to the top of Signal Mountain, 800 feet above the valley. At the top, enjoy a breathtaking view of Jackson Lake, Jackson Hole and the entire Teton Range. The road has some overlooks. Jenny Lake Scenic Drive starts north of Jenny Lake and continues southwest. Enjoy a great view of the Grand Teton and Mt. Owen from Cathedral Group Turnout. A mile west of Jackson Lake Junction on Teton Park Road, Jackson Lake Dam Overlook affords a view of Jackson Lake and Mount Moran.

Boating. Explore Jackson Lake in a pontoon, paddleboat, canoe or water-ski boat rented from Signal Mountain Marina. For more information call 307-543-2831. Dornan's Grocery Store also rents canoes. Motorboats are permitted on Jenny Lake, Jackson Lake and Phelps Lake, but there are some restrictions. Hand-propelled craft are permitted on Jackson, Jenny, Phelps, Emma Matilda, Two Ocean Taggard, Bradley, Bearpaw, Leigh and String Lakes. Dock at Leek's Marina, Signal Mountain Marina or Colter Bay Marina, all on Jackson Lake.

Water Sports. Sailing, windsurfing, jet skiing and water-skiing are only allowed on Jackson Lake. Floating the Snake River is only allowed in hand-propelled boats and rafts, not inner tubes. If you are on the

water in the early morning or at dusk, you may spy a moose along the river or in the meadows. Park and independent outfitters, such as Baker-Ewing (307-733-1800), offer float trips and fishing trips on Snake River. If you prefer to go it alone, rent equipment in Jackson.

Wildlife Viewing. The Willow Flats Turnout is six miles south of Colter Bay. Here you can observe birds, moose and beaver in a freshwater marsh, with Jackson Lake and the Teton Range as the background. Oxbow Bend is a bend of Snake River that attracts a variety of wildlife. There is also a good view of massive Mount Moran. Burnt Ridge and Signal Mountain offer the best vantage points to see elk. Also check the National Elk Refuge near the park's south entrance.

Fishing. There are many high mountain lakes, including large Jackson Lake and Jenny Lake. A Wyoming fishing license is required for fishing in the park. Licenses may be purchased in fishing stores in Jackson, Dornan's and at park marinas. Check at the visitor centers for special regulations and restrictions.

Hiking. There are 200 miles of trails in the park and parkway range shared by hikers and horses. Easier trails are on the valley floor with the trails growing more strenuous as you climb into the mountains. Rangers at the visitor center can recommend hikes and trail guides. Teton Crest Trail is a 4000 foot climb from the valley floor to major peaks. Paintbrush Canyon Trail offers a view of wildflowers. High country trails are open by late June.

South Jenny Lake. Carved by glaciers, Jenny Lake is nestled at the base of the towering Tetons. You can circle the lake on a six-mile hiking trail. During summer, shuttle boats travel to the west shore of the lake and trails to Hidden Falls, Inspiration Point and Cascade Canyon. Park rangers recommend visiting early or late in the day to avoid crowds on the trail and parking problems.

Bicycling. Cyclists will delight in the wide shoulders and superb views offered by Teton Park Road. The Antelope Flats – Kelly Loop is popular with cyclists. Bicycles are not allowed on trails or backcountry. Bikes can be rented and repaired at Dornan's in Moose from mid-May to mid-September. Call 307-733-3314.

Horseback Riding. Trail rides depart from Colter Bay Village Corral from mid-May through September (307-543-2811) and Jackson Lake Lodge Corral from mid-June through mid-September (307-543-2811). Teton Trail Rides on Jenny Lake also rents horses from June through September (307-733-2108).

Mountaineering. There are 16 routes leading to the summit. Jackson Hole Mountain Guides & Climbing School offers a variety of classes at different levels, including mountaineering, rock climbing and ski mountaineering training. Classes are small and guides are experts on the Tetons. Beginners should consider the four-day climber course that features an ascent of the Grand Teton summit. For more information call 800-239-7642.

Skiing and Snowshoeing. Jackson Hole's trails, wide bowls, alpine meadows and steep mountain passes are enjoyed by skiers and snowmobilers. Experienced trail-runners who are in great shape may choose the high country in the Gros Ventre region and tackle the cross-country run to Yellowstone National Park. Moose Visitor Center distributes a map of ski trails and snowmobile routes.

Snowmobiling. Snowmobiles can be rented outside the park. Togwotee Mountain Lodge, high in the pines northeast of Jackson Hole, is the departure point for snowmobile trips. There is also great sledding and a good chance to view bison and elk. For more information call 307-543-2847. Another snowmobile trip from this lodge is offered by Sno-World Snow Tours. Contact them at 800-676-5801.

Near Grand Teton National Park

John D. Rockefeller, Jr., Memorial Parkway. This 23,000-acre parkway links Grand Teton and Yellowstone National Parks. Snow coach rides into Yellowstone National Park run from mid-December to mid-March. Other visitor activities include float trips, cross-country skiing, snowmobiling, backcountry camping and fishing. Some activities, such as boating and snowmobiling, require permits, licenses or registration. For more information call 307-739-3300.

For More Information

Superintendent
Grand Teton National Park
PO Drawer 170
Moose, WY 83012
Tel. 307-739-3300

GREAT BASIN NATIONAL PARK

Nevada ♦ **Established 1986**

Great Basin National Park bears little resemblance to the barren desert many expect to find in Nevada. The park encompasses aspen, spruce and pine groves as well as 13 looming peaks of the southern Snake Range. Visitors will also discover mountain streams, lakes and Lehman Cave, a huge limestone cavern system. The park's highest point is Wheeler Peak, its summit at 13,063 feet.

The Great Basin, for which the park is named, stretches from the Wasatch Mountains in Utah to the Sierra Nevada in California. It is a sagebrush covered valley with narrow peaks and no outlet to the sea. This desert area was formed 10,000 years ago when the climate warmed. Lakes dried up and alpine glaciers at the tops of the mountains melted.

Dating back nearly that far is the park's bristlecone pine forest, with many trees at the highest elevations. Because of the high resin content in the wood, these trees do not rot, they erode. Scientists have found a piece of bristlecone wood they believe is 9000 years old.

The park has been inhabited continuously. The Fremont peoples hunted and farmed here from A.D. 1100 to A.D. 1300. You may spot some of their rock art. The Shoshone and Paiute peoples settled near streams in the park. They relied on the piñon nut for survival. Some of their descendants remain in this area today.

The Lehman Cave, which attracts many visitors, is actually a single cavern that extends a quarter-mile into the limestone and low-grade marble at the base of the Snake Range. It was discovered in the late 1800s by Absalom Lehman, a rancher and miner. The cavern is one of the most richly decorated caves in the country.

Tour the cave to wonder at its stalactites, stalagmites, columns, draperies and flowstone. The delicate designs are the result of rainwater finding its way below the earth's surface to the limestone, which it dissolved. Lehman is most famous for the rare and mysterious structures called shields. Shields are two roughly circular halves that suggest flattened clamshells. No one is sure how they are formed.

PLANNING YOUR VISIT

Park Open
The park is open year-round. The visitor center is closed on major holidays. Because this is a mountain park, snow does close roads and trails. If you want to visit the high country, come during the summer when there are also more frequent cave tours. Peak visitation is in July.

Seasons
This is an arid region and the humidity averages 10 percent year-round. Winters are cool. Average daytime temperatures are 25° to 30°. Nighttime temperatures drop to 5°–10°. At higher elevation expect much colder temperatures. Summers are mild. Average daytime temperatures range from 85°–95° with evening lows in the 40s. Caves remain a constant 50°.

Entrance Fees
There are no entrance fees at this time.

Permits and Licenses
A Nevada fishing license and trout stamp is required to fish the streams. Permits from the visitor center are required for the cave tours. Backcountry hikers and campers are encouraged to register with the visitor centers for their own safety, but this is voluntary.

Access and Transportation
Park headquarters is 10 miles from U.S. 6-50 near the Nevada-Utah border.

From Las Vegas. Take U.S. 93 north for 290 miles, then go east on U.S. 6-50 for 30 miles and follow signs to the park entrance. The park is five miles west of Baker on Nevada Highway 488 or 70 miles east of Ely on U.S. 6-50. There is a bus from Reno to Ely once a week. Trains serve Reno, Las Vegas and Salt Lake City. The park is 234 miles from Salt Lake City and 385 miles from Reno. The closest airports are in Reno, Las Vegas and Salt Lake City. There is a small airport in Ely. Rental cars are available from the major airports. Vehicles must use designated roads and stay off the trails.

Special Needs

Three of the four developed campgrounds have wheelchair accessible sites. The visitor center and first room in Lehman Cave are wheelchair accessible. Accessible campsites may be reserved.

Amenities

Picnic areas ◆ Scenic overlooks ◆ Junior ranger programs ◆ Guided cave tours

Travel Advisory

Wheeler Peak Scenic Drive closes progressively with changes in weather. (It is always open for three miles to Upper

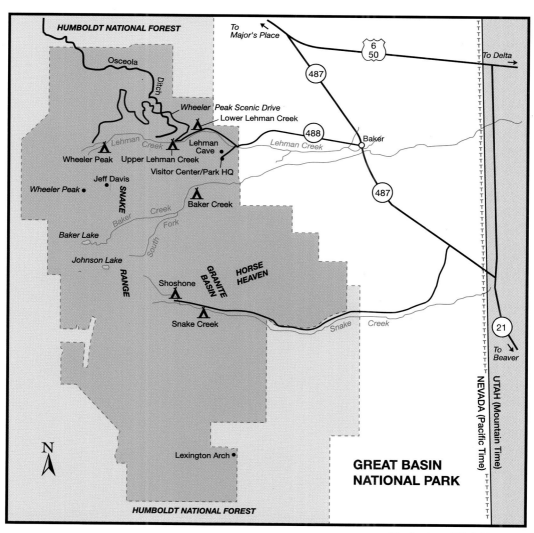

Park size: 77,100 acres

Lehman Campgrounds.) This scenic drive is not recommended for large RVs or buses.

Emergency Information

First aid is available in the park. The closest hospital is in Ely.

Visitor and Information Center

The visitor center has a slide show and exhibits. There is a bookstore in the visitor center. The center has a parking area for buses and RVs.

Campgrounds

There are four developed campsites that provide water in summer, restrooms, fire rings, tent pads and picnic tables. The Upper and Lower Lehman Creek Campgrounds are closest to the visitor center and fill up fast. Campfires are permitted in designated fireplaces only. There is a dump station near the visitor center.

Lower Lehman Creek Campground. It has 11 sites. It is open all year. The camping fee is $5 a night.

Wheeler Peak Campground. It has 37 sites. It is open only in the summer. Camping is $5 a night. This campgrounds is closest to the trails that lead to Wheeler Peak.

Upper Lehman Creek Campgrounds. It has 24 sites but is open only in summer. The camping fee is $5 a night.

Baker Creek Campground. It has 32 sites but is open only in summer. Water must be treated. Camping is $5 a night.

Primitive sites are located along Strawberry Creek and Snake Creek Roads. These have tables and pit toilets but no water. These campsites are open as snow permits.

Picnic Areas

There are two picnic areas off the main road. Campfires are permitted only in designated fireplaces. There is a dump station near the visitor center. You can buy food and supplies in nearby Baker.

Cabins, Lodges and Hotels

There are no lodges in the park but there are accommodations in Baker, Ely and Delta, Utah, 100 miles to the east.

Restaurants

Lehman Cave Café. Located at the visitor center, the cafe is open from April to October. The nearby city of Baker has a grocery store, gas station and restaurants.

THINGS TO DO AND SEE

Cave Tours. The 90-minute tours are led by rangers. They cost $4 for adults and $3 for children 6–15. Children five and under are free. Children 16 and under must be accompanied by an adult. Tours are limited to 30 people and fill up fast, on a first-come, first-served basis.

Rhodes Cabin. This log cabin was used by cave visitors at the turn of the century. It now features displays of pioneer life.

Osceola Ditch. Traces of this ditch, which brought water to gold miners in Osceola, can still be seen.

Skiing. Backcountry skiers can follow trails through the woods.

Hiking. Cross-country hiking skills are recommended. There are some easy trails that switch back through the pines, however. The easiest trail is the visitor center Nature Trail, a quarter-mile in length, just north of the center. Baker Creek Trail runs six miles from the campgrounds to Baker Lake. The adventuresome hiker can hike Wheeler Peak, the park's highest point. An eight-mile hike up Mount Wheeler takes you to over 13,000 feet and the second-highest point in Nevada. Much of the hiking is at an elevation of 9,000 feet. The Alpine Lakes Loop and Bristlecone Pine Trails lead you past pristine, glacially carved Teresa and Stella Lakes and through an ancient forest of bristlecone pines. Trail guides are available at the visitor center. Routes typically follow ridge lines or valley bottoms.

Fishing. Trout fishing is good here. Fish for rainbow and brown trout in Baker Lake, brook trout in Johnson Lake and rainbow trout in Snake and Lehman Creeks. You must have a Nevada fishing license and trout stamp.

Scenic Drives. Stop at the overlooks on Wheeler Peak Scenic Drive for views of the Snake Range. The drive begins near the park entrance to Lehman Creek. Then it climbs the mountain up 12 miles. The road is closed above the 7,500-foot level from October through May. Wheeler Peak Scenic Drive is not recommended for large RVs or buses. All other park roads are unpaved.

For More Information

Superintendent
Great Basin National Park
Baker, NV 89311-9702
Tel. 702-234-7331

A FEW TIPS

♦ *Many park trails reach elevations of 7,000 to 12,000 feet. Do not overexert.*

♦ *Do not enter mine shafts or tunnels.*

♦ *When in the caves you should stay on the trails, watch your head and use handrails.*

GREAT SMOKY MOUNTAINS NATIONAL PARK

Tennessee ◆ *North Carolina* ◆ Established 1934

Great Smoky Mountains National Park is our most visited national park, largely because of the beauty of its highlands, the spectacular fall colors and wildflowers in the spring. There are more than 800 miles of trails to explore.

This park is a sanctuary, not just for wildlife, but for flowering plants. Ninety-five percent of the park is wooded. The park's virgin forests with old growth, rivers and streams and smoke-blue Appalachian ridges provide beautiful views in all directions. The wildflowers are worth a special visit in the spring. The park has more than 1,500 species of flowering plants, including thickets of rhododendron.

Great Smoky Mountains National Park is one of the largest protected areas in the east. It is a haven for wild boars, black bears and mountain lions.

Uplifted 225 million years ago, the Great Smoky Range is among the oldest mountains on earth. The highest peak is Clingmans Dome, which stands near the center of the park, thrusting up 6,643 feet. The Cherokee tribe lived in the mountains for hundreds of years until white settlers displaced them. Some of the log cabins and barns of early settlers have been restored and are museums dedicated to pioneer life. An 88,000-acre Cherokee reservation borders the southeast side of the park.

The evergreen forests and broadleaf trees drew logging and pulpwood companies to the park. These companies heavily logged the area, which continues to be restored.

PLANNING YOUR VISIT

Park Open

The park is open year-round. Two of the three visitor centers are open all year, except Christmas Day.

Seasons

Park elevations rise from 800 feet to well over 6000 feet. Temperatures are often 20 degrees cooler on the peaks. Precipitation averages 65 inches in the lowlands to 88 inches in the high country. Spring brings unpredictable weather. Summer is hot and humid but cooler at higher elevations. Fall has warm days and cool nights and is dry. Frosts begin in late September. Winter is moderate but at higher elevations winds can be piercingly cold.

Entrance Fees

There is no entrance fee.

Permits and Licenses

A free backcountry camping permit is required. Pick one up at a ranger station or visitor center. A Tennessee or North Carolina fishing permit is required.

A Few Tips

♦ *Stay off cliff faces and keep to the trails.*

♦ *Ticks are common in summer. Use repellent and check yourself after a hike.*

♦ *Park streams are not suitable for swimming or water sports because of the risk of flash floods, rapids and submerged debris.*

♦ *Do not approach or feed wildlife, even if the animals appear to be tame.*

♦ *Do not leave valuables, such as cameras, in your car.*

♦ *Camping is permitted only at designated sites. A fee is charged. Backcountry stays require a free permit.*

Access and Transportation

The park is in eastern Tennessee and part of North Carolina.

From Knoxville. Take U.S. 129 south to Marysville, then take U.S. 321 north to Townsend.

From Asheville. Take I-26 north to I-40 west, then take U.S. 19 south to U.S. 441 for 60 miles.

There is no train or bus service to the park. The closest major airports are in Knoxville, Tennessee and Asheville, North Carolina. Rental cars are available at the airports and in Sevierville and Gatlinburg, Tennessee.

Special Needs

Restrooms and major campgrounds are wheelchair accessible. Parking and restrooms at visitor centers, picnic areas and major campgrounds are accessible. From mid-May through mid-October you may reserve an accessible site. An audio-tape and visitor publications are available at the Sugarlands Visitor Center, which will loan cassette players. A quarter-mile nature trail south of this center is accessible. Wayside exhibits are tactile.

Amenities

Park newsletter ♦ Nature walks ♦ Picnic areas ♦ Horseback riding ♦ Camp store ♦ Exhibits of pioneer life ♦ Backcountry shelters ♦ Observation tower

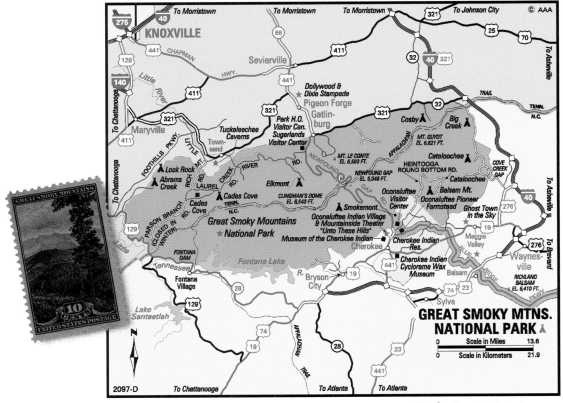

Park size: 520,269 acres

Travel Advisory

Main roads, picnic areas and camp-grounds may close during winter storms.

Emergency Information

First aid is available in the park. There are hospitals and clinics close to the park.

Visitor and Information Centers

Headquarters and Sugarlands Visitor Center are on U.S. 441, two miles south of Gatlinburg. The Oconaluftee Visitor Center is two miles north of Cherokee, North Carolina. There is an exhibit on mountain life in the 1800s here. There is also a visi-tor center in Cades Cove near Townsend, Tennessee. This center is among historic buildings that provide a glimpse into farm-ing communities of the 1800s. *Smokies Guide* is a publication available at the visitor centers.

Campgrounds

There are three developed campgrounds where you may reserve a site. There are seven additional campgrounds with sites available on a first-come, first-served basis. There is a seven-day limit between May and October and a 14-day limit between

November and April. All campgrounds have water, fire grills, tables and flush toilets. Camping fees range from $10–$15 a night.

Cades Cove and Elkmont, located in Tennessee and Smokemount in North Carolina are open year-round and do accept reservations from mid-May to the end of October. Call DESTINET at 800-365-CAMP.

Budget restrictions have forced the closure of campgrounds in the past.

Abrams Creek Campground has 16 sites for tents and trailers up to 16 feet.

Balsam Mountains Campground has 46 sites for RVs and tents.

Big Creek Campground 12 sites for tents.

Cades Cove Campground has 161 sites for RVs and tents. There is a dump station.

Cataloochee Campground has 27 sites for tents and trailers up to 16 feet.

Cosby Campground has 175 sites for RVs and tents. There is a dump station.

Deep Creek Campground has 119 sites for RVs and tents. There is a dump station.

Elkmont Campground has 220 sites for RVs and tents. There is a dump station.

Look Rock Campground has 92 sites for RVs and tents.

Smokemont Campground has 140 sites for RVs and tents. There is a dump station.

There are more than 100 backcountry sites, including some along the Appalachian Trail. Backcountry camping is free but requires a permit. Most campsites use self-registration at visitor centers or ranger stations. There are 18 shelters. Some sites require reservations in advance. Call 423-436-1231 for more information.

Picnic Areas

There are 10 picnic areas with tables next to main park roads. You can buy limited food and supplies from a campgrounds store in Cades Cove. Nearby towns also have picnic supplies and food.

Cabins, Lodges and Hotels

LeConte Lodge. This is the only lodge in the park. It is perched atop 6,593-foot Mt. LeConte, the third highest peak in the park. The lodge is accessible only on foot or horseback. It is open from mid-March to mid-November. Reservations are required. Call 423-429-5704.

Request a list of lodgings from the Gatlinburg Chamber of Commerce. Call 800-822-1998.

Restaurants

LeConte Lodge serves meals to overnight guests. There are no restaurants or snack bars in the park. There are many convenience stores and restaurants in surrounding communities.

THINGS TO DO AND SEE

Great Smoky Mountains Institute. This is a year-round education center that offers programs for all ages. Popular classes cover hiking, flora and fauna and mountain music. The Institute also gives wildlife demonstrations. A fee is charged. For more information, call 423-448-6709.

Smoky Mountain Field School. This school leads workshops, hikes and expeditions for adults. A fee is charged. For more information, call 800-284-8885.

Pioneer Exhibits. There is a collection of authentic pioneer structures throughout the park. The Mingus Mill operates from mid-April through October. The remains of Cataloochee, the biggest settlement in the Smokies includes a barn, chapel, school and houses. Take the 11-mile Cades Cove Loop to see pioneer barns, churches and homes.

Scenic Drives. There are 170 miles of paved roads and more than 100 miles of gravel roads. Backroads take you into more remote areas of the park. Newfound Gap is a scenic mountain road that crosses the crest of the Smokies, connecting Sugarlands and Ocunaluftee visitor centers. There are several scenic pullouts, such as the view from Newfound Gap, where the Appalachian Trail crosses this road. There is a seven-mile spur road here leading to Clingmans Dome, the highest point in the park. A half-mile hike from the parking lot takes you to an observation tower that offers a beautiful panoramic view.

Cycling. Bicycles are not permitted on trails but may be ridden on roads. Be warned: it's steep terrain and traffic can be heavy. The 11-mile Cades Cove Loop is popular with cyclists. You can rent a bike from the campground store in Cades Cove.

Hiking. There are 800 miles of trails including a 70-mile section of the Appalachian Trail. Treks through the Smokies reward you with lovely views of waterfalls, rivers and coves. Challenging but beautiful hikes take you through Alum Cave Bluffs, Chimney Tops, Cove Hardwoods and Snake Den Ridge. There are also less strenuous nature walks along self-guided trails.

Fishing. There are 300 trout streams in the park. They are filled with rainbow trout as well as steelhead, smallmouth and rock bass. Fontana Lake is a good spot for smallmouth, walleye and rainbow trout. You may not fish for brook trout because they are protected. Check park regulations at a ranger station or visitor center. You may fish with either a Tennessee or North Carolina license.

Horseback Riding. There are five stables in the park. Most rent horses from April through October.

Near Great Smoky Mountains National Park

The Blue Ridge Parkway. The Blue Ridge Parkway runs nearly 500 miles from the Virginia border to the park. It is the longest scenic highway in America and many motorcyclists feel the beauty of this route rivals the Pacific Coast Highway.

To plan a motorcycle trip along this route, consult this web site on the Internet: http://magenta.com:80/brmc/.

For More Information

Superintendent
Great Smoky Mountains National Park
107 Park Headquarters Road
Gatlinburg, TN 37738
Tel. 423-436-1200

GUADALUPE MOUNTAINS NATIONAL PARK

Texas   **Established 1972**

Though Guadalupe is highly evocative of the Old West, not many people outside of the Lone Star State know about this surprising, history-laden country. Perhaps Guadalupe National Park's fame has been overshadowed by the more popular Carlsbad Caverns, 50 miles to the northeast. This is ironic, for the mountains and the caverns are both the creations of the same vanished sea.

Most of the park can only be seen from the 80 miles of hiking trails. The Guadalupe Mountains are the central attraction of the park, but McKittrick Canyon is also impressive.

The centerpiece of the park is Guadalupe Peak, the highest in the Guadalupe Mountain chain. It is also the tallest in Texas, towering 8,749 feet. The Guadalupe Mountains have served as beacons for conquistadors, Apaches, homesteaders and stagecoach drivers. The mountains are really the exposed remains of one of the most extensive and ancient marine fossil reefs on the planet.

About 250 million years ago, during the Permian era, all the land in this region was submerged — covered by an enormous tropical sea — which was rich in various algae, sponges and other forms of marine life. Lime-producing marine organisms, in concert with calcium carbonate precipitated in the water, slowly built up the 400-mile long horseshoe-shaped reef, now known as Capitan Reef.

The seas retreated and the reef was completely covered in salt and sediment. Millions of years later, an uplift of the earth took place. As the Guadalupe

A FEW TIPS

♦ *Don't undertake a long hike without a topographic map, available from the visitor center.*
♦ *Wear sturdy walking shoes, a hat and sunscreen.*
♦ *Visit McKittrick Canyon from mid-October to mid-November to enjoy fall colors.*
♦ *Remember, there is no water available in most of the backcountry, so carry plenty with you — at least one gallon per person, per day.*

Mountains thrust upwards, erosion raised and exposed part of the reef. Although the greater part of the reef is still buried, paleontologists still frequently discover Permian marine fossils embedded in the exposed reef rock.

McKittrick Canyon is perhaps the best example of how diverse life can be in the canyons.

As you walk into the canyon, you will be entering Capitan Reef from the seaward side. A four-and-a-half mile, one-way trail leads up the 2,000-foot ridge, hemmed by layers of ancient reef exposed by the cutting of McKittrick Creek.

Near the mouth of the canyon you will encounter small animals and desert shrubs. Pressing on, the vegetation becomes lush, with deciduous trees, alligator juniper, wildflowers and maidenhair ferns making their appearance. Finally, at the top of the ridge, the terrain turns into a high mountain forest of ponderosa pine, southwestern pine, Douglas fir and aspen. The forest is especially luxuriant in the Bowl, a two and a half mile wide depression at the top of the mountains.

The evergreens here are vestiges of the days when the temperature was much cooler. Now these conifers can only survive at the higher elevations. Elk, mule deer, wild turkeys and black bears roam in these mountains. So do sleek mountain lions, locally known as cougars. Spotting a cougar or even hearing its cry is a fairly infrequent occurrence for visitors, but it has been known to happen. The park is also a sanctuary for more than 200 species of bird.

Anthropologists have discovered spear tips and pottery shards which suggest that the mountains have sheltered human visitors for 12,000 years or more. Those ancient people hunted camels, mammoths and other long-vanished species of the late ice age, as evidenced by prehistoric petroglyphs in the park.

This land was the home of the Mescalero Apaches. The Apaches camped near springs at the base of the mountains and climbed into the highlands to hunt and gather mescal, the succulent heart of the agave plant. At several points in the park, the blackened fire pits where they roasted the plant can still be seen just off the trails. Mescal was a staple of their diet and gave the tribe its name.

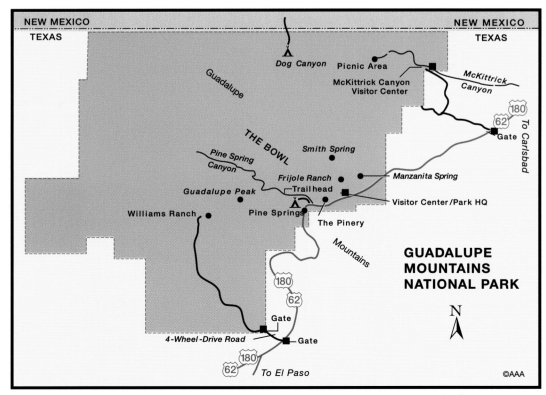

Park size: 86,416

When the Spaniards arrived in the mid-sixteenth century, they were intrigued by Apache legends of rich veins of gold running through the mountains. White settlers began encroaching upon Apache lands in the mid 1800s and the United States Army intermittently clashed with the tribe for the next 30 years.

At around the same time, stagecoaches were beginning to cross the United States on the first transcontinental mail route. John Butterfield established the Pinery Stagecoach Station within the modern park's boundaries. The Pinery Station was a place where the driver could rest and hitch up fresh horses. Eventually, Butterfield discovered an easier route to the south and abandoned the Pinery Station. But part of it is still standing today, as are several ranches of the period. Echoes of pioneer and Apache life in these mountains give the visitor a real sense of what life was like in the rugged American West.

PLANNING YOUR VISIT

Park Open

The park is open year-round. The road to McKittrick Canyon is closed at the entrance from U.S. 62-180 every night. Visitor centers are closed on Christmas Day. Peak visitation to the park is in March.

Seasons

Sudden changes in the weather are common. Blasts of wind can reach 80 miles an hour, especially in the spring. Summer brings extreme temperatures, with thunderstorms and the danger of lightning. Spring is warm, with highs in the 80s and lows in the 60s. Winter is cool and rainy, with highs in the 50s and lows in the 30s.

Entrance Fees

There are no entrance fees.

Permits and Licenses

A free permit is required for overnight backcountry camping and is available at

serve El Paso, Texas. Commercial airlines serve Carlsbad, New Mexico (50 miles from the park), El Paso, Texas (115 miles) and Midland-Odessa, Texas (170 miles). Rental cars are available at Carlsbad, New Mexico, El Paso, Texas and Midland-Odessa, Texas.

Special Needs

One RV site and the restrooms at Pine Springs campgrounds are accessible. The Pine Springs Visitor Center is fully accessible. There is a one-third mile long fully-accessible trail from the Pine Springs Visitor Center to the ruins of the Pinery Stagecoach Station. The McKittrick Canyon Visitor's Center and its restrooms are fully accessible. There are plans to make Frijole Ranch accessible. There is a bilingual park ranger on staff.

Amenities

Hiking ◆ Corrals ◆ Ranger-led activities ◆ Natural history exhibits

Travel Advisory

The Guadalupe Mountains are not suitable for rock climbing. The rock here is brittle and unsuitable even for technical climbers. Hikers and campers should watch out for cacti, rattlesnakes and desert centipedes.

Emergency Information

Limited first aid is available at Pine Springs and Dog Canyon. The closest hospital is in Carlsbad, New Mexico, 50 miles away.

Visitor and Information Centers

The park headquarters and visitor centers feature a flora and fauna exhibit, orientation slide show, and books and maps

either the visitor center at Pine Springs or the Dog Canyon ranger station. Vehicles are restricted to established roads and are prohibited from park trails. No firearms are permitted in the park. Pets are not allowed in buildings, on trails or in the backcountry. They must be leashed in the developed areas of the park. Wood or charcoal fires are not permitted in the park. Self-contained stoves may be used.

Access and Transportation

Guadalupe Mountains National Park is in west Texas, near the northern border with New Mexico. Take Highway 62-180 for 55 miles southwest of Carlsbad, New Mexico. Roads into the park are severely limited. Most of the park can only be seen from trails. Bus service is available to Pine Springs, Texas, from TNM&O Lines. For more information call 806-765-6641. Trains for sale. Pick up keys for the Williams Ranch here. McKittrick Canyon Visitor Center offers a ten-minute slide show about the canyon and outdoor exhibits. This center is closed in winter.

Campgrounds

There are two developed campgrounds available on a first-come, first-served basis for a 14-day stay.

Pine Springs Campground. Pine Springs has 20 tent sites and 18 RV sites. The campground has water, restrooms and tables. Cooking is allowed on camp stoves only. Camping fee is $7 a night.

Dog Canyon Campground. Dog Canyon has nine tent sites and five RV sites. The campground has water, restrooms and tables. Cooking is allowed on camp stoves only. Camping fee is $6 a night.

Group sites are available for $2 per person, check with the visitor center. Reservations are accepted for groups of 10 or more. There are 10 backcountry campgrounds. A free backcountry permit is required. Cook only on camp stoves.

Picnic Areas

There are several picnic areas with tables. You can buy food and supplies outside the park in Whites City or Carlsbad, New Mexico or El Paso, Texas.

Cabins, Lodges and Hotels

There is no lodging in the park. The closest accommodations are 35 miles northeast in Whites City, New Mexico.

THINGS TO DO AND SEE

Self-Guided Tours. You'll want to inspect the Pinery Stagecoach Station ruins, which are less than a 100-yard round trip from the main park road. The Williams Ranch is a historic site on the remote west side of the Guadalupes. It is reachable by four-wheel drive vehicle, but you'll need to ask for a key to the entrance gate at the park headquarters. The Frijole Ranch is a fine

example of a typical 19th century, west Texas cattle ranch.

Hiking. The park's main trailhead is located at the Pine Springs Campground. There is easy access to most trails from there. Many trails, especially those leading into the high country are steep and rough. The ascent on some of these may be as much as 3,000 feet. The trails in the canyons and other lowlands are less strenuous.

McKittrick Canyon. The canyon is a popular spot for a day hike but some parts of the canyon are off-limits. Obey the signs. Trails range up to nine miles round trip. To observe the marine fossil wealth of the park, take the canyon's Permian Reef Geology Trail.

Frijole Ranch. There is a popular two-mile round trip around the Smith and Manzanita Springs, two small oasis with freshwater springs. Trails to the Bowl, 2,500 feet above the desert floor, are 11 miles and longer, round trip.

Horseback Riding. Horses are allowed on most trails but there are no rental stables nearby. There are free corrals in the park. Horses are not allowed in backcountry overnight.

Near Guadalupe Mountains National Park

See the entry for Carlsbad Caverns National Park.

For More Information

Superintendent
Guadalupe Mountains National Park
HC 60, Box 400
Salt Flat, TX 79847
Tel. 915-828-3251

HALEAKALĀ NATIONAL PARK

Maui, Hawaii ✦ **Established 1916**

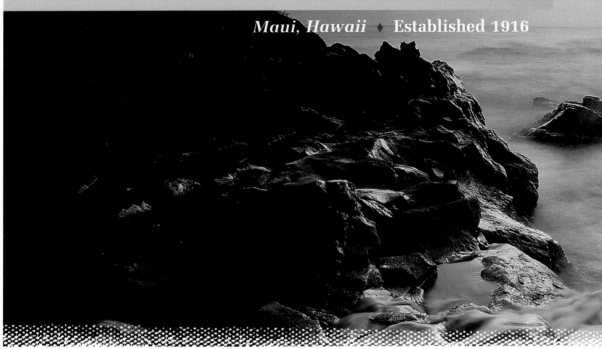

Like her sister Hawaiian islands, Maui was born in a fiery tumult of volcanic activity. A million years ago, two separate volcanoes on the ocean floor repeatedly erupted. An accretion of lava, ash and cinder eventually rose from the sea in two peaks. The peaks were linked by an isthmus and formed Maui, the "Valley Isle." Haleakalā National Park, encompassing the basin and portions of the volcano's flanks, represents the eastern bulwark of the island of Maui.

A thousand years before the arrival of Captain Cook, the volcano was a place of deep spiritual significance to the Hawaiians. Here, in ancient lore, the demi-god Maui held the sun prisoner. The island is named for him.

Haleakalā, or "The House of the Sun," is the greater of the two ancient volcanoes. The largest dormant volcano in the world, its peak towers 10,023 feet into the sky. It's crater, streaked in shades of red, yellow and black, makes the park's Crater District unique among all the wilderness areas on earth. The park encompasses starkly contrasting worlds of mountain and coast.

The 19-square mile, 2,720-foot deep crater is the park's major attraction. The road leading to the summit rises from near sea level to 10,000 feet in just 38 miles. Making this ascent will take you through several climate and vegetation zones, from humid, tropical lowlands to a sub-alpine desert resembling the surface of the moon.

Rainfall caused streams to runnel down the volcano's slopes, carving deep gouges that eventually met, forming the long erosional "crater." When a phase of volcanic activity resumed, lava funneled into these stream valleys, nearly filling them. Then, cinders,

ash and volcanic spatter were expelled from new vents in the crater, fashioning a series of symmetrical, multi-colored cones as high as 600 feet. When lava and cinder filled this water-hewn basin, it began to take on the appearance of a true volcanic crater.

In 1790, two minor lava flows along the southwest flank of the volcano burned their way down to the sea and altered Maui's coastline. Although this eruption was fairly recent when reckoned in geologic time, Haleakalā is now considered dormant. Even though no volcanic activity is visible in the crater or anywhere else on the island, seismic adjustments are still taking place beneath the volcano, deep in the earth's crust. Haleakalā could erupt again. There is simply no way to determine if or when that might happen.

Haleakalā National Park has been named a United Nations International Biosphere Reserve. In a million years of isolated evolution, plants and animals found nowhere else on earth have come forth on Maui. The

A FEW TIPS

♦ *Bring a light raincoat, sunhat and suntan lotion for hiking.*
♦ *Be prepared for weather changes.*

Golden Plover, present on the island from September to May, migrates between Maui and Alaska. The 'i'iwi bird, with it's vermilion body, black wings and tail and inch-long curved bill, is especially distinctive. Lucky visitors might also catch a glimpse of the bloodred nene, the native Hawaiian goose, which is the state bird.

Silversword is one of the more spectacular plants to be seen at Haleakalā. Its native name means "gray-gray." The silversword will grow for 5-20 years before blooming, sprouting many dagger-like silver leaves.

The abundant waters and lush greenery of the Kipahulu District are an abrupt transition from the red, brown and black hues of the crater. Sparkling pools of various sizes are linked by a small waterfall. The water is usually placid except for 'Ohe'o, a stream joining the pools, 'Ohe'o sometimes becomes a torrent of white water. At it's terminus, the streams collect together and plunge toward the ocean.

Rolling, grassy fields and forested valleys of native kukui surround the pools, as do imported plants like ginger, mango, guava and bamboo. A vast and ancient native rain forest occupies the higher elevations. Thousands of years old, it receives up to 300 inches of rainfall a year.

PLANNING YOUR VISIT

Park Open

The park is open year-round. Peak visitation is in February.

Seasons

Temperatures vary little from month to month, although winter is rainy. Weather varies at the higher elevations and can change from very hot to cold, windy and rainy in the same day. Temperatures can drop to freezing inside the crater. Snow is rare.

Entrance Fees

Per vehicle ....$4 per car per day
Tour group.................$2 per group member

Permits and Licenses

Free permits for wilderness camping are available in the summit area and at headquarters. No permit is needed in the coastal area.

Access and Transportation

Fly directly to central Maui from the mainland, or another Hawaiian Island. To reach Haleakalā Crater and summit, follow Hawaii Highways 36, 37, 377 and 378 along the well-marked 38-mile route.

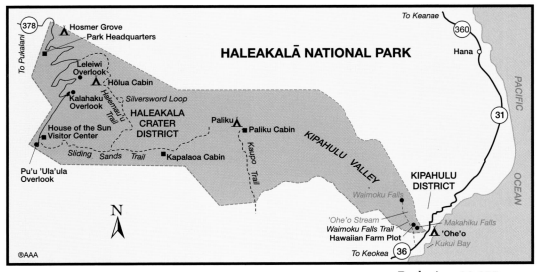

Park size: 28,655 acres

Amenities

Free nature walks
♦ Interpretive talks
♦ Hiking ♦ Horseback riding
in the crater ♦ Swimming in
'Ohe'o stream

For the 62-mile drive to Kipahulu, take Highway 36 from Kahului around the northeastern side of the island to the town of Hana. Go past Hana on Highway 31 for about seven miles. There is no public transportation on Maui, but rental cars and bus tour companies operate from Kahului.

Special Needs

There are accessible restrooms at park headquarters, the visitor center, the ranger station, the summit, Hosmer Grove and in the coastal area. There is parking and ramp access at headquarters, the visitor center and at the summit. There is ramp access in the ranger station. A free brochure is available from the Commission on the Handicapped, Old Federal Building, 335 Merchant Street, No. 215, Honolulu, HI 96813.

Travel Advisory

Pregnant women and persons with cardiac or respiratory difficulties should be forewarned that crater hikes are at high altitudes where the air is thin. Strong ocean currents make swimming in the ocean inadvisable. Be prepared for unpredictable weather. Call 808-572-7749 for recorded information on weather and roads.

Emergency Information

First aid is available in the park. The hospital nearest to the summit area is Maui Memorial Hospital. Kaiser Clinic in Kahului is 32 miles away. In the coastal area, the Hana Medical Clinic is ten miles away.

Visitor and Information Centers

The main visitor center, 11 miles from the park entrance, is open year-round. Information is also available from park

Author Mark Twain was one of the American missionaries, seafarers and journalists to visit Haleakalā in the mid-1800s. The natural grandeur he saw there remained with him for the rest of his life. In 1881 he wrote to a friend, "If the house would burn down we would pack up the cubs and fly to the isle of the blest and shut ourselves up in the healing solitudes of the eroded valley of Haleakalā and get a good rest…"

headquarters, one mile from the park entrance. Rangers provide information year around in the Kipahulu- 'Ohe'o Stream area. Call 808-248-8260.

Campgrounds

Only tent camping is allowed at Hōlua and Palikū campsites. Required free permits are issued at park headquarters on a first-come, first-served basis. There are three small primitive cabins reachable by trail only. Each contains 12 bunks and minimum equipment. Written reservation requests must be received before the first of the month, three months prior to desired stay. Assignments are made by lottery and you must give an alternate date.

There are two drive-in campgrounds available, both with a three-day limit. Hosmer Grove and 'O'heo are open all year, first-come, first-served. There are no fees, no showers, tent and RV sites and no hookups.

Cabins, Hotels and Lodges

There is no food or lodging available within the park. There are various hotels and restaurants in nearby Hana and Kahului.

THINGS TO DO AND SEE

Guided Saddle Tours. Pony Express runs guided saddle tours into the crater. Call 808-667-2200 for reservations.

Scenic Drive. Take the scenic drive leading to the summit. Scenic overlooks with orientation panels and exhibits are dotted along the road. There is a separate road with many scenic vistas, outside the park around East Maui to the Kipahulu District.

Whale Watching. Investigate one of the commercial whale watching tours available in Hana during mid-December through mid-April. The waters between Maui, Molakai, Kahoolawe and Lani are the birthing and nursing grounds for magnificent humpback whales.

Exhibits. Linger in the House of the Sun Visitor's Center on the crater's rim for exhibits and talks about the geology, ecology and archaeology of the park.

Near Haleakalā National Park

Waianapanapa State Park. Low volcanic cliffs and a native pandanus forest line the coast in this remote, rugged 120-acre park. There is a large seabird colony and an ancient coastal hiking trail. Enjoy the fishing, swimming and picnic areas. There is one campground with 12 cabins. Waianapanapa State Park is about 35 miles from Haleakalā off the Hana Highway, Hawaii 360. Call 808-244-4354 for more information.

Iao Valley State Park. Spiky moss-covered cliffs surround the cool and verdant Iao Valley, a sacred site to the people of Maui. In this jewel-like six-acre park, there are pools for swimming, hiking trails and an observation pavilion. The

park is 40 miles from Haleakalā, on Iao Valley Road off Hana Highway (also called Hawaii Hwy. 30). For more information call 808-244-4354.

For More Information

Headquarters
Haleakalā National Park
PO Box 369
Makawao, HI 96768
Tel. 808-572-9306

HAWAII VOLCANOES NATIONAL PARK

Hawaii ♦ **Established 1916**

Thirty miles southwest of Hilo on the island of Hawaii, Hawaii Volcanoes National Park is the site of two of the world's most spectacularly active volcanoes. All of Kilauea and a portion of the flank and summit of Mauna Loa are within the park's boundaries.

These are young volcanoes, perhaps thrust up from the earth's crust as recently as one million years ago. Kilauea, 4,090 feet high and still rising, sits adjacent to the southeastern slope of the older and larger Mauna Loa.

The summit of Mauna Loa stands some 13,680 feet above sea level. More than 10,000 cubic miles in volume, Mauna Loa's gently sloping bulk makes it the earth's most massive single mountain. If measured from its base, some 18,000 feet below sea level, Mauna Loa would handily exceed Mt. Everest in height. Its Hawaiian name means "Long Mountain."

Kilauea's name means "much spewing," a description it has more than lived up to,

erupting more than fifty times since 1980. Repeated eruptions between 1983 and 1985 provided awesome views of nature's wrath and did extensive damage along the park's eastern boundary. As it destroyed, it also created. A new cone over 700 feet tall rose. In 1989, Kilauea swept away the Wahaula Visitor Center in a torrent of molten rock.

Mauna Loa has been less dramatic, but has demonstrated more sustained power. Its lava flow covers more than 2,000 square miles of the Big Island. Erupting in 1949, it

steadily spewed smoke and lava for five continuous months. In 1950, Mauna Loa produced one of the most copious lava flows ever recorded: over 600 million cubic yards of lava within 23 days. On July 5th, 1975, Mauna Loa erupted again, with a six-mile sheet of fire at the Mokuaweoweo Crater, sending a twin-forked lava flow from Pohaku Hanalei and enveloping the upper portion of the summit trail. Earthquakes at the rate of one or two a minute rattled the big island for five days. In 1984, Mauna Loa erupted for 21 consecutive days.

As active as Kilauea and Mauna Loa have been, their eruptions are characteristically more of a controlled release of energy than a violent explosion. Consequently, very few lives have been lost. No one should be afraid to visit the park. Your chances of being surprised by a sudden eruption are almost nil.

Geological upheaval has made Hawaii Volcanoes

A Few Tips

♦ *Be prepared for intense sunlight.*
♦ *Persons with heart or respiratory problems should avoid sulfur fumes.*
♦ *Stay on marked trails; vegetation may conceal unstable, thin-crusted lava.*
♦ *Coastline collapse can occur suddenly. Do not go beyond barriers.*
♦ *Strong winds and unpredictable surf make swimming along the coast inadvisable.*

National Park a unique natural laboratory. In Mauna Loa's rugged high altitude wilderness area, the visitor can inspect cinder cones, gaping chasms and barren lava wrought into fantastic shapes.

On Kilauea's more accessible slopes, patches of vegetation thrive amid lava deposits. Here, a forest can be observed in all of its formative stages, from early regrowth lichens and ferns to dense groves of mature trees. Nearby, a forest trail reveals devastation dating back to an eruption in 1959.

On the hot, dry, southwestern slope of Kilauea, the Kau Desert resembles the surface of Mars. Visitors can peer across the dramatic Kilauea caldera, the great depression that marks the volcanic summit, or walk through the Thurston Lava Tube, a natural tunnel in the mountain formed when the exterior of a lava flow cooled to a crust while the still molten interior lava continued to flow.

Many varieties of plant and animal life have evolved on the isolated Hawaiian islands. Because of the volatile manner of the island's birth, each of its profusion of life forms had to find their way there on winds, currents, or as seeds carried by birds.

The ancient Polynesians, who arrived 1,500 years ago, brought domestic pigs, goats and chickens with them. They also imported plants such coconuts, bananas, ginger, mango, cassava and bamboo. In doing so, they unwittingly began a struggle for survival between delicate native plant-life and the plants and animals they introduced.

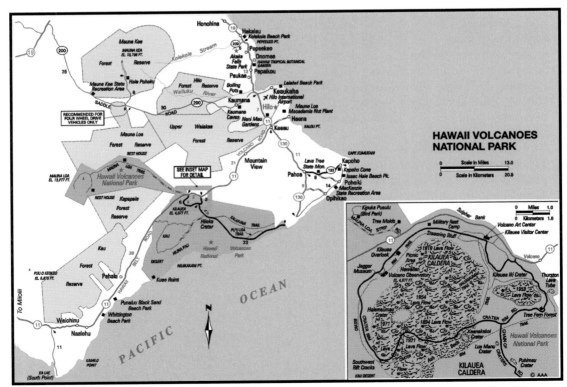

Park size: 229,177 acres

The park also includes the ruins of the 13th century Temple of Wahaula Heiau, the red-mouthed God, making this site one of Hawaii's most sacred places.

Today, Hawaii Volcanoes National Park is a unique laboratory and a preserve for rare plants and animals. The park has been named a United Nations International Biosphere Reserve and a World Heritage Site.

PLANNING YOUR VISIT

Park Open

The park is open year-round.

Seasons

In semi-tropical Hawaii there is little seasonal variation. Temperatures at the higher elevations of the park are often cool and precipitation is sudden and frequent. Peak visitation is in February.

Entrance Fees

Per vehicle..$10
Per individual $5
  Fees are valid for seven days.

Permits and Licenses

Permits are required for all overnight backcountry trips and are available from the visitor center.

Access and Transportation

The park is 30 miles southwest of Hilo, or 95 miles southeast of Kailua-Kona off Highway 11. The closest airport is in Hilo. Buses serve Hilo. There is no train service on the island. Rental cars are available at Hilo.

Special Needs

The Visitor Center, Jaggar Museum and Volcano Art Center are accessible to people in wheelchairs with some assistance. One trail and many scenic overlooks along Crater Rim Drive are also accessible. A free brochure about visiting the Big Island is available from the Commission on the Handicapped, Old Federal Building, 335 Merchant Street, No. 215, Honolulu, HI 96813.

Amenities

Nature walks ♦ Slide shows and exhibits on volcanoes ♦ Hiking ♦ Backcountry fishing ♦ Art center

Travel Advisory

Volcanic fumes in some areas of the park may present a health hazard to infants, young children, pregnant women and persons with cardiac or respiratory problems.

Altitude sickness is common when hiking at high altitudes. Pace yourself. Stay on the

trails. There are many deep cracks hidden by vegetation on the surface of Kilauea. Recent lava flow areas are thin-crusted and collapse easily. The Chain of Craters Road is closed by lava flows at its eastern end, beyond Kamoamoa Campground.

Emergency Information

First aid is available in the park. The nearest hospital is in Hilo. For eruption bulletins call 808-967-7977.

Visitor and Information Centers

The Kilauea Visitor Center is a quarter-mile from the park entrance, just off Highway 11 on Crater Rim Drive. The Thomas A. Jaggar Museum is also on Crater Rim Drive, three miles from the park entrance. Both facilities are open all year.

Campgrounds

Three campgrounds, Kamoamoa, Kipuka Nene and Namakani Paio, are open year-round. Reservations are on a first-come, first-served basis for a limit of seven days. There are no fees. These are tent sites only with no showers.

Two cabins on the Mauna Loa Trail and one at Kaipuka Pepeiao are available free of charge, on a first-come, first-served basis. Visitors must register at the park headquarters.

Picnic Areas

There are two picnic areas. The Crater Rim Road site has a table. The other spot is near Bird Park.

Cabins, Lodges and Hotels

There is a hotel and cabins in the park. The historic Volcano House is on Crater Rim Drive. For reservation information, call 808-967-7312. There are ten Namakani Paio cabins off of Highway 11. For information about the cabins and nearby accommodations, please call the Hilo Chamber of Commerce at 808-935-7178.

Restaurants

There is a diner in the park and a restaurant in Volcano House.

MADAME PELE, HAWAII'S FIRE GODDESS

The summit of Kilauea is considered the sacred home of Madame Pele, the goddess of fire. Daughter of the earth and sky, Pele fled from her cruel older sister, the goddess of the sea, taking refuge in the heart of the volcano. She is revered by Hawaiians to this day. Offerings of food, flowers and liquor are frequently left for her at the summit.

A word of warning: Pele takes a dim view of tourists who steal lava or pumice souvenirs from her mountain. Hawaiian folklore holds that she punishes such transgressors with bad luck. Park rangers will tell you Pele's reach extends to the mainland and beyond. Every day they receive boxes of purloined souvenirs in the mail, along with letters describing the revenge Pele has exacted. The sadder but wiser souvenir-hunters plead with park officials to return the souvenirs to Madame Pele's custody, with heartfelt apologies.

THINGS TO DO AND SEE

Thomas A. Jagger Museum. The museum exhibits maps, models and drawings highlighting the history of the park and volcanic and seismic occurrences.

The Volcano Art Center. The center, housed in the historic 1877 Volcano House, features a gallery of paintings, sculpture and workshops.

Near Hawaii Volcanoes National Park

The Mauna Kea Observatory. The observatory is located about 55 miles from Hilo off Hawaii Highway 200. Located on the world's highest island mountain and open year-round, Mauna Kea is one of the world's leading astronomical centers. Six nations maintain telescopes on this dormant 13,796-foot high volcano summit. A visitor center at 9,200 feet offers thrilling astronomical displays and a stargazing program on Friday nights.

Akaka Falls State Park. This 65-acre park is the site of the splendid 442-foot Akaka Falls. A paved, self-guided footpath takes visitors through a lush jungle with many scenic overlooks. The park is located 15 miles north of Hilo, on Hawaii Highway 220. Call 808-961-7200.

For More Information

Headquarters
Hawaii Volcanoes National Park
Hilo, HI 96718
Tel. 808-985-6000

HOT SPRINGS NATIONAL PARK

Arkansas ◆ **Established 1921**

The smallest national park is famous for its 47 natural hot springs. Hot Springs National Park, which earned the area the nickname "Spa City," is nestled into the Ouachita Mountains of Arkansas.

The springs and eight bathhouses on Bathhouse Row, dating back to the 1920s, are the park's main attractions. For years, visitors have flocked to Hot Springs to "take the waters" as therapy for rheumatism and for relaxation. Only the Buckstaff Bathhouse remains open for traditional baths today. It is operated by a private company and monitored by the National Park Service.

The hot water from the springs is unlike mineral water. It is relatively soft with a pleasant taste and no odor. There are two thermal-water fountains and two cold-water fountains where you can bring your own container and collect water to sample.

The springs flow out of Hot Springs Mountain at a rate of 850,000 gallons a day. After percolating up from more than 6,000 feet below the earth's crust, the water temperature reaches 143 degrees. Only three of the springs are now open for visitors to see. Others are covered to keep the water pure. It is piped to an underground reservoir and used by all the bathhouses. Four area hotels, the Arlington, Majestic, Downtowner and Hot Springs Hilton, have thermal water bathing facilities that are regulated by the National Park Service.

Unlike other parks, Hot Springs National Park overlaps a downtown area. Bathhouse Row is on Central Avenue with the mountains of the park on either side of the street. The park and the city are so intertwined it's difficult to know when you've left one and entered the other.

The area's mountains have a lot to offer, especially to novice hikers. There are more than 35 miles of trails through beautiful pine, oak and hickory forests and among flowering trees such as dogwoods and southern magnolias.

PLANNING YOUR VISIT

Park Open

The park is open year-round.

Seasons

The weather is mild in spring and fall, humid and hot in the summer. Winters are cold but variable, with temperatures ranging from freezing to the 60s. Visitation is highest June through October.

Entrance Fees

There are no admission fees. At Fordyce Bathhouse, which is the visitor center, you can make a donation to continued restoration efforts.

Permits and Licenses

There are no permits or licenses.

Access and Transportation

Southeast: Take U.S. 270 from Glenwood, Arkansas.

East: Take U.S. 70 from Benton, Arkansas.

North: Take Highway 7 from Holis, Arkansas.

Greyhound provides bus service to Hot Springs.

Amtrak serves Little Rock (60 miles away) and Malvern (20 miles away). Rental cars are available in Hot Springs.

Hot Springs has an airport three miles from downtown.

The park does not have a parking lot. There are several private lots with pay parking near the visitor center and some parking on the street. Mountain bikes are banned from the trails.

Special Needs

Fordyce Bathhouse Visitor Center is accessible and has wheelchairs on loan. There is a model of Bathhouse Row avail-

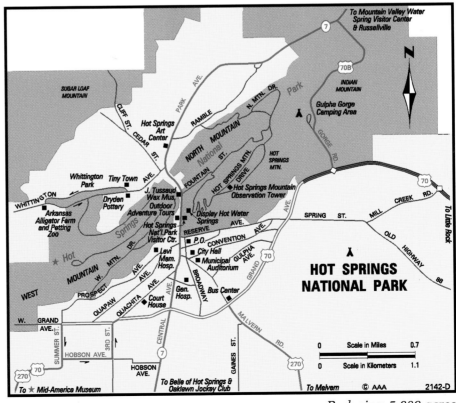

Park size: 5,839 acres

A FEW TIPS

♦ *The view from the Hot Springs Mountain Tower is worth the small fee. It's spectacular, especially when the flowering trees of Hot Springs are in bloom.*

able for visually impaired visitors. The park brochure is available in large print and on cassette. An American Sign Language interpreter can be available with advance notice. For more information ask for the park accessibility bulletin.

Amenities

Baths ♦ Hiking trails ♦ Picnic areas ♦ Walking tours ♦ Self-guided tours ♦ Summer campfire programs ♦ Video on Bathhouse Row ♦ Bookstore in Fordyce Bathhouse

Travel Advisory

Mountain trails cover uneven terrain. Be alert for stinging insects, ticks and snakes. There is poison ivy in the mountains.

Emergency Information

There are two hospitals in Hot Springs.

Visitor and Information Centers

Fordyce Bathhouse. This building serves as the visitor center. It is open year-round except Thanksgiving, Christmas Day and New Year's Day. It has a museum and 24 furnished rooms with period pieces. There is a video on bathing.

Campgrounds

Gulpha Gorge Campground. This area is on the east side of the park, along a creek. It has 42 campsites. The fee is $8 per night. Campsites are available on a first-come, first-served basis. There are no hookups or showers. Groups must reserve well in advance.

Picnic Areas

There are picnic tables on Grand Promenade, Hot Springs Mountain, West Mountain and Gulpha Gorge. Most picnic areas have tables, grills and restrooms. Water is available at Hot Springs Mountain.

Cabins, Lodges and Hotels

The Arlington Resort Hotel and Spa.
The hotel was built in 1875 and renovated in the 1920s. Water from the hot springs is pumped into the bathhouses, lodging and restaurants. Call 501-623-7771. There are several other hotels and motels in downtown Hot Springs.

Restaurants

Because the park and the downtown area overlap, there is a wide selection of restaurants.

THINGS TO DO AND SEE

Historic Bathhouse Row. There is a two-hour tour of the 1920s era Bathhouse Row on Central Avenue. Fordyce Bathhouse features three floors of tile, marble and stained glass as well as period furniture, steam cabinets and tubs from the 1900s. The spring is in the basement.

Baths. No appointment is needed to visit Buckstaff Bathhouse in the park. You can purchase a ticket for a private bath or sitz bath, a steam session in a full steam cabinet or head-out cabinet, hot packs and cool-down showers or a full-body Swedish massage. Call Buckstaff Bathhouse at 501-623-2308.

Hiking. This is the perfect park for new hikers. The Grand Promenade Trail is one of the easiest, leading from the bathhouse area to the mountains. The brick walkway begins behind the visitor center, and travels behind Bathhouse Row on Central Avenue and past several covered springs. The Peak Trail is more strenuous, ending at the summit of Hot Springs Mountain and the Mountain Tower. Dead Chief Trail is less than two miles. It starts at the visitor center and intersects Short Cut Trail, which leads to Hot Springs Mountain and the Gulpha Gorge Trail.

Driving Tours. There are two tours, both roughly 40 minutes long, that depart from the visitor center. Both point out picnic areas, hiking trails and overlooks. They offer a good orientation to the area. Hot Springs Mountain Drive is a 21-mile drive with several overlooks. The 216-foot Hot Springs Mountain Tower offers a view of the park. There is a fee.

Special Events. The city has a number of lakes for water sports as well as galleries, concerts and festivals. For a schedule of events call 1-800-SPA-CITY. In October, the city holds a Volksmarsch sanctioned by the American Volkssport Association.

For More Information

Superintendent
Hot Springs National Park
PO Box 1860
Hot Springs, AR 71902-1860
Tel. 501-783-3961, ext. 640

ISLE ROYALE NATIONAL PARK

Michigan ◈ Established 1931

Isle Royale is the largest island in the largest freshwater lake on earth. Visitors are drawn to this secluded get-away spot by the unspoiled beauty of spruce and fir forests, a rugged shoreline and hundreds of tiny islands just 500 miles from Chicago.

The island is just 45 miles long and nine miles wide, but it teems with fox, moose, beaver, mink and packs of Eastern timber wolves. The wolves crossed an ice bridge from Canada during the severe winter of 1949 and today they keep the moose population in check – which in turn controls the beaver population.

Isle Royale is on the northwest corner of Lake Superior. Nearly 75 percent of the park is water. Of 38 lakes, at least 31 contain brook, lake and rainbow trout, walleye and yellow perch. Fishermen report the biggest catches in spring and fall.

Numerous small coves and bays make for varied sailing expeditions. There are historic lighthouses and shipwrecks to investigate. Many visitors explore the island, lakes and ponds by canoe.

There are 165 miles of trails for hikers. A special treat for those on foot are the 17 varieties of wild orchid on the island, including calypso and yellow lady's slipper. Lookout tours are at Feldtmann Ridge, Ishpeming Point and Mount Ojibway.

Native Americans once mined copper on the island. Island Mine, Todd Harbor, Siskowit Mine, Daisy Farm and Minong Mine are abandoned shafts. Learn more about early mining by visiting one of the bookstores operated by the Isle Royale National History Association. There are bookstores in the visitor centers at Rock Harbor, Windigo or Houghton.

A FEW TIPS

♦ *Bring warm clothes, even in summer. It's chilly on the water.*

♦ *Do not attempt to cross Lake Superior in a small boat (20 feet or less).*

♦ *Get lake charts and maps before you go out on the water.*

♦ *U.S. citizens returning from Canada must clear U.S. customs at Rock Harbor, Amygdaloid or Windigo ranger stations.*

PLANNING YOUR VISIT

Park Open

The park is only open from mid-April to October 31. Full transportation services are available from mid-June through Labor Day. The park is closed November 1 to April 15.

Seasons

Lake Superior cools Isle Royale throughout the year. Even in summer, temperatures

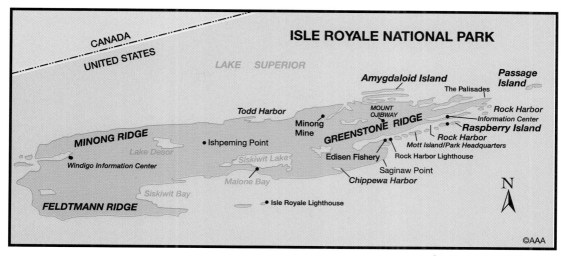

ISLE ROYALE NATIONAL PARK

CANADA
UNITED STATES

LAKE SUPERIOR

Amygdaloid Island | *Passage Island*
The Palisades

Todd Harbor | MOUNT OJIBWAY | Rock Harbor
Minong Mine | Information Center
MINONG RIDGE | GREENSTONE RIDGE | *Raspberry Island*
Ishpeming Point | Rock Harbor
Lake Desor | Mott Island/Park Headquarters
Windigo Information Center | *Siskiwit Lake* | Edisen Fishery | Rock Harbor Lighthouse
Malone Bay | Saginaw Point
Siskiwit Bay | *Chippewa Harbor*
FELDTMANN RIDGE | Isle Royale Lighthouse

N

©AAA

Park size: 539,300 acres

rarely top 80 degrees. However, you will be cool on the ferries. Lake Superior's waters are quite cold. Evening temperatures range from the high 30s to low 40s. Dense fog is common in spring. Thunderstorms occur throughout the summer. Peak visitation is in late July through August.

Entrance Fees

There are no entrance fees and no camping fees. Cost for transportation to and from the island varies depending on your point of departure.

Permits and Licenses

You must get permits at Windigo or Rock Harbor for camping, boating and scuba diving. A Michigan fishing license is required for all Lake Superior waters. No license is required for fishing in the park's inland lakes.

Access and Transportation

Transportation from the mainland to the park is by boat or seaplane only. Reservations are recommended.

From Houghton, Michigan. From June through Labor Day, take a six-hour boat ride on the Ranger III, the National Park Service boat. It departs from Houghton to Rock Harbor. For more information, call

906-482-0984. From May through September, take a half-hour seaplane ride with Isle Royale Seaplane Service. Flights depart from Houghton to Rock Harbor and Windigo. Call 906-482-8850.

From Copper Harbor, Michigan. From May through September, take a four-hour boat ride on the Isle Royale Queen. It departs from Copper Harbor to Rock Harbor. Call 906-289-4437 (in summer) or 906-482-4950 (in winter).

Ferry rides cost about $45.

From Grand Portage, Minnesota. From May through October, contact GPIR Transport Lines to book a passenger vessel. Call 715-392-2100.

On Your Own Boat. Use Lake Survey Chart 14976, "Isle Royale," to guide you from Keweenaw Peninsula. The map can be purchased in the park. Boats less than 20 feet in length should not attempt to cross Lake Superior. Ranger III transports boats.

Water charter service is scheduled through Rock Harbor Lodge, National Parks Concessions, Inc. Call 906-337-4993 (in summer) and 502-773-2191 (in winter). The closest airport is Houghton/Hancock.

There are no roads within the park. All wheeled vehicles are banned.

Special Needs

There is a park brochure on handicapped access available from Isle Royale Park headquarters.

Amenities

Boat tours ♦ Backpacking ♦ Hiking ♦ Scuba diving ♦ Canoeing ♦ Kayaking ♦ Boat, canoe and motorboat rental ♦ Water taxis ♦ Fishing guides ♦ Self-guided trails ♦ Ferry ♦ Artist in residence program

Travel Advisory

You may not bring pets, firearms or wheeled vehicles onto the island. There is no telephone service on the island. Use insect repellent. Mosquitoes are heavy.

Emergency Information

First aid is available at the ranger stations. The nearest hospital is in Rock Harbor.

Visitor and Information Centers

Park headquarters is on Mott Island. Windigo Information Center is on the western side of the island. Rock Harbor Information Center is on the eastern side of the island. There is a historical exhibit at Rock Harbor Lighthouse.

Campgrounds

There is no camping fee, but a permit is required to stay at any of the 36 campsites on the island. The Huginnin Cove Campground is a rustic site right on the shoreline. Three types of camping are available. Three-sided shelters accommodate six people, tent sites accommodate six people in one to three tents and group sites accommodate from seven to 10 people. Sites are available on a first-come, first-served basis. Stays at each campground are limited. Bring a self-contained stove. Open wood fires are prohibited. Quiet hours are enforced.

Picnic Areas

There are picnic areas on the island. Food, supplies and fuel are available at camp stores in Windigo and Rock Harbor. A snack shop and marina grocery at Rock Harbor sell souvenirs and camping supplies.

Cabins, Lodges and Hotels

There is only one hotel on the island. Rock Harbor Lodge is on the shore. The lodge is open late June through Labor Day. Call 906-337-4993 (in summer) or 502-773-2191 (in winter) for reservations.

Restaurants

Rock Harbor Lodge serves breakfast, lunch and dinner.

THINGS TO DO AND SEE

Mine Tour. The Minong Mine tour departs from Rock Harbor Lodge once a week. The tour, led by a ranger, includes a 21-mile cruise along the north shore.

Edisen Fishery. This commercial fishery hosts two tours a week, departing from Rock Harbor Lodge. The fishery is a landmark on the scenic boat cruise.

Hiking. There are nearly 170 foot trails on the island. Stick to the trails because the island has dense vegetation, bogs and swamps. Starting from Windigo or Rock Harbor, a good five-day hike takes you the entire length of the island. Sidetrips to Malone Bay, Chippewa Harbor or Siskiwit Bay give you beautiful views of the water and a chance to enjoy cooling breezes. Off Malone Bay, you can catch a glimpse of Isle Royale Lighthouse.

Nature Walks. Rangers lead nature walks starting at Rock Harbor and Windigo, from June through Labor Day.

Fishing. Michigan regulations apply to all Lake Superior waters, including inland lakes and streams. You may not use traps, seines or nets. You may not dig for bait or use live bait. Arrange guided fishing trips through Rock Harbor Lodge.

Boating. Visitors can rent canoes, motorboats and kayaks at Windigo and Rock Harbor and from National Park Concessions, Inc. Call 906-337-4993 (in summer) and 502-773-2191 (in winter). Popular destinations are Raspberry Island and Passage Island. Motorboats are not allowed on the inland lakes.

The marina at Rock Harbor Lodge is open from the end of May through mid-September. Park docks accommodate cruisers of moderate draft. Overnight docking is allowed at some campground and docks. Check the park map available at the visitor centers.

For More Information

Superintendent
Isle Royale National Park
800 East Lakeshore Drive
Houghton, MI 49931-1895
Tel. 906-482-0984

JOSHUA TREE NATIONAL PARK

California ♦ **Established 1994**

Joshua Tree National Park is about 140 miles east of Los Angeles, near the booming resort and retirement region around Palm Springs. Situated at the eastern end of Southern California's Transverse mountain ranges, two larger deserts meet and overlap within the park's boundaries. Each of the adjoining deserts imparts something unique to this desolate but beautiful landscape. For this reason, Joshua Tree has sometimes been called the "in-between desert." More than a million people a year visit the park.

The eastern side of the park is bounded by the low lying Colorado Desert. In this region the elevation is generally below 3,000 feet. The western side of the park is Mojave desert country, with elevations above 3,000 feet. Because of the western segment's higher elevations, this half of the park is cooler and rainier, with lush plant life. Most of the park's thousands of namesake joshua trees are found in the Mojave sector.

Folklore has it that early Mormon settlers named the *Yucca Brevifolia* the joshua tree because its hoary beard and upraised arms reminded them of the prophet Joshua beckoning them into the promised land. No two joshua trees are alike. Some naturalists have found the entire species hard to love. Writer Charles Francis Saunders, taking fussy exception to its twisted limbs, shaggy trunk and dagger-shaped leaves, denounced this large member of the lily family as looking "grotesque as the creation of a bad dream."

It is nearly impossible to determine the age of a joshua tree. Unlike most trees, its trunk is composed of countless tiny fibers. It has no growth rings. At infrequent intervals between February and April, when the precipitation and temperature are just right, the joshua tree shyly discloses seldom-seen white and pale yellow blossoms. Many visitors revisit the park for years in hopes of seeing them.

The wildflowers which grow in the park are equally elusive. They bloom spectacularly, but only once every 20 years or so. The last great bloom was in 1995.

In the southern and eastern Colorado Desert sections of the park, there is a stunning profusion of desert flora. There are 17 varieties of cactus alone. Cholla cactus, also known as teddy bear cholla grows waist high. A variant, known as the jumping cholla is notorious for its diabolical ability to leap onto the pants legs of any passersby. There are also creosote bushes, ocotillo cactus, ironwood, smoketree and native California fan palms.

A FEW TIPS

♦ *Water is available at only four locations within the park: Cottonwood Springs, Black Rock Canyon Campground Indian Cove Ranger Station and Oasis Visitor Center.*

Geological instability is responsible for the park's striking landscape. A handful of mountain ranges rise abruptly from the desert floor. Land that now comprises the park has sunk beneath sea level at least ten times in the last 800 million years. Each time it resurfaced as a result of a radical uplifting of surface rock. The park is ringed with the dramatic proof of these events. The Pinto Mountains form the northern boundary and the little San Bernadino Mountains hem the southwestern edge. The Hexie Mountains occupy the center of the park. The Cottonwood, Eagle and Coxcomb Mountains loom to the south and east. The San Andreas Fault runs along the park's southwestern border.

Monzogranite intrusions, or large boulder gardens full of multi-ton granite blocks, are another geological oddity. Scattered haphazardly, these giant building blocks got their shape through a complicated process of chemical and hydrological weathering, along with accumulations of minerals, water and lichens. The Wonderland of Rocks is a good example of this phenomena, which scientists call spheroidal weathering. It is

also responsible for the creation of Skull Rock in the Jumbo Rocks Area.

After sunset, when the air cools, the park's animals emerge to hunt and forage. Wildlife here includes kangaroo rats, burrowing owls, yucca night lizards, bobcats, sidewinders, coyotes, road runners, bighorn sheep, golden eagles and tarantulas. The desert tortoise, a rare and protected species, makes its home throughout the park. Visitors are seldom lucky enough to spot one.

PLANNING YOUR VISIT

Park Open

The park is open year-round. Peak visitation is in April.

Seasons

Cacti and wildflowers are most likely to bloom in March. Rainfall is usually around three quarters of an inch for an entire year. July is the hottest month with temperatures averaging 104°. Summer nights cool down to 65° or 70°. Average high temperatures are 85° in October, 62° in January and 90° in May. Between November and March,

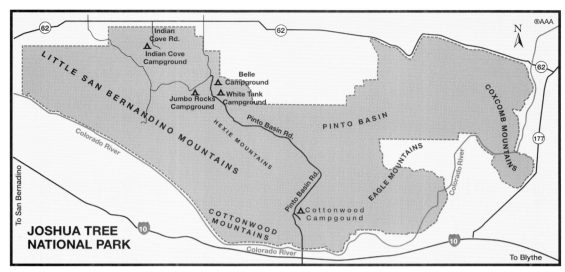

JOSHUA TREE
NATIONAL PARK

Park size: 794,000 acres

overnight lows reach the low 40s. There is an average 81 days above 100° a year. Temperatures routinely run from 5 to 10 degrees cooler in the higher elevations.

Entrance Fees

Per vehicle $10
Per individual $5

Permits and Licenses

Backcountry use is allowed if you register at the visitor center or ranger stations. Vehicles are restricted to established roads.

Access and Transportation

The park is east of Los Angeles, near Palm Springs.

From the West. Take I-10 (U.S. Highway 60) and Twentynine Palms Highway (Highway 62) to the west entrance at the town of Joshua Tree and the North entrance at the town of Twentynine Palms.

From the East. The Cottonwood Springs entrance is 25 miles east of Indio, California via I-10, 10 (U.S. Highway 60). Amtrak serves Palm Springs and Indio. Greyhound serves Palm Springs. The Morongo Basin Transit Authority serves Yucca Valley, Joshua Tree and Twentynine Palms. The closest airport is 50 miles from the park in Palm Springs. Rental cars are available in Palm Springs and Twentynine Palms.

Special Needs

The Cap Rock Nature Trail and Twentynine Palms Oasis Nature Trail are accessible.

Amenities

Hiking ◆ Interpretive walks ◆ Picnicking ◆ Wildlife watching ◆ Camping

Travel Advisory

Stay clear of posted mine shafts. Be careful around cacti. Dress for wide temperature fluctuations.

Emergency Information

First aid is available in the park. The closest hospital is in Joshua Tree.

Visitor and Information Centers

The Oasis Visitor Center is located at the Twentynine Palms entrance. The Cottonwood Visitor Center is at the south entrance. The Black Rock Canyon Visitor Center is at the campground southeast of Yucca Valley.

Campgrounds

There are nine primitive campgrounds scattered throughout the park. All are open year-round. Campers must bring their own water and firewood. Most sites have picnic tables and pit toilets. Six of the nine are available for free on a first-come, first-served basis. There is an $10 per night fee at the Cottonwood Campground and a $12 per night fee at Black Rock Campground.

To reserve a site at Black Rock Campground call 800-365-2267. There are also three group camping sites which may be reserved at that number.

Picnic Areas

There are picnic areas near the nine park campgrounds.

Cabins, Lodges and Hotels

There is no lodging in the park. There are many hotels in nearby Joshua Tree, Yucca Valley and Twentynine Palms.

Restaurants

There are no restaurants or snack bars in the park. There are a variety of restaurants and markets in nearby Joshua Tree, Yucca Valley and Twentynine Palms.

THINGS TO DO AND SEE

Ranger-Led Hikes. In spring and fall, rangers lead nature hikes. The Twentynine Palms Oasis Hike covers three miles in three hours. The three-mile Mastodon Peak

trek explores a gold mine and the Cottonwood Peak area in 2 1/2 hours. The Ryan Mountain Hike, at three hours and three miles, offers some of the best scenery in the park.

Keys Ranch Tour. The Keys Ranch, also called the Desert Queen Ranch, is one of few homesteads to prevail over this terrain for any length of time. A 90-minute tour is free. The tour covers about a mile. Participation is limited to the first 20 applicants.

Cactus Garden Tour. Rangers lead quarter-mile tours through the cholla cactus garden.

Geology Walk. A one-half mile hike leads visitors to some of the park's most famous rock formations. The hike takes about an hour and a half.

Scenic Drives. Stop at the Twentynine Palms Visitor Center for road maps to chart your course into the northern and western sections of the park. Here you'll be able to see the largest rock formations of monzonite and the thickest stands of joshua trees. The Jumbo Rocks and Hidden Valley offer marvelous scenery and photo opportunities. At Key View Point, you can look out over the entire Coachella Valley, including Indio, Palm Springs and the adjoining Anza-Borrego National Forest, including the Salton Sea.

Rock Climbing. Joshua Tree is one of America's best climbing sites, especially in winter. The park's natural walls feature the sharp edges, cracks and high friction that experienced climbers favor. There are also several routes of varying difficulty. Beginners should choose Echo Rock. More experienced climbers can tackle Headstone Rock and Saddle Rock. Vertical Adventures, a leading guide service, can help you plan a climbing expedition in Joshua Tree. Call them at 714-854-6250.

For More Information
Superintendent
Joshua Tree National Park
74485 National Park Drive
Twentynine Palms, CA 92277
Tel. 619-367-7511

DESERT RATS LOOT WILDERNESS

During the 1920s, Rudolf Valentino's smoldering silent film portrayal of a desert sheik sparked a landscaping craze for cactus gardens in Los Angeles and Palm Springs. Environmental looters poured into Joshua Tree in droves, uprooting hundreds of cholla and ocotilla cacti. They even set fire to joshua trees to mark a blazing trail into the nighttime desert.

These greedy entrepreneurs seemed determined to strip the Mojave clean. Wealthy socialite Minerva Hoyt fought back. She founded the International Desert Conservation League. In 1936, she was the first conservationist to lobby Congress to protect Joshua Tree. Her efforts belatedly paid off in 1994, when the California Desert Protection Act upgraded Joshua Tree to national park status.

KATMAI NATIONAL PARK

Alaska • **Established 1980**

Three hundred miles southwest of Anchorage is a land of volcanoes, glistening waterways and dense forest growth that is some of the world's most unforgettable scenery. Katmai National Park is a true wilderness, with breathtaking views of nature at its most commanding and pristine. This remote locale, lush with vegetation, is interrupted only by a series of lakes and streams.

Katmai attracts an estimated 55,000 visitors annually, many of whom come to enjoy a supreme vantage point for watching the world's largest gathering of brown bears. The post-hibernation appearances by the bears is a first time outing for cubs born each winter. As many as 30 bears, weighing up to 900 pounds, can be seen fishing for their meals during prime salmon spawning season. Viewing areas have been established to keep visitors from harm's way.

Equally impressive is the sight of salmon leaping six feet in the air as they make their way upstream to spawn. By mid-summer, millions of the fish pass through these waters.

Virtually undeveloped, Katmai serves as home to red foxes, moose, minks, wolves and beavers. There are more than 40 different species of bird. Coastal areas offer breeding turf for the peregrine falcons that nest among the cliffs. They are not alone. Eagles, hawks and owls find this zone to be prime nesting ground. Sea lions and sea otters splash on the rocks below them.

The land is alive too. There are 15 active volcanoes here, ranging along the Shelikof Strait off the Katmai coast. In

1912, Novarupta unleashed its power. When explorers arrived four years later, they dubbed this area of smoke and ash the Valley of Ten Thousand Smokes. Congress has since deemed the valley a national monument.

In more recent times, man's own deeds have proven devastating. Traces of the 1989 Exxon Valdez oil spill remain in Katmai's beaches. Park rangers still monitor the long-term effects on wildlife.

Katmai has much to offer hikers. A 23-mile route wends through the valley, from Brooks Camp to the Valley of Ten Thousand Smokes. The trek is rough and includes three rivers, but it is rewarding terrain. Less athletic visitors can opt for the view from a tour bus.

A Few Tips

♦ *Be sure to pack rain gear at all times.*
♦ *Bear-proof food utensils are available at the visitor center.*
♦ *Make tour arrangements in advance.*
♦ *Make noise while walking or hiking.*

PLANNING YOUR VISIT

Park Open

The park is open year-round.

Seasons

Peak visitation is between June and mid-September. This is when the brown bears come out of hibernation and sockeye salmon spawn.

Entrance Fees

No entrance fees are charged at Katmai National Park and Preserve.

Permits and Licenses

The McNeil River, Katmai's most popular bear watching area, issues 10 permits a day to visitors. Permits are issued by lottery entered with a $50 fee sent to the Alaska Department of Fish and Game. For more information call 907-344-0541. Applicants can be placed on standby and pay a $25 fee to camp near the ranger station.

Access and Transportation

There is no road access into Katmai, except for a 9-mile dirt path to the park's edge at Lake Camp. Visitors arrive by floatplane or plane. Commercial flights from Anchorage to King Salmon run daily and charters are available during the peak season. Charters should be arranged in advance. Book your charter flights from Anchorage, Homer or Kodiak. Many charters also arrange transportation to area lodges.

Special Needs

Lodging and viewing platforms are accessible for those with disabilities. However, officials warn that bears roam freely. Coming into contact with bears is not uncommon. Visitors must be able to move quickly to avoid confrontations, so those who cannot move quickly are urged to remain in designated areas for their own safety.

Amenities

Camp store ♦ Canoe and kayak rental ♦ Guided fishing ♦ Bear-viewing platforms ♦ Nature walks ♦ Tour bus

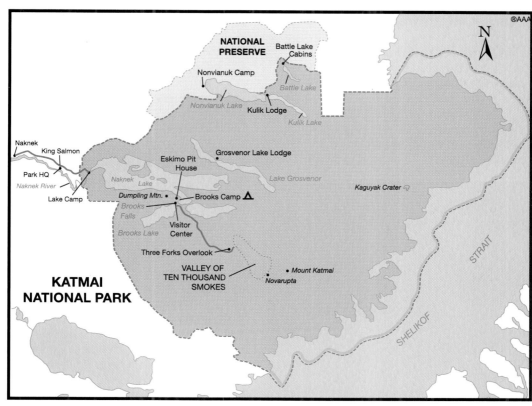

Park size: 4.1 million acres

Travel Advisory

Summer is chilly. Temperatures range from lows in the mid-40s to highs in the mid-50s and mid-60s during the day. The area is windy and sudden gusts are common. Warm, sunny days can suddenly become overcast, windy and rainy. Light rains can seem constant. Be sure to carry always pack rain gear. Climate changes can be sudden and extreme. Summer nights are cold. Daylight lasts less than eight hours during the winters, which are cold.

Emergency Information

First aid available in the park is limited. The closest hospital is in Anchorage. A clinic in Nanek is staffed in the summer.

Visitor and Information Centers

The King Salmon Visitor Center is a first stop for most travelers headed for Katmai. The center offers information and exhibits. Brooks Camp Visitor Center is open from June to mid-September. Since bears are a major attraction, the center offers instruction on sharing the park with bears.

Campgrounds

Brooks Camp Campground is located on Naknek Lake and offers amenities such as firepits, tables, water, pit toilets and food-storage caches. Maximum capacity is 60 and guests can stay no more than seven nights. Cooking facilities are available in three shelters which are shared by all campers.

Campers 13 and older are charged $10 a night for camp use June 1 through September 17. Overnight permits are limited to six people. Additional permits are available for larger groups. Reservations are required and can be made through DESTINET at 800-365-2267.

Picnic Areas

Buy supplies and groceries before entering the park.

Cabins, Lodges and Hotels

Accommodations are available at Brooks Lodge, Grosvenor Lake and Kulik Lodge from June through late September. For reservation information call 800-544-0551. More rustic accommodations are available from June to early August at Chenik Camp, which is popular with bear watchers. For reservation information call 907-235-8910.

SHARING KATMAI WITH BEARS

As a visitor in Katmai National Park you are a guest in the natural habitat of the American Brown Bear, a member of the same species as the grizzly. Park officials warn that bears seem oblivious to their audience because they are accustomed to being watched, have not associated humans with food and they enjoy an abundance of salmon. However, bears are dangerous when they feel threatened or startled.

Visitors must not deliberately confront any animals in the park, especially bears. When not on the viewing platforms, you must keep a minimum distance of 50 yards from individual bears and at least 100 yards from groups of bears.

Restaurants

Family-style meals are served at Brooks Lodge. There are also dining facilities at other lodges.

THINGS TO DO AND SEE

Valley of Ten Thousand Smokes. A daily bus takes visitors along a 23-mile route through the park that ends at the Valley of Ten Thousand Smokes. The tour is led by nature experts.

Nature Walks. Rangers lead daily nature walks, pointing out Katmai's bird life, wildlife and geological points of interest.

Flightseeing. Dramatic sightseeing tours by air are also available and can be arranged in King Salmon.

Bear Watching. Almost every visitor wants to see the massive brown bears hunt for salmon at the river's edge. Large groups of bears can often be spotted from the platforms at Brooks River Falls.

Fly Fishing. Katmai is one of the greatest fly fishing spots in Alaska. Lodges are available in remote — but legendary — fishing spots. Guides can lead you to the best spots if you have an Alaska fishing license. Catch-and-release fishing is encouraged; and required for rainbow trout fishing in the Brooks River, where only fly fishing is permitted. Anglers are cautioned to beware of bears.

Hiking. Katmai offers a range of long and short hikes. Most are rugged and follow waterways. Brooks Lodge offers drop-off and pickup.

Boating. Katmai's rocks and unpredictable weather presents boating challenges for even experienced sailors. Familiarize yourself with any craft you take on the waters. Independent outfitters offer guides.

For More Information

Katmai National Park and Preserve
PO Box 7
King Salmon, Alaska 99613
Tel. 907-246-3305

KENAI FJORDS NATIONAL PARK

Alaska ◆ **Established 1980**

Kenai Fjords National Park offers visitors a dramatic landscape and seascape, with mountains, icefields, misty canyons and fjords. The fjords are natural sculptures formed by glacial scouring, much like the fjords in Norway. This landscape is still shifting and changing gradually, with an occasional dramatic jolt. Glacial plates continue to push the Kenai Mountains upward.

Glaciers are the result of snowfall exceeding snowmelt while new snow piles up on the old. In turn, masses of snow push glaciers to move or stretch. As the ice moves, it takes with it land from underneath, carving and gouging out the landscape.

No better example can be found of such natural activity than the 300-square-mile

A FEW TIPS

♦ *Pack rain gear. Rainfall is frequent and heavy during the peak summer travel months.*

♦ *Much of the park's coastline is privately owned. Check with rangers or park headquarters.*

♦ *Hikers should be prepared for sudden storms, extreme temperatures and blinding sunlight.*

Harding Icefield, the most significant feature of this national park. This icefield is one of only four in the United States. It measures a massive 35 by 20 miles and serves as the source for most of the other glaciers within the park boundaries. Appearing to rise from the sea, icefields with waterfalls or green foliage are a startling and beautiful sight. Sea mammals can sometime be spotted riding icebergs through the fjords.

Visitors most often visit Exit Glacier, an ice point that emanates from Harding Icefield. The glacier descends an estimated 2,500 feet and spans about three miles. The edge of this icy turf is bordered by bare land with patches of green vegetation.

The park's rugged coastal region extends to a lush rain forest. Animal life includes mountain goats, moose, bears, marmots and wolverines. High up in the spruce and hemlock trees, bald eagles nest. Along the rocks and shore, sea lions and harbor seals play, while in the water, porpoises, sea otters and whales including grays, humpbacks, killers and minkes, move through the fjord waters. Seabirds, puffins and gulls breed and feed among the cliffs.

Sadly, this area, was damaged by the 1989 Exxon Valdez oil spill at nearby Prince William Sound. Rangers monitor the area to identify any possible long-term effects on the park's flora and fauna.

To appreciate Kenai Fjords National Park takes several perspectives requiring several modes of transportation. The ideal way to see the park is by foot and by plane, boat tour and kayak.

PLANNING YOUR VISIT

Park Open

The park is open year-round. Peak visitation is in July. The park can be crowded during the summer months.

Seasons

Despite season changes, visitors should always be prepared for rain. The seaside climate ranges from heavy rain alternating with cool, as well as sunny, and warm days from spring through fall. Not until mid-June do daytime highs begin reaching the mid-50s to mid-60s. May is the driest period. September marks the start of the storm season. Winter weather is rainy and cold with daily temperatures resting in the 30s. The fjords can get anywhere from 35 to 65 feet of snow annually.

Entrance Fees

There are no entrance fees.

Permits and Licenses

If you plan to fish, an Alaska fishing license is required.

Access and Transportation

Kenai Fjords National Park is located in south-central Alaska, 127 miles from Anchorage on the Seward Highway. Major airlines fly into Anchorage. Car rentals are available at the airport. Commuter flights and bus service are available between Anchorage and Seward. The Alaska Railroad runs during the summer between Seward and Anchorage. The Alaska Marine Highway ferry connects Homer and Seldovia with Seward via Kodiak. It also serves Valdez and Cordova.

Special Needs

Exit Glacier Trail is accessible to wheelchairs and is located just a quarter mile from the glacier. The public use cabins are also accessible.

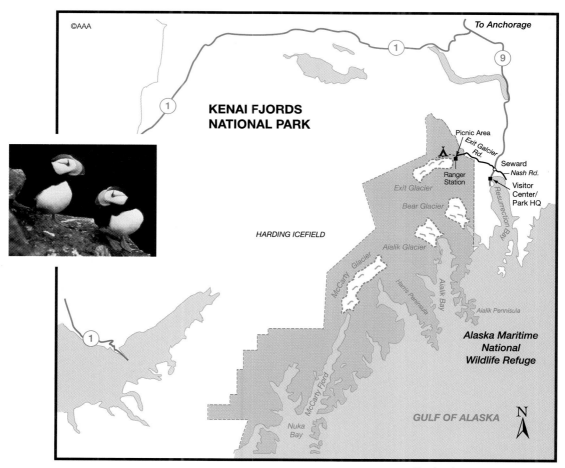

©AAA

KENAI FJORDS NATIONAL PARK

To Anchorage

Picnic Area
Exit Glacier Rd.
Ranger Station
Seward
Nash Rd.
Visitor Center/ Park HQ
Exit Glacier
Bear Glacier
HARDING ICEFIELD
Aialik Glacier
McCarty Glacier
Harris Peninsula
Aialik Bay
Aialik Pennisula
Alaska Maritime National Wildlife Refuge
McCarty Fiord
GULF OF ALASKA
N
Nuka Bay

Park size: 650,000 acres

Amenities

Flightseeing ♦ Brown bear watching
♦ Kayaking ♦ Fishing ♦ Hiking ♦ Boat tours

Travel Advisory

Much of this park area is covered in ice, making travel difficult. Only one short road allows for auto travel. Touring is best accomplished via charter boats or kayaks.

Emergency Information

Rangers are stationed at Exit Glacier. There is a hospital in Seward.

Visitor and Information Centers

Park headquarters and the visitor center is located in Seward at the Small Boat Harbor. Visitors can get information as well as see a photo exhibit and slide program about the fjords. Exit Glacier Ranger Station serves as an information source, complete with exhibits about the glacier and Harding Icefield. The center is open during the summer.

Campgrounds

There is a tents-only campsite at Exit Glacier Campground, three-quarters of a mile from Exit Glacier. There are cabins at Aialik and Exit Glacier.

Picnic Areas

There are picnic tables near Exit Glacier Ranger Station. Supplies are available in Seward.

Cabins, Lodges and Hotels

There are accommodations in Seward.

Best Western Hotel. Some rooms have waterfront views. The hotel provides transportation to the harbor. For more information call 800-528-1234.

Great Alaska Fish Camp. There are guides available from this fish camp. It also offers hiking, river rafting, sightseeing and educational programs. For more information call 800-544-2261.

Kenai Princess Lodge. The lodge overlooks the Kenai River and has a restaurant, hot tubs, and RV parking. For more information call 800-426-0500.

Restaurants

There are no restaurants in the park. The closest restaurants are in Seward.

THINGS TO DO AND SEE

Seward Walking Tour. Visitors can take a scenic walking tour of the historic port district and see homes dating back a century.

Boat Tours. Seward serves as launch site for chartered half-day or full-day boat tours from mid-May through mid-September. Boat tours highlight glaciers, birdwatching and seal, otter and whale spotting. Overnight trips to the fjords are also available.

Flightseeing. Sightseeing by air is available via charters originating from Seward or Homer. One-hour flights provide an awe-inspiring view of Harding Icefield and the fjords. Kachemak Air Service offers tours of Kenai Fjords as well as other area sites. Call 907-235-8924.

Other Tours. In summer months, bus excursions from Seward take travelers to Exit Glacier. Kayaking tours provide a dramatic look at the fjords. Mariah Tours & Charters guides travelers through the fjords. For more information call 800-270-1238. Also call Kenai Coastal Tours (800-770-9199) or Kenai Fjords Tours (800-478-8068).

Ranger-led Activities. Naturalists lead hikes to the glacier's base and day-long hikes to the ice field from the ranger station at Exit Glacier. Rangers host Saturday night campfire programs and interpretive programs in the visitor center.

Hiking. A half-mile trail marked with trailside exhibits starts at the Exit Glacier ranger station. For experienced hikers, the rugged route is highlighted by a steep, rough-cut, three-mile trail that climbs the north side of Exit Glacier. The reward is reaching a site that overlooks Harding Icefield. Backpacking in this terrain requires good physical condition and experience. Commercial operators offer camping guides.

Scenic Drive. Exit Glacier is the only park area accessible by vehicle, via a nine-mile gravel road leading from the Seward Highway to the Exit Glacier ranger station.

Fishing. Fishing opportunities abound.

Saltwater fish can be found in the waters off the park's coast. Species include halibut, lingcod and a variety of rockfish. Freshwater fish include trout and silver salmon. Fishing guides and boat charters can be arranged at Resurrection Bay.

Boating. Even the most experienced boaters must be prepared for anything when entering the strong winds and rough seas of the Gulf of Alaska. Information on landing sites, weather conditions and navigational hazards is available from the visitor center.

Kayaking. Fjords are a popular destination for kayakers. Guided trips are strongly recommended although you can simply rent a kayak.

For More Information
Superintendent
Kenai Fjords National Park
PO Box 1727
Seward, AK 99664
Tel. 907-224-3175

KOBUK VALLEY NATIONAL PARK

Alaska ◆ **Established 1980**

North of the Arctic Circle, Kobuk Valley nestles between the Baird and Waring Mountains. This national park encompasses the central section of the 125-mile Kobuk River and the looming Kobuk Sand Dunes.

The 25-square mile sand dunes are an amazing sight and well worth the easy hike from the Kobuk River. Buff-colored sand, formed by glaciers grinding down the earth, was carried here by wind and water more than 30,000 years ago. Smaller dunes cover another five square miles in the park.

Kobuk Valley is the primary nesting place for more than 100 species of birds. The park is also home to wolves, bears, foxes, wolverines and weasels. A migratory herd of caribou spends late August through early October in their fall range here.

It's easy to believe man has made no mark on this wild country, but that's not quite true. Recent archaeological finds at Onion Portage date back to prehistory.

Artifacts prove humans have hunted here for at least 10,000 years. At least seven different cultures have called this land their own. Nearby Kotzebue is Alaska's biggest Eskimo community with more than 3,000 residents.

This is a remote site with rugged terrain and harsh weather. There are no campgrounds or trails. Visitors come to enjoy primitive camping and backpacking, wildlife observation and photography and water sports on the Little Kobuk and Hunt Rivers. Smaller rivers, the Ambler, Salmon and Noatak, are increasingly popular for river-running. The rivers yield salmon and sheefish, a freshwater tarpon.

PLANNING YOUR VISIT

Park Open
The park is open year-round. Peak visitation is in August.

Seasons
This area is subject to high winds year-round. Summers are mild and cool with extended daylight. Winters are extremely dark and harsh. The Kobuk River typically thaws by early June and freezes by the last week of September.

Entrance Fees
There is no entrance fee.

Permits and Licenses
Fishermen must have Alaska fishing licenses. Licenses are available in Kotzebue or Anchorage. Sport hunting is prohibited in the park but it is legal to carry a firearm for protection from bears.

Access and Transportation
The park is in northwest Alaska, 26 miles north of the Arctic Circle. There are no roads or rail service. You must fly into Kotzebue from Anchorage or Fairbanks and then air taxi to a nearby village. In summer, you can travel the park on foot or watercraft. In winter, you can hike or snowmobile.

Special Needs
There are no facilities in the park itself. Park headquarters is accessible, as is the Interagency Kotzebue Public Lands Information Center. Braille and large print brochures about the park are available. An orientation video is close-captioned.

Amenities
There are no amenities. This park is a perfect site for primitive hiking, fishing and backcountry camping.

Travel Advisory

This is untamed country. Encounters with wild animals are possible. You must have good backcountry skills for wilderness survival. All visitors should be off the river before it freezes, around the end of September.

Emergency Information

There is no first aid available in the park. There are search and rescue groups in nearby villages. The closest hospital is in Kotzebue.

Visitor and Information Centers

There is no visitor center or facilities within the park. For information about the park, visit the Public Lands Information Center in Kotzebue. This office is open year-round, except on federal holidays. Hours of operation are limited in the winter.

Campgrounds

There are no campgrounds. Visitors can camp on the tundra, except in archaeological areas or on private property along the rivers. A camp stove is recommended. You may not cut live trees. Set campfires using downed wood.

Picnic Areas

There are no picnic tables, grills or fire pits in the park.

Cabins, Lodges and Hotels

There are no accommodations in the park. Lodging is available in the villages of Kiana and Ambler during the summer and

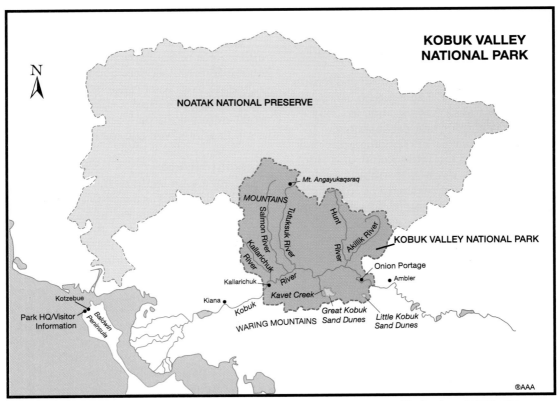

Park size: 1,750,421 acres

in Kotzebue year-round Nullagvik Hotel in Kotzebue is a modern hotel with a view of Kotzebue Sound. For more information call 907-442-3331.

THINGS TO DO AND SEE

Flightseeing. Alaskan tour companies can arrange package tours that include visits to the Kobuk River and the Great Kobuk Sand Dunes.

Floating the Rivers. Motorboats, kayaks and canoes are permitted on the rivers. Count on covering no more than 15 miles a day and allow extra time for bad weather. The Kobuk is not a whitewater spot, it is a slow and winding river. Much of the land along the river is privately owned so you will probably encounter people involved in subsistence hunting and fishing.

Hiking. There are no trails in the park but the wildflower-dotted tundra covers permafrost. Hikers can reach the northern tip of the Great Kobuk Sand Dunes by an easy cross-country hike from the Kobuk River, following the uplands near Kavet Creek. Hiking guides are available outside the park.

Fishing. For the best catch, fish near or in the Kobuk's tributaries. Fishing guides can show you the best spots for grayling, arctic char, trout, sheefish, salmon, pike and whitefish. Alaska fishing seasons and regulations apply.

Near Kobuk Valley National Park

Living Museum of the Arctic. This million dollar museum was established in the early 1970s. It preserves traditional stories and folk art. The museum sponsors exhibitions of native crafts, Eskimo subsistence ways and traditions. There is a slide show highlighting the wisdom of the elders. For more information about the museum call 800-478-3301.

For More Information
Kobuk Valley National Park
PO Box 1029
Kotzebue, AK 99752
Tel. 907-442-3890

A FEW TIPS

♦ *Wear insect repellent to ward off biting flies and mosquitoes.*
♦ *Do not trespass or disturb the fishnets and camps of people living within the park.*
♦ *Guard against hypothermia. Dress in waterproof clothing and layer it.*
♦ *Do not camp near the river. Water levels can rise without warning.*

LAKE CLARK NATIONAL PARK

Alaska ♦ **Established 1980**

This dazzling peninsula stretches from the coastline at Cook Inlet to the 10,000-foot peaks of Mt. Redoubt and Mt. Iliamna, both active volcanoes. The park and preserve encompasses more than 4 million acres of spruce, balsam and poplar forests with wild roses blooming in their shadows. Other sights include waterfalls that cascade to the sea and a glacier-fed, turquoise gem that spans 50 miles, Lake Clark. The park is framed by the Chigmit Mountains.

The parks natural residents include wolves, caribou, lynx, wolverines, moose, Dall sheep and foxes. Like all of Alaska's parks, this is bear country. Offshore, look for seals, sea otters and beluga whales. Native fish include Arctic grayling, Dolly Varden trout and northern pike.

♦ *Much of this area is privately owned. Check with rangers before setting out for the backcountry. Local residents fish the lakes here. Respect their property and privacy.*
♦ *Pack extra food and supplies. Store food in bear-proof packaging.*
♦ *Like the other wildlife in this area, insects are prolific. Use insect repellent to fend off mosquitoes and biting flies.*

Red salmon use this area as a spawning ground. During a three-week period in June, as many as nine million salmon travel from Iliamna Lake up to Newhalen River to Lake Clark. This creates a visible swath of red across the width of the lake. The lucky salmon not caught by fishermen — or bears — will return to the exact spot where they were born.

This land has been continuously occupied since prehistoric times. The Tanaina tribe lived here until the early part of this century. Archaeological studies are underway to determine more about the early inhabitants here. There are residents who live off the park lands. Respect their rights and privacy during your visit.

PLANNING YOUR VISIT

Park Open
The park is open year-round. Peak visitation is in August.

Seasons
This region is warmest between June and August, when temperatures range between 50 and 65 degrees. Colder weather begins in late September or early October

when frost and snow are common. Winter is long, typically from October through April. Temperatures in the interior can plummet well below zero. Rainstorms strike suddenly throughout the year. The coastline is cooler. Winds can be quite strong in the mountain passes.

Entrance Fees

There are no entrance fees.

Permits and Licenses

Park rangers encourage a voluntary registration at headquarters in the interest of safety. If you are going to fish Lake Clark you must have an Alaska fishing license.

You can get a license in Anchorage or Port Alsworth. Hunting is allowed in the preserve only.

Access and Transportation

The park is in south-central Alaska, 150 miles southwest of Anchorage. Visitors reach Lake Clark by commercial flights or charters. There is no roadway access to the park or roadways in the park. Flights originate from Anchorage, Kenai or Homer. Flight time is less than two hours from Anchorage. The closest commercial airport is in Iliamna.

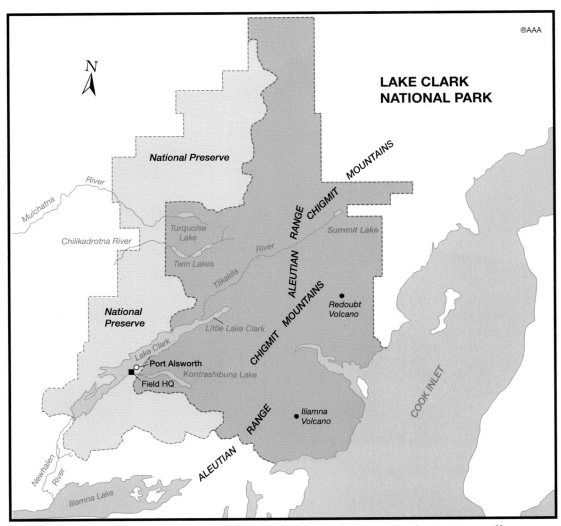

Park size: 3.4 million acres

WHAT IS LOW-IMPACT CAMPING?

Camping in Alaska's national parks is often backcountry camping. Before setting out in search of a campsite, campers should contact the park headquarters for any advice or restrictions. Some parks, such as Lake Clark, encourage a voluntary registration for the sake of camper safety. Others keep track of hikers and campers by issuing permits.

Low-impact camping is the use of techniques to minimize damage to the environment. A low-impact camper: packs out all garbage, avoids trampling fragile plant life when hiking or making camp, washes himself and his gear at least 100 feet from the water source and buries human waste well away from camp, trails and the water.

Special Needs
This is rugged terrain. Most of the facilities and tours in this area are not handicapped accessible.

Amenities
Guided nature hikes ♦ Slide programs ♦ Boat rentals ♦ hiking ♦ Mountaineering ♦ Whitewater rafting ♦ Flightseeing

Travel Advisory
Weather conditions can change suddenly and drastically. Carry raingear and have a backup plan when weather postpones your original plans. Backpackers must carry extra food and supplies. Winter stays should only be undertaken by people experienced with cold-weather camping.

Emergency Information
The closest clinic is in Iliamna. The nearest hospitals are in Anchorage and Kenai.

Visitor and Information Centers
Information about Lake Clark is available at a small visitor center located at the park's headquarters in Port Alsworth. The Alaska Natural History Association sells materials in the park. There is also an exhibit on Lake Clark at Kenai National Park's Bicentennial Visitor Center.

Campgrounds
There are no developed campgrounds in the park. Primitive camping is allowed on the shores of Lake Clark and in Port Alsworth. No permits are required. Backpackers who stay in the park are expected to be self-sufficient and highly skilled at wilderness camping. Food should be stored in bear-proof containers. Cache all food and scented items away from campsites and use low-impact camping techniques.

Picnic Areas

There is no store in the park. Food and supplies are available on a limited basis.

Cabins, Lodges and Hotels

There are fishing lodges, cabins and bed and breakfasts around the lakes. Other lodging is available at Port Alsworth. Farm Lodge is a comfortable, modern lodge with duplexes that offers several sleeping arrangements, including bunk beds. Home-style meals are served. Guest services include fishing and hiking guides. For reservation information call 800-662-7661

Restaurants

There are restaurants in Port Alsworth. Meals are served in the park's lodges.

THINGS TO DO AND SEE

Guided Tours. Guide services and boat rental are available on the coast and at Port Alsworth. Alaska Adventures offers rafting,

canoeing and kayaking trips. Call 907-457-8907 for more information.

Fishing. Lake Clark is prized for sockeye salmon. Other common catch is grayling, Dolly Varden trout and lake trout. Fishing trips can be arranged with independent outfitters.

River Trips. The Chilikadrotna River is gaining popularity as a whitewater rafting spot. Float trips can be arranged on Mulchatna, Tlikakila and Chilikadrotna as well as other rivers in the area.

Hiking. There is one maintained trail in the preserve. It begins at the ranger station at Port Alsworth and leads to Tanalian

Falls and Kontrashibuna Lake. Other hikes traverse the western slopes which are higher and drier than the eastern portion of the park and the mountains themselves. Guides can be hired in Port Alsworth.

Near Lake Clark National Park

Katmai National Park. Please see the entry on Katmai National Park. Bear-watching is the number one attraction here.

McNeil River State Game Sanctuary, McNeil Falls. This sanctuary on the Alaska Peninsula is a haven for brown bears. Reservations are available through a lottery system conducted by the Alaska Department of Fish and Game in March. For more information call 907-267-3305.

For More Information

Lake Clark National Park and Preserve
4230 University Drive, Suite 311
Anchorage, AK 99508
Tel. 907-271-3751

FISHING IN ALASKA

Alaska has more coastline than the Lower 48 states combined. Her many lakes lure fishermen from all over the world. Lake Clark is a top freshwater fishing destination. The summer salmon run is from June to August.

However, before you land that 50-pound salmon or monster halibut, you must get your license from the Alaska Department of Fish and Game (907-465-4180). Fishermen under 16 do not require a license. Most charter-boat operators and fishing lodges can also sell licenses and stamps.

Fees for nonresidents range from $10 for a one-day permit to $50 for an annual license. If you are after king salmon and want to keep your catch, you must get an additional stamp, ranging from $10 for one-day's worth of fishing to $35 for an annual stamp.

Limits and special provisions vary from area to area. The Department of Fish and Game can provide up-to-date information, or you can take advantage of a sportfishing package tour. One of the more established fishing guide services is Alaskan Experience. Call 800-777-7055 for more information.

LASSEN VOLCANIC NATIONAL PARK

California ◆ **Established 1916**

Lassen Volcanic National Park stands at the juncture of the Cascade range and the Sierra Nevada Mountains in northeastern California. Lassen Peak, the volcano for which the park is named, is one of the world's largest plug dome volcano. It soars 10,457 feet above sea level.

Lassen Peak was a vent in the side of the ancient and powerful Tehama volcano. Tehama's peak eroded over the centuries Lassen Peak is thought to have been born at least 27,400 years ago.

Lassen Peak was the site of an eruption on June 19, 1914. Its active period con-

sisted of more than 150 eruptions and lasted for the following seven years. The greatest eruption took place in 1915, when the volcano rocketed an enormous plume of ash, cinder and gas over 30,000 feet into the air. The fallout from the blast had a cataclysmic effect on the surrounding landscape, aftereffects can still be observed today. Although the volcano's last eruption dates back to 1921, scientists believe it will one day erupt again.

Lassen Peak is one of the so-called Ring of Fire volcanoes, which nearly encircle the boundaries of the Pacific Ocean. Until the eruption of Mount St. Helens in 1980, Lassen's 1921 eruption had been the most recent volcanic eruption in the continental U.S.

The park is of intense interest to scientists, who are using it as a model in order to predict what the future of the devastated terrain around Mt. St. Helen's might be. The devastated area of the park is a good example of the way plant life gradually returns to a barren area.

Notable volcanic features of the park include lava pinnacles, huge mountains created by flowing lava, cinder cones and a lava plateau more than a mile above sea level.

A FEW TIPS

◆ *Advise rangers of all trips.*
◆ *Terrain and snow conditions are usually ideal for cross-country skiing.*
◆ *Keep children on trails and paths at all times. Carelessness can lead to accidental burns at geothermal sites.*

Rich in scenic beauty, Lassen Volcanic National Park is graced with forests, lakes, meadows and streams. The park is also a hive of geothermal activity, with fumaroles, mud pots, steaming sulfur vents and hot springs. Bumpass Hell, the largest center of geothermal activity in the park, has acres of boiling pools, mud pots and steam vents. There, spring water bubbles out of the ground at temperatures of 212 degrees, well above the boiling point. Scientists say the water has been getting hotter in recent years.

There are over 700 different species of plantlife and 250 species of animal life in the park, a kind of fusion of the wildlife of both the Cascades and the Sierra Nevadas. Beautiful Lake Manzanita is ringed with pines and fir trees and surrounded by meadows full of wildflowers in the spring.

The vicinity of the park was the ancestral home of the Atsugewi, Yana, Yahi and Maidu Native American peoples. White settlers were drawn to the region by the California gold rush of the late 1840s. Traces of the Nobles Emigrant trail can still be seen in the park.

PLANNING YOUR VISIT

Park Open

The park is always open, but the Lassen Park Road is closed from November to mid-June. Most of the park trails are covered with snow in winter. Peak visitation is in August.

Seasons

Summer temperatures range from highs in the mid-80s to lows in the low 30s. Winter temperatures range from the 40s to the teens. Most precipitation is in winter. The annual snowfall can reach 700 inches.

Entrance Fees

Per private vehicle $5
Per individual...$3
Fees are valid for seven days.

Permits and Licenses

A California fishing license is required to fish in the park. A permit is required for backcountry camping. Free permits are available at visitor centers.

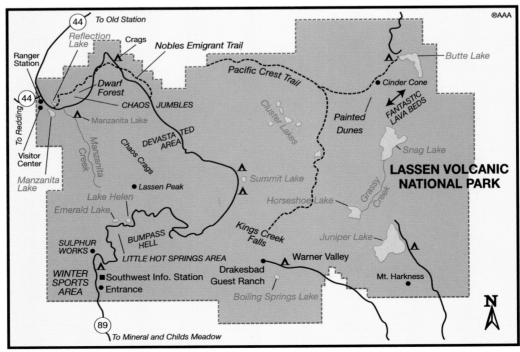

Park size: 106,372 acres

Special Needs

The following areas are accessible: Manzanita Lake Visitor Center restrooms, the amphitheater, Summit Lake Campground, southwest entrance, Information Center, chalet restrooms, Butte Lake Campground and restrooms and Lassen Peak portable restrooms (with assistance).

Access and Transportation

From the West. Take Highway 44 for 48 miles east from Redding to Manzanita Lake.

From the South. Take Highway 36 west and Highway 89 north for 65 miles from Susanville or 52 miles east and north from Red Bluff to southwest entrance.

Also From the South. Travel 13 miles on a paved and gravel dirt road from Chester to Juniper Lake entrance.

From the South. Drive 17 miles northwest of Chester on a paved and gravel road to Warner Valley entrance.

From the North. Take Highway 44 for 26 miles north and east of Manzanita Lake, than six miles south on dirt road to Butte Lake entrance.

Greyhounds and Trailways buses serve Red Bluff (52 miles away), Redding (48 miles away), daily from Sacramento (162 miles away) and San Francisco (262 miles away). Greyhound operates between Reno, Nevada (150 miles away) and Susanville (65 miles away), daily. Buses serve Mineral from Red Bluff (52 miles) and Susanville.

Amtrak serves Redding and Chico. Airlines serve Redding, Reno and Chico. Private planes land at Chester and Red Bluff.

Rental cars are available at Redding, Red Bluff, Chico, Susanville and Reno.

Amenities

Scenic drives ♦ Hiking ♦ Corrals ♦ Fishing ♦ Boating ♦ Winter sports ♦ Naturalist programs

Travel Advisory

Bears live in the park, although they are not often encountered. Keep your distance and store food properly.

Volcanic rock is crumbly and unsuitable for rock climbing. Boiling water may be near the surface in thermal areas. The crust of ground cover in such areas may be brittle. You could plunge through if not careful. Stick to trails and boardwalks. Make sure children do, too.

The park's high elevations can leave you short of breath. Pace yourself.

Emergency Information

First aid is available in the park. The nearest hospital is in Chester, on Route 36, 35 miles from the south end of the park. Another hospital is in Burney, on Route 44, 45 miles west of the north end of the park.

Visitor and Information Centers

Both the Loomis Museum near Manzanita Lake on Highway 89 and the Southwest Information Station are open daily from mid-June to Labor Day.

On June 9, 1914, three men climbed Lassen Peak, previously thought to be a dead volcano. They wanted to see for themselves why the ground was rumbling. They saw more than they bargained for. Peering down into a newly formed crater, the earth began to rock and pitch beneath their feet. As they turned and began a mad scramble for their lives down the steep slope, Lassen erupted. Boxcar sized rocks, ash and sulfur fumes filled the air. One man was struck by a hurtling projectile and knocked unconscious. But miraculously, the eruption stopped as abruptly as it had begun. The three hikers escaped with their lives.

Campgrounds

There are six campgrounds. Summit Lake North and Summit Lake South have a seven-day limit. All others have a 14-day limit. Weather permitting they are usually open in June or July through September. Fees range from $8 to $12 a night. Showers are at Manzanita Lake. There are RV sites except at Juniper Lake and Southwest. Make a reservation for one of two group campgrounds.

Picnic Areas

There are picnic areas at Manzanita Lake, Kings Creek and near Bumpass Hell. All have tables.

Cabins, Lodges and Hotels

The Drakesbad Guest Ranch is 47 miles southeast of headquarters in Chester, California. Request the long distance operator for Susanville. Then ask for Drakesbad, number 2. There are six lodge rooms and four cabins. The ranch is open from mid-June to early October.

Outside the park, hotels, motels and lodgings are available in Mineral and Redding. For more information, call the Redding Chamber of Commerce at 916-225-4433.

THINGS TO DO AND SEE

Scenic Hike or Drive. Lassen Peak can be toured by car or ascended on foot. Check out the Sulphur Works, a roadside exhibit off of the twisting climbing summit road. Here you can observe hissing fumaroles, sputtering mud and gurgling clay daubed in pastel colors by the minerals in the soil. This is all that remains of the vent of the once imposing Mt. Tehama. The nearby peaks are the remnants of its rim.

Bumpass Hell. There is a large balanced rock at the edge of the parking lot which was left high and dry by an ancient glacier. This geothermal zone is named after an unfortunate area guide. A hundred and thirty years ago, K.V. Bumpass plunged through the thin crust of earth, badly burning his leg in the boiling mineral water just beneath the surface. Ever after, the indefatigable Bumpass bragged about his premature descent into hell.

Further up the road the Devastated Area is mute testimony to the awful power of the 1915 eruption. Still, there are signs of renewal amid the scorched and fallen trees and blasted earth.

At nearby Chaos Crags and Chaos Jumble you can walk around the site where a volcanic dome collapsed 300 years ago. The enormous landslide which resulted, involving millions of tons of rock, veered into the course of a nearby creek, damming its flow. Lovely Manzanita Lake is the result.

Hiking. The park's 150 miles of trails include a 17-mile section of the Pacific Crest Trail. This is a beautiful, varied hiking area that takes you through coniferous forests, alpine tundra and along waterways. A *Lassen Trails* booklet available at visitor centers describes popular hikes.

Fishing. Fish for rainbow trout in Manzanita Lake. There are catch and possession limits and some waters are off-limits to fishermen, so check the signs. You may not dig for bait or clean fish in the park.

Boating. You may enjoy many park lakes in unmotorized boats, rowboats or canoes. Boats are banned from Reflection Lake, Emerald Lake, Helen Lake and Boiling Springs. There are no boat rentals in the park.

Trail Rides. Pack and saddle stock may stay overnight in the corrals at Butte Lake, Summit Lake and Juniper Lake. Reservations are required. Call the park at 916-595-4444, ext. 5155. There is also a small corral near the northern park boundary for Pacific Crest Trail users.

Near Lassen Volcanic National Park

Lassen National Forest. About 40 miles from the park in Susanville is a lush, evergreen mountain forest with many active geothermal spots. There are lakes and streams on its 1,100,000 acres. It features handicapped access, hiking, boating, boat ramp, summer and winter sports and 1,200 campsites. Most campsites are open mid-May to mid-October. For information call 916-257-2151

Whiskeytown-Shasta-Trinity National Recreation Area. The Whiskeytown headquarters is on California Highway 299 off I-5, 60 miles west of Lassen Volcanic National Park. This is historic gold rush country and in addition to three impounded lakes that offer unlimited water recreation, you can try your hand at panning for gold in its 254,388 acres. There are 1,156 campsites, houseboats and cabins. Reservations are required. This area is open year-round. For more information call 916-241-6584 or 916-246-5222.

For More Information

Superintendent
Lassen Volcanic National Park
PO Box 100
Mineral, CA 96063-0100
Tel. 916-595-4444

MAMMOTH CAVE NATIONAL PARK

Kentucky ♦ **Established 1941**

The land surface of Mammoth Cave National Park is about 80 square miles. But the real attraction of the park is an eerie underworld hundreds of feet below the sun dappled Kentucky hills and hollows. It consists of more than 330 miles of cave. Mammoth Cave is the world's largest cave system. No one can say precisely how large it is. New caves are still being discovered and explored.

Native Americans used parts of the cave system nearly 4,000 years ago. Well preserved artifacts of that time, including clothing and even mummies have been discovered. Modern exploration of the cave began in the 1790s. One of the early guides was Steven Bishop, a young slave who found and mapped some of Mammoth's passages armed only with a flickering lard-fat lamp. Bishop died in 1857. He was laid to rest in the guide's cemetery near the cave's entrance.

The underground landscape of Mammoth Cave is full of pits, domes, rivers and animals especially adapted to living there. Two layers of stone underlie the topsoil covering Mammoth Cave. A sandstone and shale cap, nearly 50 feet thick in places, arches over limestone ridges. Slightly acidic surface water seeps through this cap, eroding the limestone deeper underground into a honeycomb of caverns and passages.

The upper passages of the cave were carved out ten million years ago. They are dry today. The flowing waters of the Echo River and a host of other underground streams are still enlarging the lower passages. The many beautiful rock formations in the cave are the result of groundwater trickling underground. The dissolved calcium carbonate remains after the groundwater evaporates. Drop by drop, the resulting crystallization of the residue

A FEW TIPS

♦ *Groups wishing to explore the caves on their own need a permit.*

♦ *Pets are permitted on leashes except in the caves and the visitor center. Kennels are available at the Mammoth Cave Hotel.*

♦ *Watch for wild deer while driving in the park.*

♦ *Reserve cave tours early.*

creates stalactites, which form on the ceilings and stalagmites, which form on the floor. They also include flowstone, draperies and even gypsum "flowers" in the dry passages. The latter are so delicate that many people mistake them for living blossoms.

Unusual animals make their home in the dark coolness. The rivers and streams support colonies of small, albino, eyeless fish. There are also eyeless shrimp, crayfish, spiders and crickets. These creatures, living in the blackness of the caves, have developed extra-sensitive organs on their head and body. They can detect movement nearby.

Most visitors to Mammoth Cave take one of the ranger-guided tours of the 12 miles of the caves open to the public. There are over 600,000 visitors a year to the caves.

When underground explorers emerge from the darkness, the aboveground section of the park offers forests full of oak and hickory, the Green and Nolin Rivers, rugged hillsides, prairies and bogs. Combine a cave tour with a nature hike to truly appreciate Mammoth's unique blend of history and natural beauty.

PLANNING YOUR VISIT

Park Open
The park is open year-round, except for December 25. Peak visitation is in July.

Seasons
Underground, the temperature remains in the mid-50s to low 60s all year. Aboveground, summer temperatures range from 45° at night to 100° during the day. The average temperature is 90°. July and August are the hottest months. Winter temperatures range from 0° to 70°. The average daily temperature is 34°. Most snow falls in January and February. Fog is possible.

Entrance Fees
There is no entrance fee. Fees are charged for cave tours and Green River boat trips.

Permits and Licenses
Free permits for backcountry camping are available at the visitor center and headquarters.

Access and Transportation:
The park is in central Kentucky, about 90 miles from Louisville or Nashville.
From Louisville. Take I-65 south to exit 53, Cave City exit, then take Route 70 into the park.
From Nashville. Take I-65 north to exit 48, Park City, then take Route 255 west to the park.
There is no train service. Greyhound serves Cave City. Taxi service from the bus station to the park is available. The closest airport is in Louisville, Kentucky (81 miles

from the park) and Nashville, Tennessee (85 miles from the park). Rental cars are available at the airports.

Special Needs
A special cave tour is offered for physically impaired persons. The visitor center is fully accessible. Loop D of the main campground, including restrooms, is wheelchair accessible. The picnic area is minimally accessible. The Heritage Trail is designed to accommodate people with disabilities.

Amenities
Cave tours ♦ Hiking ♦ River trips ♦ Horseback riding ♦ Fishing ♦ Ranger-led activities ♦ Bicycle trail ♦ Environmental education and elderhostel programs

Travel Advisory
Wear sturdy, low-heeled walking shoes in the caves. Persons with heart or respiratory conditions should consult a ranger before taking a cave tour. These underground visits can be strenuous.

Emergency Information

First aid is available in the park. The nearest hospital is Caverna Hospital at Horse Cave, U.S. 31W, 15 miles from the park.

Visitor and Information Centers

The park's visitor center sells cave tour tickets, presents orientation programs and movies and features exhibits. The visitor center is nine miles northwest of Park City and 10 miles west of Cave City.

Campgrounds

There are four developed campgrounds at Mammoth Cave. They are open year-round. Campsites are available on a first-come, first-served basis. The sites near Green River are particularly popular. Backcountry camping is permitted on the north side of the park. There are designated sites along trails.

Picnic Area

There is a picnic area near the visitor center. It has grills and restrooms. Supplies are available at the service center at park headquarters. This store is only open weekends in the spring and fall. A concessioner provides food service in the park.

Cabins, Lodges and Hotels

Mammoth Cave Hotel is in the park. It is open year-round. There are 107 air-conditioned units. The hotel has a restaurant and kennels. For reservation information call 502-758-2225. Woodland Cottages, near the hotel, are open from spring to early fall. Sunset Point Motor Lodge is open year-round.

Restaurants

The restaurant at Mammoth Cave Hotel is open year-round. For unique atmosphere, eat lunch underground at the Snowball Dining Room. It is in the cave.

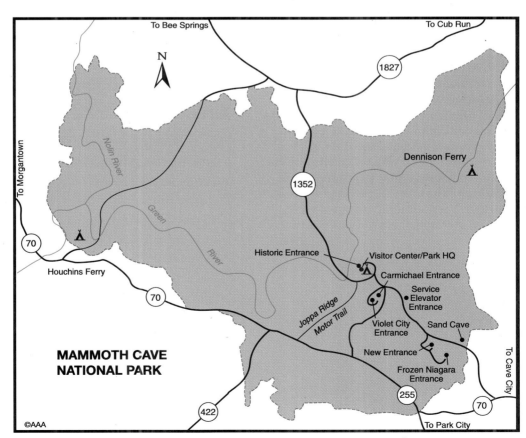

Park size: 52,700 acres

THINGS TO DO AND SEE

Cave Tours. A variety of guided cave tours are offered. Four tours are available in the summer. The shortest cave tour is the Discovery Tour, a 45-minute guided tour. Other options include the two-hour Historical Tour, which traces the long history of the cave. The Frozen Niagara Tour lasts two hours and highlights fine examples of flow-stone in the Niagara Room. The Lantern Tour, given only in summer, is led by guides with old fashioned kerosene lanterns.

Cave tours sell out quickly. Park officials strongly urge you to make reservations through DESTINET. Call 800-365-2267 no earlier than 56 days and no later than one hour before the tour. Fees ranging from $3.50 to $25 are charged, depending on your age and the tour you choose.

Boat Cruise. From April through October, an hour-long cruise along the Green River is available aboard the Miss Green II. For reservations call 502-758-2243. You can also canoe on the Green and Nolin Rivers. Canoe rentals are available from private outfitters outside the park.

Any one of several different guided tours will give you a good overview of stalactites, stalagmites, flowstone, gypsum flowers and other features of the park. There is also much natural beauty above-ground, on and around the Green River.

Hiking. There are 70 miles of trails in the park. The Kentucky Department of Parks can provide detailed information

about the trails. Call 502-564-5410. Sixty miles of trail on the north side of the park are backcountry. The remaining 10 miles are nature trails near the visitor center, on the south side of the park. The paved Heritage Trail begins near the Sunset Point Motor Lodge and is lighted for evening walks.

Fishing. You may fish in the Green River and Nolin River. You must have a Kentucky fishing license. Check at the visitor center for additional information and regulations.

Riding. There are 60 miles of trails open to horses. Guided trail tours are conducted by local outfitters such as Jesse James Riding Stables. Call 502-773-2560.

For More Information
Superintendent
Mammoth Cave National Park
Mammoth Cave, KY 42259
Tel. 502-758-2328

MAMMOTH CAVE GOES TO WAR

A hundred and forty feet underground, the cave still bears the scars of being hastily pressed into service as a nitrate mine during the War of 1812. Slaves hauled in logs, fabricated bleaching vats and filled them with soil from the cave's floor. They poured water over the vats and allowed the runoff to trickle into troughs as brine. Two pipelines fashioned from hollowed-out logs conveyed water into the cave and the nitrate-rich brine out of it. When the water evaporated it left a residue of nitrate crystals. In this labor-intensive fashion, slave labor produced gunpowder used against the British.

MESA VERDE NATIONAL PARK

Colorado ✦ **Established 1906**

There is a legend about Mesa Verde. In 1888, two cowboys rode through a snowstorm in the Four Corners country; the converging state boundaries of Colorado, Arizona, New Mexico and Utah. They were out in the harsh weather hunting for stray cattle. History doesn't record whether they found their missing livestock or not. They did however, see something absolutely astonishing.

Looming through the snow flurries like a hallucination, the empty windows and facades of a deserted city appeared high over their heads. It looked like an entire community, a fantastic ghost town built of stone.

Unwilling to believe their eyes, the cowhands created a makeshift ladder and went exploring. They walked through a honeycombed network of rooms and storehouses and handled pottery and stone tools still lying where the owners had left them seven centuries before.

These pre-Columbian cliff dwellings had once belonged to a people called the Anasazi, or "the ancient ones." Originally a tribe of nomads, the ancestral Puebloans became expert dry country farmers and city planners. Starting about 800 years ago, these mysterious Native Americans began erecting a spectacular series of cliff homes 2,000 feet above the Montezuma Valley. Many of these dwelling places are miraculously well preserved. They are the central attraction of Mesa Verde National Park.

Archaeologists believe the Anasazi originally lived in pithouses before they began to build conventional post and adobe homes for themselves. They left no written records. No one knows what prompted them to make their homes high in the side of cliffs. It must have been an incredibly difficult and time-consuming task. Tree ring dates gleaned from lumber used in the "Cliff Palace" found by the cowboys indicates that the construction job took about 70 years.

The basic building materials were rectangular blocks of sandstone, mortared together with a mixture of mud and water. There appears to be no standard plan to the houses. All of the building materials must have been hand-carried down the sides of cliffs to the construction sites. The structures seem to arise naturally from the cliffs, as if they had grown there.

The dwellings were built at around 7,000 feet above sea level, often several hundred feet above the mesa floor and one hundred feet below the mesa tops. The could only be reached by ladders or handholds and toeholds built into the canyon walls. Most structures were single family homes, but one cliff building has over 200 rooms. Anthropologists think the people were probably a matriarchal society.

The inhabitants lived in the front rooms of their cliff houses, usually in living spaces which averaged six feet by eight feet. The back rooms were mostly storage areas. Women made pottery or ground corn in the courtyards out front. Men fashioned tools out of stones and bone. In every house there was a kiva, or special room reserved for religious or ceremonial use. The kivas were round, and inside them the people gathered to pray for rain, rich harvests and good luck for their hunters.

On top of the mesa the men tended fields of corn, squash and beans. They also hunted for deer, rabbits and squirrels, cooking the wild game over fires they fed with juniper and piñon wood. It was a precarious life in more ways than one, with survival dependent upon the weather and the harvest. Every year enough food had to be cultivated and stored to keep everyone alive during the long winters.

The ancestral Puebloans were once known as expert basket weavers, but with the advent of pottery, they virtually forgot about baskets and elevated their everyday clay vessels into an art form.

Many surviving relics show the characteristic decoration of the artisans: intricate black designs painted on white pottery. Sometime during the late 1200s, the Anasazi people abandoned the incredible cliff communities it had taken so long to build.

Some people believe it was an extended drought that finally forced them to go elsewhere. Or perhaps it was soil exhaustion or famine arising from rapid population growth. For whatever reason, by the end of the 13th century the culture had vanished from the plateau, never to return.

PLANNING YOUR VISIT

Park Open
The main park road is open all year. There is limited access in winter. Peak visitation to the park is in July.

Seasons
Summer high temperatures reach the 90s. Evening temperatures fall to the mid-60s. Thundershowers are possible. In fall and spring, daytime temperatures reach the 60s and evening temperatures are in the 30s. Winter temperatures range from the 40s to the teens at night. There is an average 80 to 100 inches of snowfall.

Entrance Fees
Per vehicle...$10
Per individual $5
Fees are valid for 7 days.

Permits and Licenses
There is a fee for tours of Balcony House and Cliff Palace. Vehicles are allowed only on roads, turnouts or parking areas. Bicycles are not allowed on Wetherill Mesa Road. Mountain bikes are not permitted on hiking trails. Hiking is restricted to five trails within the park.

Access and Transportation
The park is in southwest Colorado, 35 miles west of Durango off U.S. 160.

From Durango. Take U.S. 160 for 10 miles east of Cortez or for eight miles west of Mancos. Note: It is 21 miles from the park entrance to the Chapin Mesa ruins.

A FEW TIPS

♦ *Hold on to your children on cliff trails and canyon rims.*

♦ *Visiting the cliff dwellings is strenuous. Elevations reach more than two miles above sea level. Exercise caution if you have cardiac or respiratory problems.*

♦ *Slopes can be slippery. Wear sturdy shoes with good tread.*

♦ *It is a federal offense to remove artifacts from the park.*

There is bus service from Grand Junction, Colorado and Galllup, New Mexico to Durango.

Trains serve Grand Junction, Colorado and Gallup, New Mexico and Durango. There are daily scheduled flights to Cortez, 10 miles from the park and Durango, 35 miles from the park. Rental cars are available in Durango and Cortez.

Special Needs

Scenic overlooks are accessible with assistance. The Chapin Mesa Archaeological Museum has accessible restrooms and a portable ramp. The Spruce Tree House and Step House cliff dwellings are accessible with assistance. Morefield Village

Campground has accessible restrooms, parking, paved walks and gravel trails. The visitor center has parking and ramps. Wetherill Mesa has accessible restrooms.

Amenities

Scenic drives ◆ Hiking trails ◆ Bus tours ◆ Ranger-led tours ◆ Tram

Travel Advisory

You will be cited and fined for entering a cliff dwelling without a park ranger present. Trailers and towed vehicles are prohibited beyond Morefield Village Campground.

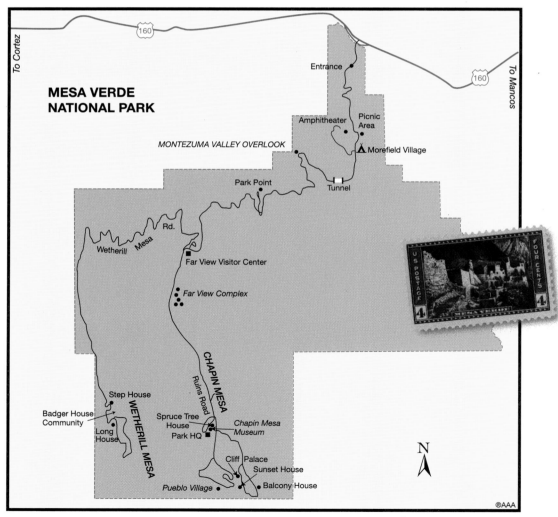

Park size: 52,085 acres

Emergency Information

First aid is available within the park. The closest hospital is in Cortez, Colorado, ten miles away.

Visitor and Information Centers

The Far View Visitor Center provides information and arts exhibits. It is closed fall to spring. Chapin Mesa Museum also exhibits arts and crafts.

Campgrounds

Camping is permitted only in a designated campground. Morefield Village Campground is four miles south of the main park entrance. There are 477 sites and toilets, tables, grills, utility hookups and a dump station. Campsites are available from mid-April to mid-October on a first-come, first-served basis. No backcountry camping is allowed. The gathering of firewood is prohibited. Camps should not be left unattended for more than 24 hours.

Picnic Areas

There are seven picnic areas off main roads. Picnic spots are at Wetherill Mesa, the Museum area on Chapin Mesa, both loops of Top Loop Road, Morefield Village Campground and two overlooks.

Cabins, Lodges and Hotels

Far View Motor Lodge is open May through October. For reservation information, call 303-529-4421 (summer) or 303-533-7731 (winter.)

Restaurants

Four restaurants in the park are open from May through October. You can get light meals and snacks at the restaurant in the Far View Motor Lodge, at Wetherill Mesa, at Far View

Terrace or in Morefield Village at the Knife Edge Café. Spruce Tree Terrace is open year-round.

THINGS TO DO AND SEE

Cliff Dwellings Tour. A daily six-hour tour of Chapin Mesa leaves from Far View Motor Lodge at 9 a.m., late May through mid-September. You will see pithouses, pueblo sites and cliff dwellings, with a stop at the museum for lunch. A fee is charged.

Spruce Tree House. The cliff dwelling is open on a self-guided basis in the summer. In the winter, three ranger-led tours are conducted daily.

Cliff Palace. Rangers guide tours of the dwelling in the summer, and sometimes in late spring and early fall, weather permitting. Tickets must be purchased at Far View Visitor Center.

Balcony House. This ranger-led tour requires climbing a 32-foot ladder and wriggling through an ancient crawlspace. Tours are conducted in summer only. Tickets must be purchased at Far View Visitor Center.

Far View Complex. The sites are open on a self-guided basis from mid-April to mid-November. A guide to the mesa-top pueblos is available at the visitor center and the museum.

Wetherill Mesa. Vehicles are allowed on the 12-mile stretch of road from the visitor center to the parking area on the mesa. From there, take the mini-tram to Long House for a ranger-led tour. The Badger House community of mesa-top villages and Step House are open for self-guided tours. They offer superb views of the surrounding area. The Wetherill Mesa is open only in the summer. Tickets must be purchased at Far View Visitor Center.

Scenic Drives. Many cliff dwellings can be viewed from canyon-rim viewpoints. There are wayside exhibits describing the development of the culture. Mesa Top Loop Road offers two six-mile, self-guided loops on Chapin Mesa. Park Point offers a panoramic view of the Four Corners region.

Hiking. Hiking is restricted to five trails in the park to protect the fragile sites. No hiking is permitted in winter. Register at the ranger's office before setting out on a hike. You'll need to register unless you opt for the one-mile loop from Soda Canyon Overlook to Cliff Palace-Balcony House. Two trails lead from Spruce Tree House Trail into Spruce Canyon. Petroglyph Point Trail and Spruce Canyon Trail are both a little more than two miles. Prater Ridge Trail is nearly eight miles. Two trails start at Morefield Village Campground.

Bicycling. You may ride a bike on all park roads except those on Wetherill Mesa. Lanes are narrow and crowded, especially in summer.

Near Mesa Verde National Park

Aztec Ruins National Monument, Aztec, New Mexico. This 319-acre site is in New Mexico, off U.S. 550, is about 60 miles southeast of Mesa Verde National Park. Facilities include exhibits and picnic areas. Misnamed by early settlers, this timber and masonry group of dwellings shows the influence of Anasazi peoples. This monument contains the only restored great kiva, or ceremonial chamber in the Southwest. The monument is open year-round. For information, call 505-334-6174.

San Juan National Forest, Durango, Colorado. This national forest is on U.S. 550, about 50 miles east of Mesa Verde National Park. There are more than 900 campsites and opportunities for a very wide range of activities. Visitors can fish, swim, hunt, ride, take a llama trek, boat, canoe or kayak and enjoy winter sports. Facilities are open all year. There is plenty to interest nature lovers and history buffs. Vegetation ranges from high alpine desert to piñon desert in this rugged San Juan mountains area, studded with lakes and rivers. There are also archaeological sites to explore.

For More Information

Superintendent
Mesa Verde National Park, CO 81330
Tel. 970-529-4554

PROTECT YOURSELF AND THE PARK

Some hiking rules are meant to protect you — such as the admonition to stick to designated trails — and some are meant to protect a fragile environment.

For your own safety, have a realistic idea of your limitations. Don't push yourself to hike a trail that is too steep, precarious or long. Walk at a moderate pace, preferably with others. If you must go solo, leave your itinerary with the rangers and let them know your expected return time. If you become lost, stay where you are until help arrives.

Know the signs of hypothermia and heat exhaustion. No matter what the climate, take water along — even for short hikes. The rule of thumb is to carry one gallon of water per person per day. Start your return trip before half you water is gone. Do not drink the water in park streams and lakes. Untreated water may contain Giardia, Campylobacter and other harmful organisms. To kill these organisms, you must bring water to a boil.

In Mesa Verde National Park, the number of trails is restricted to protect the ruins. Please tread lightly at any historical sites you visit. In other parks, trails may be restricted to protect the land from erosion and damage to plant life. Obey park rules and try to visit environmentally fragile areas in small groups. Do not take plants, rocks, fossils or artifacts as souvenirs. The national parks exist to showcase and safeguard the natural world.

MOUNT RAINIER NATIONAL PARK

Washington ◆ **Established 1899**

♦ *Hike only in groups in the backcountry. Bring topographic maps and inform the rangers of your route and destination.*

♦ *If you visit during the peak season from May to October, avoid weekends. Parking lots at Paradise and Sunrise are full by noon on weekends.*

♦ *If you plan a scenic drive during the winter, your vehicle should be equipped with all-season tires and tire chains.*

Native Americans called Mount Rainier "Tahoma," or "the great mountain." At 14,411 feet, Rainier towers over the 6,000-foot summits that guard its flanks. It is the greatest single-peak glacial system in the U.S.

Mount Rainier National Park is less than a three-hour drive from Seattle or Portland. It offers dense evergreen forests, seemingly endless wildflower strewn meadows, cascading waterfalls and sparkling white glaciers.

Mount Rainier is one of a string of volcanic mountains in the Cascade Range, which extends from Lassen Peak in California to British Columbia's Mount Garibaldi. Scientists believe Rainier is a relatively young volcano. It first erupted approximately one million years ago. Successive eruptions spewed out vast quantities of lava, ash and pumice. Layers of this material formed the towering mountain we see today.

There are 25 named glaciers and about 50 smaller, unnamed glaciers and ice packs on the mountain. They cover nearly 34 square miles of its slopes. Emmons Glacier is the largest.

Glaciers form when snow falls repeatedly upon unmelted snow. The weight of the snow causes it to compact, driving oxygen out and turning snow into ice.

Gravity goes to work on the dense, heavy ice, slowly drawing it down the mountainside.

The valleys and foothills of the mountain are free from ice. In the Carbon River section of the park, named for its surrounding coal deposits, rain falls heavily and the forests are at their thickest. The lowland forest in the Onhanapecosh section is famous for an ancient stand of timber called the Grove of the Patriarchs. The grove is full of grand-Douglas fir, western red cedar and western hemlock. Many trees are between 500 and 1000 years old.

In the late spring and summer the park's many broad meadows come alive with glacier lilies, phlox, pink mountain heather and other brilliantly colored wildflowers. The Paradise Valley is at the foot of the Nisqually Glacier. It offers a view of rolling green hills clad in wildflowers. Towering over it all is the snowy cap of Mount Rainier.

The park is full of wildlife. Expect to see deer, chipmunks, ground squirrels, marmots and pika. There are also thriving populations of elk, black bears and mountain goats. These species are shy of humans and are much less frequently seen.

PLANNING YOUR VISIT

Park Open

The park is open year-round. Only the Nisqually entrance remains open in winter. Peak visitation is in August.

Seasons

This area is subject to such sudden and extreme weather changes it is said that Mount Rainier creates its own weather. The park has heavy rain and snowfall, with the most precipitation from October to May. Average summer temperatures range from the mid-40s to the upper-70s at Longmire and from the lower 40s to the mid-60s at Paradise.

Entrance Fees

Per vehicle $10
Per individual $5
Fees are valid for seven days.

Permits and Licenses

A free permit is required for backcountry camping. Pick up a permit at visitor centers and ranger stations. Vehicles are restricted to established roads. Climbers must register with a ranger before climbing Mount Rainier. Solo climbers must request approval from the park. (Allow two weeks for approval.) A $15 fee is charged for each person attempting a summit climb. An annual fee is $25.

Access and Transportation

The park is located in west-central Washington, about 80 miles southwest of Seattle. Access is off Highway 410, which runs from Tacoma to Yakima.

For Southwestern Access. Go south on Route 7 from Tacoma to State Route 706 through Elbe and on to Longmire. The Nisqually entrance is 47 miles southeast of Tacoma.

From the Southeast. Take U.S. 12 to Highway 123 to Stevens Canyon entrance.

From the North. Take Highway 410 from Buckley to the White River entrance.

Greyhound and Trailways buses provide service to nearby towns and cities. Gray Line runs buses from Seattle and Tacoma to the park from mid-spring to mid-fall.

Amtrak provides service on both north-south and east-west routes stopping at Yakima, Ellensburg, East Auburn and Seattle. Major airports serve Portland and Seattle/Tacoma. Rental cars are available in Portland, Seattle, Tacoma and Yakima.

Special Needs

Paradise Visitor Center is fully accessible. Other visitor centers have limited access. The Longmire Museum and lodges are accessible. Cougar Rock Campground has a limited access campsite and restroom. Self-guided trails have limited access. Wheelchairs are available for short-term use at visitor centers. There are

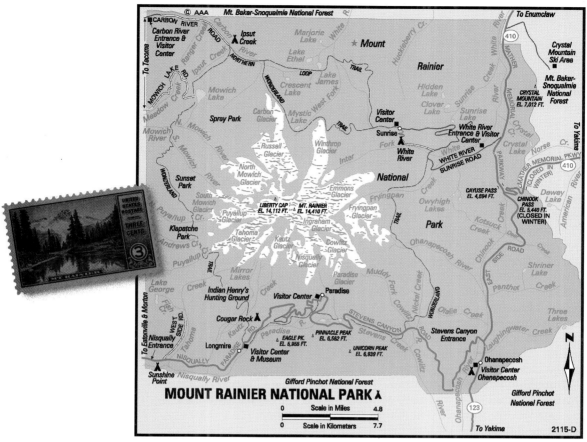

Park size: 235,404 acres

handicapped accessible rooms at the National Park Inn at Longmire.

Amenities

Scenic drive ♦ Hiking ♦ Guided mountaineering ♦ Horseback riding ♦ Winter sports ♦ Fishing ♦ Bicycling ♦ Guided snowshoe walks ♦ Winter sports equipment rental

Travel Advisory

Expect road closings in winter. Always carry rain gear. Be prepared for sudden weather changes. Only physically fit, well trained and well equipped climbers should attempt to scale Mount Rainier. Elevations in the park range from 1,880 feet at the Carbon River rain forest to 14,411 feet at the summit. Bicycles are not allowed on trails. Winding park roads are narrow and difficult to maneuver.

Emergency Information

First aid is available in the park. Hospitals are in Morton (40 miles away), Enumclaw (45 miles away) and Puyallup (60 miles away).

Visitor and Information Centers

There are four visitor centers. Longmire Visitor Center and Henry M. Jackson Visitor Center provide information and exhibits. Paradise Visitor Center presents audio-visual programs on the park. Ohanapecosh Visitor Center features an exhibit on the northwest forest. Sunrise Visitor Center features exhibits on the subalpine and alpine environments.

Campgrounds

Five drive-in campgrounds provide a total of 682 individual campsites and seven group sites. Developed campsites are available on a first-come, first-served basis for 14 days from mid-June through Labor Day. From Labor Day through June 15, there is a 30-day limit. Reservations are accepted for group sites up to 90 days prior to arrival. Make fires only in fire rings or grills at designated areas.

Sugar Rock. This area has 200 sites with RV hook-ups, water, firepits and restrooms. A trailhead for the Wonderland Trail is nearby.

Cougar Rock Campground. Cougar Rock has 200 sites and five group sites with water, flush toilets and a dump station. The campground is open late May to mid-October. Camping fee is $6 a night.

Ipsut Creek Campground. This campground has 29 sites and two group sites with water. The campground is open May through October. Camping fee is $5 a night.

Ohanepecosh Campground. It has 205 sites with water, flush toilets and a dump station. The campground is open late May to late October. Camping fee is $8 a night.

Sunshine Point Campground. It has 18 level sites with water and firepits. The campground is open all year. Camping fee is $5 a night.

White River Campground has 117 sites with water and flush toilets. The campground is open late June to late September. The camping fee is $6 a night.

Backcountry camping is allowed with a permit. Campers are required to pack out everything and use a portable camp stove. There are 20 designated campsites along the Wonderland Trail that circles Mount Rainier.

Picnic Areas

There are nine picnic areas. They are located at: Carbon River, Sunshine Point, Longmire, Cougar Rock, Paradise, Stevens Canyon, White River, Sunrise and Tipsoo Lake. Limited food and supplies are available at National Park Inn and Longmire, Sunrise Lodge and in the communities near the park.

Cabins, Lodges and Hotels

There are two accommodations in the park. National Park Inn at Longmire was built in 1917 and renovated in 1990. Two rooms are handicapped accessible. The inn's cozy lounge with oversized fireplace is inviting. It is open year-round. Paradise Inn at Paradise was also built in 1917. It is open mid-May to early October. The large, rustic lobby has two oversized stone fireplaces. There is also a gift shop.

For reservations at both inns, call Mount Rainier Guest Services, 360-569-2275.

Restaurants

The dining room at National Park Inn is open year-round. Dining rooms at Paradise Inn and Sunrise Lodge are open in the summer. There is also food service at Jackson Visitor Center in the summer.

THINGS TO DO AND SEE

Longmire Museum. Take a self-guided tour through a museum dedicated to the history of the park. Longmire Museum is located at the site of the old Mineral Springs Resort opened by James Longmire in 1884.

Mountain Guide Service. Mount Rainier covers eight miles and a vertical gain of more than 9,000 feet. Mountaineers are encouraged to use the long-established mountain guide service in the park. The school offers a one-day climbing class and leads summit climbs. Get current information on rates, reservations and equipment by contacting Rainier Mountaineering at 206-569-2227 (summer) and 206-627-6242 (winter).

Hiking. The park has 300 miles of hiking trails. The central feature of the park is its namesake, Mount Rainier. You can see the mountain throughout the park. The 93-mile Wonderland Trail encircles it. A complete circuit takes 10 days to two weeks. Paradise Valley is the center of most activity in the park. Silver Falls Loop is a good choice for hikers who prefer to stay at lower elevations. Also of interest is the lowland forest and the Grove of the Patriarchs.

Scenic Drives. Major roads run from the southwest entrance to the southern and eastern parts of the park. There is a spur to Sunrise on the northeast side of the mountain. Sunrise, the highest point you can reach by road, offers splendid views of Emmons Glacier. The section between the entrance and Longmire is one of the world's most beautiful mountain roads. There is also a separate road to Carbon River on the northwest. These roads were designed to make the least environmental impact possible. They are extremely narrow, with trees growing very close to the berm. All but the 18 miles of road between the southwest entrance and Paradise are closed in the winter.

Horseback Riding. Saddle and pack stock are permitted on more than 100 miles of trails. Most of these trails are in the lower forest.

Winter Sports. Snowshoeing, cross-country skiing and snowboarding are popular at Paradise, the primary winter sports area in the park. Some winter sports equipment can be rented at Longmire.

Fishing. You may fish the park's lakes and streams with a Washington fishing license. However, there are some restrictions, so check with a ranger. Catch-and-release fishing is encouraged. The daily limit is six pounds plus one fish, not to exceed a total of 12 fish.

For More Information

Superintendent
Mount Rainier National Park
Tahoma Woods, Star Route
Ashford, WA 98304
Tel. 360-569-2211

NORTH CASCADES NATIONAL PARK

Washington ◆ **Established 1968**

North Cascades National Park is isolated and rugged, a mountain wilderness in the far northwest reaches of Washington State. It is a land of subalpine meadows and countless waterfalls, of streams and rivers. Glacier-clad peaks spring up almost vertically from forested valleys. The hundreds of snowcapped mountains in the park's proximity are part of the Cascade Range, sometimes called the American Alps. The Cascade range extends from British Columbia to Northern California.

The park is part of the North Cascades National Park Service Complex which contains the Lake Phelan and Ross Lake National Recreation areas. The three facilities are separated only by an invisible border. In fact, the Ross Lake Recreation area cuts right through the middle of North Cascades and serves as the dividing line between the National Park's North and South units.

The North Unit borders Canada and encompasses Mount Shuksan and the Picket Ridge, known for glaciers, high peaks, mountain valleys and remote valleys. The South Unit includes the so-called "Eldorado High Country" and the Stehekin River Valley, one of the most impressive glacier-carved canyons in the Cascades.

Although some of North Cascades National Park near Ross Lake is well traveled, sections of the park are seldom seen. This is not for any lack of scenic splendor, but simply because these isolated areas are difficult for anyone but an experienced wilderness hiker to visit. Still, the main road through Ross Lake National Recreation Area and more than 360 miles of trails allows vacationers to enjoy the peaceful solitude of the forests and the dramatic impact of North Cascade's mountains and glaciers.

Scientists have charted more than 300 active glaciers in the park. This is more than half the glaciers in the lower 48 states. Meltwater from the glaciers flows down the mountainsides, eventually joining with streams to become a river, or cascading over a high cliff as a waterfall.

Sometimes the silence of the woods is shattered by deep rumbling sounds as glacier ice breaks off and crashes down into the valley. The crevassed ice masses present special

A FEW TIPS

♦ *Take cold weather gear. It can snow in mid-summer.*

♦ *Crossing snowfields may require special equipment.*

♦ *In the backcountry, hang your food out of reach of bears.*

♦ *Check stream conditions with park rangers before starting wilderness trips.*

challenges to even the most experienced mountain climbers.

Moist air blowing in from Puget Sound and the Strait of Juan De Fuca feeds the glaciers. Blowing in from the west, the ocean air condenses into snow and rain over the mountain tops. This depletes most of its moisture. The remaining air is much warmer and drier when it reaches the eastern slopes.

Western red cedar, hemlock and Douglas fir thrive on slopes drenched by 110 inches of rain a year. By way of contrast, perhaps 35 inches of rain a year fall in Stehekin at the head of Lake Chelan. You can see the results in the different vegetation. Only Ponderosa pine and sagebrush flourish in the rain shadow of the peaks.

More than 1,500 different species of plants thrive in the park. The evergreen forests of the lowlands are relieved by open meadows at higher elevations. In spring, the meadows shed their snow mantle and come alive with brilliant mountain wildflowers. You might also see yarrow, thimbleberry, elderberry and serviceberry.

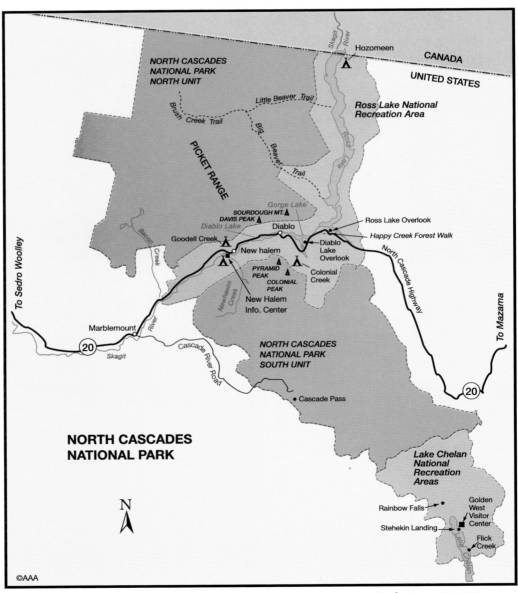

Park size: 504,780 acres

The park is especially rich in animal life. Many species live here, including bears, wolves, mountain lions, blacktail deer, river otters, spotted owls and marmots. Bald eagles are often seen feeding on salmon from the streams. Observant hikers will spot a profusion of other birds, reptiles and amphibians.

In the late 1800s, prospectors searched these mountains for lead, gold and platinum. Some made promising strikes at first. In the long run, travel to this out of the way land proved too much of an impediment for profitable mining. The mines were abandoned by 1910. Logging operations proved equally difficult.

The one successful commercial endeavor in the park has been at the initiative of the Seattle City Light Company. The utility built three dams on the Skagit River. The dams created the Ross, Diablo and Gorge Lakes. These lakes and the creeks in the region are favorites with trout fishermen.

PLANNING YOUR VISIT

Park Open

The park is open year-round. Many areas are inaccessible in the winter due to snowfall. Peak visitation is in August.

Seasons

The North Cascades get more rain on their western side than the eastern side. Therefore, expect more cold weather and cloudy days west of the range. Summer temperatures may reach almost 100° at drop to the 40s and night. Average summer highs are in the 70s, with lows in the 50s. Average winter highs are in the 30s with lows in the 20s.

Entrance Fee

There is no entrance fee.

Permits and Licenses

Free backcountry camping permits are required. They are available at park headquarters and ranger stations. Grazing is not permitted in the park. Adequate feed should be carried for horses. A locally available Washington State fishing license is required. No hunting is permitted. No pets are allowed on the trails or in the cross-country areas except the Pacific Crest Trail, where leashes are required. Mountain bikes, trail bikes and other motorized equipment are prohibited on trails.

Access and Transportation

The park is in north-central Washington. From I-5, take Route 20 east. Highway 20 crosses the park through the Ross Lake district. To reach the Stehekin area of the park, you must hike or take the Chelan ferry or a floatplane.

There are no paved roads into the park.

From Burlington. Take Highway 20, the North Cascades Highway, to Ross Lake National Recreation Area and trailheads into the park. Vehicle access to Ross Lake is by unpaved road from Canada only. Stehekin is reachable only by boat or floatplane from Chelanor by trail.

Amtrak serves Seattle. Greyhound and Trailways both provide bus service to Seattle. Rental cars are available at the airport in Seattle.

Special Needs

Most information facilities are wheelchair accessible. The Happy Creek Forest Walk and the Washington Pass Overlook are also wheelchair accessible.

Amenities

Scenic drives ♦ Hiking ♦ Mountaineering ♦ Boating ♦ Fishing ♦ Bicycling ♦ Naturalist hikes ♦ Boat tours

Travel Advisory

The park lakes are cold. Swimming is not recommended. Be cautious when crossing streams and traveling outside of developed areas.

Emergency Information

First aid is available at ranger stations. The nearest hospital is in nearby Sedro Woolley.

Visitor and Information Centers

There are three visitor centers: Sedro Wolley, Newhalem Creek (off North Cascades Highway) and Golden West (at Steheken on Lake Chelan).

Campgrounds

There are 13 campgrounds in the park. Sites are available on a first-come, first-served basis. Fires are permitted only at designated areas. Only downed or dead wood may be used for fires.

Gooddell Creek Campground. This area has 22 sites, tables water, vault toilets and is accessible off the main road.

Newhalem Creek Campground. This campground has 129 sites, tables, water and vault toilets. It is accessible off the main road.

Colonial Creek Campground. It has 164 sites, tables, water, vault toilets and is accessible off the main road.

Hozomeem Campground. There are 122 sites, tables water and vault toilets. It is off Ross Lake.

There are nearly 100 backcountry campgrounds and another 30 sites for horse campers. Backcountry campgrounds accessible by trail only include: Cottonwood Campground, Flat Creek Campground, Park Creek Campground, Shady Campground, Dolly Varden Campground, Tumwater Campground, Highbridge Campground, Harelequin Campground and Purple Point Campground.

Picnic Areas

There are picnic sites at Goodell Creek, off the main road, at Hozomeem, off Ross Lake and at a dozen sites in the southern unit and the Lake Chelan area.

Cabins, Lodges and Hotels

There are no lodges in the park. There are lodges in the recreation areas that are open during summer:

Ross Lake Resort. This is accessible from the main road. Call 206-386-4437.

North Cascades Lodge. This is on Lake Chelan and is accessible only by boat, floatplane, or trail. Call 509-682-4711.

Stehekin Valley Ranch. This is in the Lake Chelan area and is accessible only by boat, floatplane, or trail. Call 509-682-4677.

Silver Bay Inn, Bed and Breakfast. This is in the Lake Chelan area and is accessible only by boat, floatplane, or trail. Call 509-682-2212.

Cabins For Rent. These are in the Lake Chelan area, accessible only by boat, floatplane or trail. For information write: Flick Creek House, Box 25, Silver Bay Guest House, Box 43, Stehekin Log Cabin, Box 288, all Stehekin, WA 98852.

Restaurants

Diablo Lake Resort, North Cascades Lodge and Stehekin Valley Ranch all have restaurants that are open in summer.

THINGS TO DO AND SEE

Mountaineering. Climbing trips can be arranged through local concessionaires. Write to the park for a list.

Boat Trips. Guided boat trips are available from Ross Lake Resort. Scenic 55-mile ferryboat trips up Lake Chelan to Steheken guarantee beautiful scenery. Call Chelan Boat Company at 509-682-2224.

Guided Hikes. Guided hikes of the 360 miles of park trails are provided by local concessionaires. Write to the park for a list.

Llama Treks. Deli Llama Wilderness Adventures leads four-day llama treks for about $500 per person. Call 206-757-4212 for more information.

Scenic Drives. The jagged peaks of the North Cascades are the central attraction of this undeveloped park. Few roads actually go into the park, but on clear days there are views of the park from the North Cascades Highway into Ross Lake Recreation Area. Called "the most scenic mountain drive in Washington," the Highway provides roadside vistas of Gorge, Diablo and Ross Lakes. Only Gorge and Diablo can be reached by vehicle from the highway.

Diablo Lake Overview offers superb views of Diablo Lake, Sourdough Mountain, Davis Peak, Colonial Peak, Pyramid Peak and spectacular features of the Skagit River. There are wayside exhibits and viewpoints (including a view of the Picket Range from Newhalem). Take the Cascade River Road, 25 miles of improved dirt and gravel, to reach the Cascade Pass Trail.

Hiking. There are 360 miles of trails in the park. A shuttle bus runs from Stehekin to major trailheads along a 23-mile road. Some of the most popular hikes are backpacking trips to Horseshoe Basin and the 11-mile Cascade Pass-Sahale Loop. This hike leads through the Stehekin River valley, passing the Sahale Glacier.

Near North Cascades National Park

Skagit River Bald Eagle Natural Area. This 924-acre refuge for bald eagles is located off Washington Highway 20, about ten miles from North Cascades National Park in Rockport. There are no visitors facilities, but viewing areas do accommodate wheelchairs. Eagles can be observed feeding on chum salmon along the Skagit River. The eagle population is at its peak in mid-January. The refuge is operated by the Nature Conservancy.

Mount Baker-Snoqualmie National Forest. More than a million acres of national forest adjoin North Cascades National Park and Mount Rainier National Park. This forest has 1,596 campsites, trails, boat ramps, scenic drives and handicapped access facilities. Visitors can enjoy both winter sports and water sports among the evergreens, lakes and streams. The forest is open all year. Campsites are only available May through October. Roads are often impassable in winter. For more information call 306-442-0170.

For More Information

North Cascades National Park
2105 Highway 20
Sedro Woolley, WA 98284
Tel. 360-856-5700

OLYMPIC NATIONAL PARK

Washington ♦ **Established 1938**

Washington State's Olympic Peninsula has been characterized as a gift from the sea. With its 57 miles of Pacific coastline, to its snow-capped, glacier-peaked Olympic Range and its four different rain forests, the peninsula is steeped in moisture.

The rock which later became the Olympic mountains was once completely submerged. To this day, marine fossils can be found embedded in their summits. About 29 million years ago, the tectonic plate under the floor of the Pacific Ocean shifted, colliding with the plate supporting the continent of North America. When the heavy oceanic plate slid under the lighter continental one, the upper layers of seabed buckled, colliding with the coastline. The ridges of seabed finally assumed the contours of the present-day Olympic Mountain range after being sculpted by glaciers, streams and eons of erosion.

Moisture-laden winds from the Pacific sweep eastward over the area, depositing rain, snow and mist. This steady replen-

ishment of moisture sustains one of the most unusual features of the park.

There are four rain forests on the Peninsula: Bogachiel, Queets, Hoh and Quinault. All of the rain forests are tucked into valleys facing the ocean. In their cool dark environments, lush vegetation thrives. The plant life is uncommonly diverse, ranging from the moss and wild mushrooms underfoot to ancient, towering trees. The forests extend throughout the Olympic Peninsula and up the mountain slopes. Moderate temperatures combined with so much moisture make for ideal growing conditions. Although these mountain slope forests receive less rain than the rain forests, they still drink in an average 100 inches of precipitation a year.

Cedar, fir and hemlock grow in dense stands. The alpine meadows of the mountain slopes are alive with wildflowers in the spring and summer. This area is also home to the largest herd of Olympic elk.

The Olympic Range extends about 40 miles. Mount Olympus, at 7,965 feet the tallest of the mountains, is actually at the center of the range. Inside the park, the

A Few Tips

♦ *Quotas have been established for visitors to Dosewallips and the Staircase areas of the park.*

♦ *Reservations can be made at the visitor center or by contacting park headquarters.*

♦ *Rain gear is recommended at any time of the year.*

♦ *Do not approach deer or bears.*

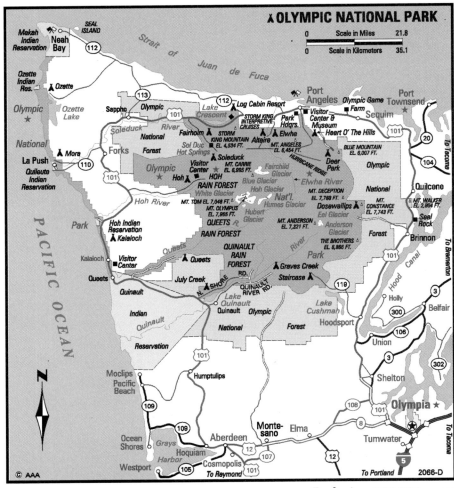

Park size: 922,626 acres

range is roughly circular. The land is contoured by 13 rivers that radiate out like the spokes of a wheel. To the north and east, the mountains drop abruptly to the waters of the Strait of Juan De Fuca and the Hood Canal. To the south and west, the slopes descend gently.

On many mountain summits, fresh snow falls on top of previous snowfalls, forming glaciers. There are 60 active glaciers with a combined total area of about 30 square miles scattered over various peaks in the park. Mount Olympus alone has six glaciers on its peak. It receives up to 200 inches of precipitation a year. The meltwater runoff from the glaciers is fed through the complex skein of rivers and streams. The result is the lushness and fertility you see throughout Olympic National Park.

Sixty miles of wild and scenic shoreline is a very different environment. This strip of land is part of the park but not directly connected to it. Here seals, sea lions and whales can be observed swimming off the rocky shores. The tide pools are alive with snails, sea urchins and star fish.

Eight kinds of plants and five kinds of animal on the peninsula live nowhere else in the world. This wilderness is as precious as it is beautiful.

PLANNING YOUR VISIT

Park Open

The park is open year-round. Peak visitation is in August.

Seasons

The park has a moderate marine climate. Summer is generally warm, but it is cooler at the higher elevations. There is more precipitation on the western side of the park than the eastern side. Rain is widespread throughout. High temperatures range from 65° to 80°, lows from 45° to 55°. Winter is colder, with afternoon highs about 32° to 50°. Higher elevations are snow covered from early November to late June. Rain is very frequent. Spring and fall are marked by highly variable weather and temperatures anywhere from 35° to 70°.

Entrance Fees

Per vehicle $10
Per person $5
   Fees are valid for 7 days.

Permits and Licenses

Vehicles of all kinds are restricted to park roads. Backcountry camping permits are free. Permits are available at all ranger stations.

Access and Transportation

The park is in the central portion of Washington's Olympic Peninsula. It also includes a narrow 63-mile strip of the Pacific Coast. The Olympic Peninsula is the northwest tip of the United States, west of Seattle/Tacoma and Puget Sound. U.S. 101 travels around the park.

There are regularly scheduled flights to Port Angeles from Seattle or Portland and to Sequim from Seattle.

Seattle is an Amtrak destination. Port Angeles is served by Greyhound Bus Lines, operating several trips daily from Seattle. Rental cars are available in Port Angeles, Sequim and Grays Harbor, as well as in all larger cities in the Puget Sound area.

In-Park Transportation

There is regularly scheduled ferry service across Puget Sound with connections to the Hood Canal Floating Bridge and Bremerton. Schedules are available from Washington State Ferries. Call 800-542-0810. Most of the year, a ferry runs between Port Angeles and Victoria (British Columbia, Canada). Call 206-457-4491 for schedule and fare information. Victoria Rapid Transit operates a seasonal, passengers-only ferry service. Call 206-452-8088.

Special Needs

An accessibility guide is available at park headquarters. There are wheelchair accessible restrooms in most of the campgrounds. Some trails are wheelchair accessible. Other trails are accessible with assistance. Sol Duc Hot Springs Resort has hot spring pools and accessible cabins. There are also accessible lodgings at Crescent Lodge and Kalaloch Lodge.

Amenities

Ferry ♦ Scenic drives ♦ Hiking trails ♦ Swimming ♦ Fishing ♦ Winter sports ♦ Naturalist programs ♦ Park newspaper ♦ Grocery stores

Travel Advisory

Be careful when hiking along the coast; rocks and logs can be slippery and unstable.

Emergency Information

First aid is available at most ranger stations. The closest hospitals are in Port

Angeles, Forks, Shelton and Aberdeen-Hoquiam.

Visitor and Information Centers

There are three main visitors centers: Olympic Park, Hurricane Ridge and Hoh, which is in the rain forest. Olympic Park, in Port Angeles, is open year-round and features a small theater/auditorium and children's activity room. The Wilderness Information Center is at the Olympic Park Visitor Center. Hurricane Ridge and Hoh Visitor Centers may be self-service during winter months. There are ranger stations at Hoodsport, Staircase, Storm King (at Lake Crescent), Ozette and Kalaloch.

Campgrounds

There are 16 campgrounds in the park and many of them are on the lake. Most are open from June through September but a few are open year-round. Campsites are available on a first-come, first-served basis for a stay not longer than 14 days. All campgrounds have toilets, firepits and grills. Only dead and downed firewood must be collected for fires. Camping fees vary with the campground and the season.

Backcountry camping is permitted with a wilderness use permit. During peak summer season, reservations may also be required up to 30 days in advance. Call the park's Wilderness Information Center at 360-452-0300. If you do camp in the backcountry, choose an established site and pack out all trash. Open wood fires are prohibited in many areas.

Picnic Areas

There are seven picnic areas located off main park roads. There are grocery and camper supply stores at Fairholm General Store, Log Cabin Resort, Sol Duc Hot Springs Resort and Kalaloch Lodge.

Cabins, Lodges and Hotels

There are four lodges in the park: Kalaloch, Lake Crescent, Log Cabin and Sol Duc Hot Springs. They are open from late April through late September. For reservation information for Kalaloch Lodge call 360-962-2271. For reservation information for Lake Crescent call 360-928-3211. For reservation information for Log Cabin Resort motel units and cabins call 360-928-3245. For reservation information for the Sol Duc Hot Springs Resort call 360-327-3583.

Restaurants

The four park lodges all have dining rooms that are open from April through September or early October. The dining room, lounge and coffee shop at Kalaloch Lodge are open year-round.

THINGS TO DO AND SEE

Interpretive Tours. Rangers lead interpretive tours from July through Labor Day. Check at any visitor center or ranger station for more information.

Hiking. There are nearly 600 miles of varied trails in the park – high passes, primitive trails, easy nature walks and rugged beach treks. The rain forests are a major feature and the Hoh Rain Forest is probably the most visited. The Pacific shoreline, including the Kalaloch, Mora and Ozette areas is scenic. Lake Crescent is the site of many recreational opportunities. Hurricane Ridge and the Sol Duc River are also of interest.

Scenic Drives. The park has 168 miles of roads which are spurs off U.S. Highway 101. Nearly half the roads are gravel. No roads cross the wilderness. The central attraction in the park is Mount Olympus, which can be viewed in the distance. It is not possible to drive very near the mountain. None of the roads into the park meet each other and none crosses the park. Therefore, to visit the different sections of the park, you must use separate roads. Heart O' The Hills Road, leading to Hurricane Ridge, offers many scenic views, especially at Lookout Rock, a turnout area just before the tunnels. Other scenic paved routes include U.S. 101 just west of Port Angeles, which travels part of the length of Lake Crescent. Hoh River Road, from the west of the park, takes you into the Hoh

Rain Forest. A road off U.S. 101 will take you past Quinault Lake. You can continue north and travel up part of the coastal area of the park, passing Kalaloch.

Near Olympic National Park

Olympic National Forest. The forest nearly surrounds Olympic National Park, so the terrain and recreational features are one in the same. The National Forest consists of 631,514 acres, with 402 campsites. It is open all year, but most campsites are open from May through October. For more information call 206-753-9534.

Nisqually National Wildlife Preserve, Olympia, Washington. This 2,818-acre preserve is off I-5, about 35 miles south of Olympic National Park. There are no campsites but there are photo blinds. Visitors come to hike, fish, boat and observe waterfowl, marsh and wading birds, including 19 species of duck and raptors that visit the river delta on Puget Sound. The preserve is open year-round, dawn to dusk. For more information call 206-753-9467.

For More Information

Superintendent
Olympic National Park
600 East Park Avenue
Port Angeles, WA 98362
Tel. 360-452-0330

PETRIFIED FOREST NATIONAL PARK

Arizona ♦ **Established 1962**

Other areas of the world have petrified forests, but Petrified Forest National Park is the largest concentration of the brightest colored petrified wood in the world.

Prehistoric Arizona was a vast floodplain covered with streams and inhabited by dinosaurs, reptiles and amphibians. Many of its trees were 200 feet tall. Those species no longer exist as living organisms, but time has worked upon their remains, fashioning what was once wood into beautifully colored stone.

When the ancient trees died, they toppled and were carried to the floodplain by heavy streams. They were shorn of their roots and branches in the fast water, ending up as solid logs. The logs were covered with silt and mud. This dramatically slowed the process of decay.

Volcanic activity in the area filled the air with ash and silica, which wafted down into the marshes. Silica-bearing water gradually seeped into the logs. These deposits crystallized into quartz. The logs were preserved, now full of semiprecious agate, jasper, rose quartz and amethyst.

When the land eventually sank, the logs once again became covered with sediment. Over the centuries, earthquakes and major upheavals of the land cracked buried logs into the smaller pieces found in the park today. When the land rose, so did the petri-

fied wood. Wind and rain washed away the sediment, burnishing the beautiful colors. In some areas of the park, as much as 300 feet of fossil-bearing material is buried.

The northern part of the park also encompasses the colorful badlands of the painted desert and Native American ruins dating from A.D. 800 to A.D. 1400.

PLANNING YOUR VISIT

Park Open

The park is open year-round.

Seasons

Expect high winds. Summers are warm and clear in the daytime. Typical highs reach the 90s, lows dip to the 50s. Thunderstorms are frequent and sudden, accounting for 50 percent of the park's annual nine inches of precipitation. Winter brings highs in the 40s and lows in the 20s. Storms may cause road closures.

Entrance Fees

Per vehicle...$10
Per individual $5
Fees are valid for seven days.

Permits and Licenses

Free wilderness backpacking permits are available. Federal law prohibits removal of any petrified wood or other natural cultural object. Heavy fines are levied against violators.

Access and Transportation

The park is in east-central Arizona, accessible from I-40 (U.S. 66) on the north end and U.S. 180 on the south end. A 27-mile paved road connects these two highways. The north entrance is 26 miles from Holbrook on I-40. The south entrance is 19 miles from Holbrook on U.S. 180. Trains stop at Winslow, Arizona and bus service reaches Holbrook. The closest airports are in Flagstaff, Phoenix and Albuquerque. Rental cars are available at the airport and in Holbrook.

Special Needs

All major facilities, including concessions, are accessible. A detailed accessibility guide is available from park headquarters.

Amenities

Scenic drives ◆ Hiking ◆ Ranger-led programs ◆ Scenic pullouts ◆ Curio shops

Travel Advisory

Do not climb on petrified logs. Stay on trails and behind barricades. There have been cases of bubonic plague in this area. Risk of exposure is slight, but check with park rangers for current information.

Emergency Information

There are emergency medical technicians in the park and an ambulance service in Holbrook. The nearest hospitals are in Winslow, Arizona and Gallup, New Mexico.

A FEW TIPS

◆ *Park elevations range from 5,100 to 6,235 feet. Beware of over-exertion at high altitudes.*
◆ *Always carry sufficient water.*
◆ *Notify park personnel before undertaking extended hikes.*

Visitor and Information Centers

Painted Desert Visitor Center is at the north entrance. It shows a 17-minute film on how wood become petrified. At the south entrance, Rainbow Forest Museum exhibits petrified wood and fossils.

Campgrounds

There are no developed campgrounds within the park. Wilderness camping is allowed in the Painted Desert area and the Rainbow Forest area. There are private campgrounds in Holbrook (25 miles from the park), Sitgreaves National Forest (50 miles south), Coconino National Forest (100 miles west) and Cholla Lake County Park (35 miles west).

PURLOINING THE PETRIFIED WOOD

Many visitors just can't resist taking petrified wood out of the park as a souvenir. Some years ago park rangers, secretly placed a number of marked petrified wood specimens beside a major trail. Two weeks later, nearly a quarter of the marked specimens had vanished.

People have always looted the Petrified Forest. In 1851, military surveyors passing through the area helped themselves to saddlebags full of souvenirs. For a time, fossilized logs were carted off by the wagonload, destined to become tabletops, mantels and decorative inserts. Gem collectors of the 1890s simply dynamited the fossilized logs in the hunt for amethyst and quartz crystals.

Please remember that there are strict regulations against removing anything from the park. Heavy fines are imposed against violators. If you must have some petrified wood as a keepsake, buy some in one of the souvenir or rockhound stores in Holbrook or other nearby communities.

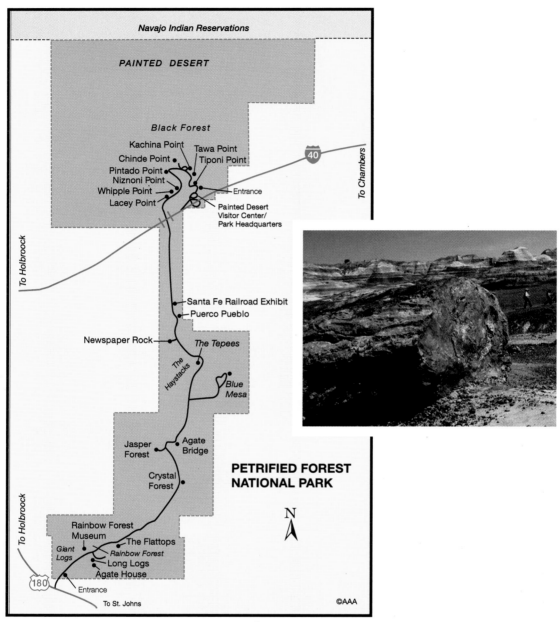

Park size: 93,533 acres

Picnic Areas

Picnic areas at Rainbow Forest and Chinde Point have water and toilets in warmer months. Food and souvenirs are sold in the park.

Cabins, Lodges and Hotels

There are no accommodations within the park.

Restaurants

A cafeteria at the park's north entrance is open all year. At the south entrance, a snack bar is open all year.

THINGS TO DO AND SEE

Rainbow Forest Museum. The museum offers excellent exhibits and explanations of how the Petrified Forest came to be and continues to change.

Popular Sites. Admire petrified wood at Rainbow Forest, Giant Logs, Jasper Forest, Agate Bridge and the Blue Mesa. The Painted Desert is also of great scenic interest. There are several Native American ruins dating before A.D. 1400. The Puerco Pueblo is the remains of a pueblo consisting of about 75 rooms surrounding a courtyard. Newspaper Rock is a block of sandstone covered with petroglyphs, signs and symbols which have never been interpreted. Agate House is a partially restored pueblo made of petrified wood chunks.

Hiking. If you're up for a rugged hike, visit Pilot Rock, the park's highest point.

Any of the paved trails such as Blue Mesa, Crystal Forest, Long Logs or Giant Logs are easier — just short jaunts off paved park roads.

Scenic Drive. The 28-mile park road will take you to all the park's main features. It winds along the rim of the Painted Desert, passes through archeological areas and leads to petrified wood sites. The road runs north-south through the length of the park, allowing you to enter at one end and exit at the other without doubling back. Allow several hours to stop at all the scenic pullouts. The six-mile road along the desert rim has eight overlooks that offer sweeping views of the Painted Desert. A three-mile spur road climbs Blue Mesa. The Jasper Forest Overlook shows the area's topography and the petrified logs strewn below. Long Logs is near the south entrance. Many trunks here are more than 100 feet long.

For More Information

Superintendent
PO Box 2217
Petrified Forest National Park, AZ 86028
Tel. 520-524-6228

REDWOOD NATIONAL PARK

California ♦ Established 1968

A FEW TIPS

♦ *Redwood Information Center loans animal-proof food canisters.*

♦ *Pack layers of clothing and rain gear at any time of year.*

♦ *Swim in Smith River or Redwood Creek. Ocean swimming is not advised due to extremely cold water and dangerous undertow.*

♦ *Be aware that ticks may transmit Lyme disease. Use insect repellent when hiking.*

Sequoia sempervirens, or Coast Redwoods, are not only the tallest trees, but the tallest living things on the planet. The world's tallest living tree, 365.5 feet tall, stands in a grove within the park on the banks of Redwood Creek. Nearby stands the third tallest tree on earth. The Redwood National Park exists to protect these majestic remnants, one time residents in a mighty forest of more than 2 million acres. Before the last ice age, thousands of redwood forests were dotted across the face of North America. Today, only a fraction survive.

At the turn of the century, the coast redwood was in grave danger of being eradicated by the logging industry. The State of California and a private organization, The Save The Redwoods League, came to their rescue, acquiring hundreds of redwood groves and placing them under the protection of 37 state parks.

In 1968, Redwood National Park was established by gathering three state parks under its new status: Jedediah Smith, Del Norte Coast and Prairie Creek.

Redwood National Park stands at the northern limit of the coast redwood's modern range. The climate of the rest of the continent is no longer conducive to the growth of the giant trees. They now flourish only on a narrow strip of land on the Pacific Coast, extending from Curry County in southern Oregon to south of Monterey, California. The growth zone is within 30 miles of the coast and exists only at elevations below 3,000 feet. Cool moist air from the Pacific Ocean is essential to the coast

redwood, as is fog, heavy rainfall and a moderate temperature year round.

The redwood's vulnerable point is its broad but shallow root system. The roots are sometimes only ten feet deep and lack a deep tap root. This can result in inadequate support for their towering trunks. High winds can be fatal to the big trees, causing them to topple. Toppling is their leading cause of death. Nobody knows why, but there seems to be no correlation between the age of a redwood and its size. The oldest trees are not necessarily the tallest or bulkiest.

The shade from these trees creates a perfect environment for azaleas, rhododendrons and lush ferns. The flowers add a blaze of color in the spring.

Animals seen in the park include mountain lions, blacktail deer and the Roosevelt elk, the second largest member of the deer family. The Roosevelt elk is found only in this part of the country. The park is the habitat of some 300 species of birds, about half of which live near the water. Beaver, mink and otter thrive in the park's freshwater lakes and streams.

Redwood National Park also includes 40 miles of rugged coastline. The beaches are wild and rocky. Gray whales are often spotted offshore, migrating from their summer feeding route in the Arctic to their winter calving area in Baja, California. The whales pass the park in December and again in the spring, when pods escort their young back north.

Harbor seals frequent the rocks off the park's stretch of coastline. Porpoises and sea lions are also spotted on a fairly regular basis. Closer to shore, the tide pools are full of sea urchins, starfish, crabs and barnacles. This tidepool is a good spot for clamming and surf fishing.

Planning Your Visit

Park Open

The park is open year-round. Peak visitation is in July.

Seasons

The coastal climate is usually moist and warm, with wet winters, cool summers and frequent fog or wind from the ocean. The ocean influences seasonal temperatures, which become more extreme inland. River and coastal valleys are warmer and less windy than the coastline. July temperatures inland are in the 70s to 90s, while on the coast they are in the 50s to 60s. Snow is uncommon.

Entrance Fees

There is a $5 a day users fee at Prairie Creek Redwoods State Park, Del Norte Coast Redwoods State Park and Jedediah Smith Redwoods State Park.

Permits and Licenses

Pick up permits for backcountry camping and vehicle access to Tall Trees Grove

trailhead at the information center. No pets are permitted on the trails. California fishing licenses are available at hardware and tackle shops. Trailers should not venture off the main roads due to steep grades and general road conditions.

Access and Transportation

The park is in northwestern California. U.S. 101 runs the length of the park. Redwood National Park begins at Orick, which is 330 miles north of San Francisco.

There are three main park entrances, Crescent City, Orick and Hiouchi.

From the North. Take U.S. 101 south for 26 miles from Brookings, Oregon to the Crescent City entrance.

From the South. Follow U.S. 101 north for 44 miles from Eureka to the Orick entrance.

From the Northeast. Take U.S. 199 southwest for 75 miles from Grants Pass, Oregon to the Hiouchi entrance.

Greyhound Bus serves Crescent City. There is no train service to the park. The nearest airports are in San Francisco. There are several passenger flights to Arcata and Crescent City, where rental cars are available.

Special Needs

An access guide is available at information centers, which are themselves wheelchair accessible. Wayside exhibits can be viewed from autos. Accessible restrooms are available at Lady Bird Johnson Grove, Requa Road, Redwood Creek Trailhead and the picnic areas at Lagoon Creek, Lost Man Creek and Crescent Beach.

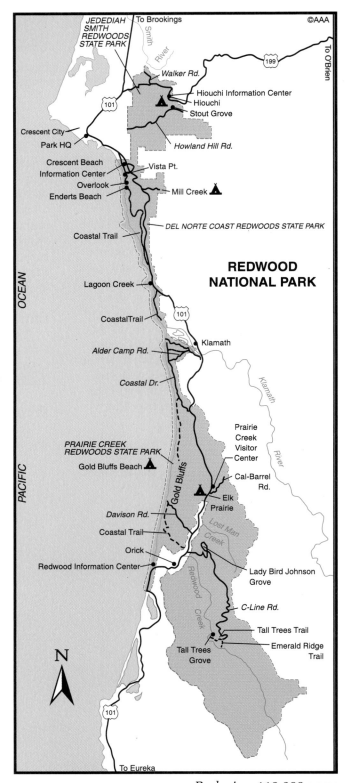

Park size: 113,200 acres

Amenities

Scenic drives ◆ Shuttle bus tour
◆ Hiking ◆ Fishing ◆ Horseback riding
◆ Bicycling ◆ Swimming ◆ Environmental
programs ◆ Bookstores

Travel Advisory

You are allowed to gather fruits and
berries for personal consumption.

Emergency Information

First aid is available within the park.
Sutter Coast Hospital is in nearby Crescent
City. Mad River Hospital is 35 miles from
the south end of the park.

Visitor and Information Centers

Park headquarters is at the corner of
Second and K Street in Crescent City. Here
you will find park information and interpretive programs.

There are five information centers.
Hiouchi Information Center, on Highway
199, houses exhibits about redwoods, the
coastline and related topics. This center is
closed October to June. Redwood Information
Center in Orick features exhibits and programs. It is open year-round except on
major holidays. Crescent City Information
Center (south of Crescent City) offers park
information and interpretive programs. It is
open year-round except on major holidays.
Prairie Creek Visitor Center is open from 9
a.m. to 5 p.m. with shorter winter hours. It
is closed on major holidays. Jedediah
Smith Information Center is also open 9
a.m. to 5 p.m. in summer, with no winter
hours. It is closed on major holidays.

Campgrounds

All developed campgrounds are operated by the state parks. (There is no
camping fee for the primitive sites in the
national park.) The camping cost is $16 a
night in summer and $14 a night off sea-
son. Walk-in or bike-in campsites cost $3 a
person. There are four walk-in campgrounds and four drive-in campgrounds in
the state parks. Camp or build fires only

where indicated. For reservations call
DESTINET at 800-444-7275.

**Del Norte Redwoods State Park, Mill
Creek Campground.** Off Highway 101, it
has 145 sites, tables, grills, toilets, dump
station and is open May to October.

**Jedediah Smith Redwoods State Park,
Jedediah Smith State Park Campground.**
On Highway 199, it has 106 sites, tables,
grills, toilets and dump station. It is open
all year. This is a drive-in camp.

**Prairie Creek Redwood State Park,
Gold Bluffs Beach Campground.** It has
tables, grills and toilets. It is open all year.
This is a drive-in campground.

Elk Prairie Campground. It has tables,
grills, toilets and dump station. It is open
all year.

There are also primitive campsites with
tables and toilets at Nichol Creek,
DeMartin, Flint Ridge, Little Bald Hills and
Butler Creek in Prairie Creek Redwoods
State Park. A permit is required.

Backcountry camping is allowed on
Redwood Creek Trail along the creek gravel
beds, except within a quarter mile of Tall
Trees Grove.

Picnic Areas

There is a wide selection of picnic sites. Choose between: Hiouchi ranger station, Jedediah Smith Redwoods State Park, Crescent Beach and Overlook, Wilson Creek, Lagoon Creek, Klamath Overlook, Fern Canyon, High Bluff Quarry, Gold Bluffs Beach, Prairie Creek Redwoods State Park, Lady Bird Johnson Grove, Lost Man Creek, Redwood Creek Trailhead, Skunk Cabbage Trailhead and the Redwood Information Center.

Cabins, Lodges and Hotels

Redwood Youth Hostel offers lodging within the national park. For more information, ask at the information centers. There are many lodges and hotels in the surrounding communities.

Restaurants

There are no restaurants in the park.

THINGS TO DO AND SEE

Trail Tours. Guided horseback trips in the southern section of the park are available from outfitters in Orick. Some trips involve overnight camping. Call Tall Trees Outfitters at 707-488-5785 for cost and schedule information.

Scenic Drives. U.S. 101 runs north and south through the park, providing a scenic drive along the coast and through the redwoods. Other roads offer scenery which is a little off the beaten path. The partially unpaved coastal drive around the mouth of

the Klamath River is scenic. Howland Hill Road, an alternative route to Crescent City, is an unpaved narrow scenic drive through a redwood forest that gives you access to Stout Grove. Walker Road is an unpaved scenic road through a redwood forest that provides access to the Smith River. Davison Road, which is unpaved and narrow, goes to Gold Bluffs Beach, where resident herds of Roosevelt elk are often seen. The Cal-Barrel road is an unpaved road through a redwood forest.

C-Line Road. Thirty-five vehicles a day are allowed to enter the C-Line Road, which takes you to the one-and-a-quarter mile trail to the Tall Trees Grove. The daily permits are issued at the Redwood Information Center. Access time is 9 a.m. to 2 p.m. only. The C-Line road closes at dusk.

Hiking. The Coastal Trail is a series of short trails totaling a 35-mile trek along the coast from Crescent Beach to Orick. This trail is in six sections, ranging in length from four to six miles. Hiking this trail you pass ancient redwoods, prairies, bluffs and beaches. A shorter but beautiful walk is the Lady Bird Johnson Grove Trail, a one-mile,

self-guided nature walk starting near Redwood Creek Trailhead. The most popular trail is the Redwood Creek Trail, an eight-mile hike that takes you past Tall Tree Groves and the "Emerald Mile." This hike is only possible in summer. It is strenuous and involves crossing two creeks.

Whale Watching. The Crescent Beach Overlook, on the Enderts Beach Road, is a promising spot for whale watching.

Fishing. Fishermen can do both freshwater and saltwater fishing in the park, with hopes of catching silver and king salmon and steelhead or cutthroat trout. Smith River and Klamath River are famous salmon and trout waters.

Bicycling. There are two designated bike trails: Ossagon Trail in Prairie Creek Redwoods State Park and Holter Ridge Trail in Redwood National Park. The bike trails wend through redwood forests to the beach.

Near Redwood National Park

Six Rivers National Forest. This 957,980-acre forest is about 15 miles from Redwood National Park in Eureka. There are picnic areas and 395 campsites and opportunities for hiking, riding, hunting and winter sports. The six major rivers that traverse the forest allow visitors to enjoy white water rafting, kayaking and excellent salmon and steelhead fishing. This national forest is open all year and for the most part, accessible. Campsites are available from May through November.

For More Information

Superintendent
Redwood National Park
1111 Second Street
Crescent City, CA 95531
Tel. 707-464-6101

REDWOOD OR SEQUOIA?

Many people confuse the redwood with its cousin, the giant sequoia. Redwoods are actually taller than sequoias, but not as large in terms of total mass. Mature redwoods average somewhere between 200 and 240 feet in height. When viewed from the ground they seem even taller, owing to the lack of branches on the lower 100 or 200 feet of trunk.

Redwoods live about half as long as giant sequoias. They have been known to live for as long as 2,000 years, but 500 to 700 years is closer to their average lifespan. Their longevity is due to their natural resistance to insects, disease and fire.

ROCKY MOUNTAIN NATIONAL PARK

Colorado ♦ Established 1915

Rocky Mountain National Park straddles the Continental Divide. It is an expanse of aspen forests, meadows and tundra studded with snow-covered peaks looming up as high as 14,000 feet. Glaciers feed lakes, streams and waterfalls and the Never Summer Mountains are the site of permanent snowfields. This majestic landscape is Colorado's most popular destination.

At the lower elevations, the park is warm and dry with forests of Ponderosa and lodgepole pine, western red cedar, Douglas fir and blue spruce. Wildflowers blanket the meadows in summer.

Higher up, tall stands of spruce, fir, aspen and pine form deep forests. Melting snow from the mountain slopes flow to the lakes and rivers scattered throughout the valley below. Above 9,000 feet, spruce, subalpine fir and limber pine are the most common trees. They bend and twist under the fierce and constant winds. Above the timberline, a rocky alpine tundra — reminiscent of northern Alaska — covers a third of the park. This tundra is strewn with grasses, mosses and dwarf plants.

Blooming season in the tundra is brief but brilliant thanks to a wealth of wildflowers, including Colorado's state flower, the blue columbine. The tundra's bouquet includes alpine buttercups, dwarf clovers, alpine forget-me-nots, yellow violets and wood lilies.

Bighorn sheep are the unofficial mascots of the park. The forests and mountains also support elk, beavers, mountain lions, moose, bobcats, marmots, coyotes, mule deer, chipmunks and squirrels. Overhead, golden eagles soar.

Cross the Continental Divide and enjoy some unforgettable scenery. Drive Trail Ridge Road, the highest continuously paved road in the country. Highway 34, as it is called on most maps, winds through 50 miles of high country, 11 miles of it above the tree line. It is open from Memorial Day through mid-October. Opening and closing dates depend on weather conditions.

A FEW TIPS

♦ *Wildflowers peak in late June and early July.*
♦ *Call ahead if you plan to drive Trail Ridge Road to make sure it is open.*
♦ *Bring rain gear and sunscreen.*
♦ *No boats or flotation devices are allowed on Bear Lake.*
♦ *Be careful not to overexert yourself at high elevations.*

PLANNING YOUR VISIT

Park Open

The park is open year-round. Roads close after heavy snowfall. The only through-road from one side of the park to the other usually opens Memorial Day and closes in mid-October. Peak visitation is in July and August.

Seasons

Summer days are sunny and pleasant with possible afternoon thunderstorms. Nights are cool. Winter brings blizzard conditions with extreme drops in temperature. In the mountains, snow and below-freezing temperatures are always possible.

Entrance Fees

Per private vehicle $10
Per individual...$5
Fees are valid for seven days.

Permits and Licenses

There is a backcountry permit fee of $15. A Colorado fishing license is available locally. Vehicles must use designated roads and parking lots.

Access and Transportation

The park is in north-central Colorado off Highway 34 and Highway 36. In the summer, Trail Ridge Road (Highway 34) takes you through the park from the western Grand Lake entrance to the eastern

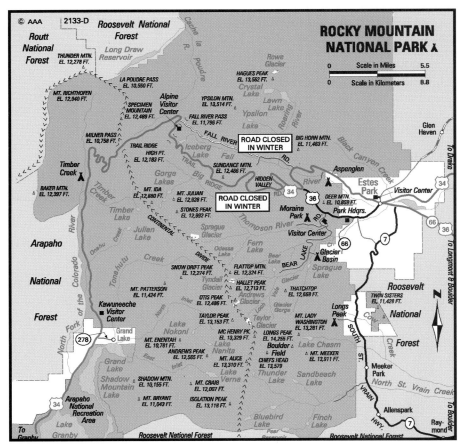

Park size: 265,727 acres

Beaver Meadows and Fall River entrances. To reach the east entrances, take U.S. 36 for 65 miles northwest of Denver. To reach the west entrance, take I-70 for 85 miles west of Denver to U.S. 40 to U.S. 34 north for 15 miles.

Amtrak serves Denver and Cheyenne. The closest airport is Denver International, 65 miles from the park. There is an airport in Cheyenne, 91 miles from the park. Rental cars are available in Denver and Cheyenne.

In-Park Transportation

Bear Lake Shuttle Buses serve Bear Lake Road. Take the road from the Estes Park entrance to the parking area.

Special Needs

Visitor centers can provide Braille and taped information. Parking lots, visitor center restrooms, Rock Cut and Rainbow Curve restrooms and Bear Lake Trail, Sprague Trail and Coyote Trail are accessible. Five Senses Trail near Sprague has handicapped access. Campgrounds have an accessible restroom. There is a backcountry campsite that is accessible. To reserve this site call 970-586-1242.

Amenities

Shuttle bus ◆ Skiing ◆ Campfire programs ◆ Naturalist walks ◆ Mountaineering ◆ Scenic drives ◆ Riding ◆ Winter sports ◆ Snowmobiling ◆ Museum

Travel Advisory

Sections of Trail Ridge Road reach elevations of more than two miles above sea level. This could pose a risk to people with heart conditions or respiratory problems. Main roads can be closed after winter storms.

Emergency Information

First aid is available in the park and in Estes Park and Grand Lake. Hospitals closest to the park are in Estes Park and Granby.

Visitor and Information Centers

Headquarters Visitor Center (near Estes Park) and Kawuneeche Visitor Center (near Grand Lake) provide orientation programs and exhibits year-round. The Alpine Visitor Center (on Trail Ridge Road) is open Memorial Day through mid-October. Also open in summer are centers at Lily Lake

(South of Estes Park), Corral Creek and Sheep Lake.

Campgrounds

There are five developed campgrounds in the park. They have a total of more than 500 campsites. Sites at Longs Peak, Aspenglen and Timber Creek are available on a first-come, first-served basis. Sites at Moraine Park and Glacier Basin can be reserved by calling 800-365-2267. Group sites are available at Glacier Basin.

Moraine Park Campground. There are 247 sites open year-round. There is water from mid-May and dump stations. The camping fee is $14 a night.

Glacier Basin Campground. There are 150 sites available throughout the summer. There is water and dump stations. The camping fee is $14 a night.

Aspenglen Campground. There are 54 sites open from mid-May. The camping fee is $12 a night.

Timber Creek Campground. There are 100 sites. It is open all year and has water in the summer and dump stations. Camping fee is $12 a night.

Longs Peak Campground. There are 26 sites available all year. There is water in the summer. No RVs or motor homes allowed. Your stay is limited to three days. The camping fee is $12 a night.

Backcountry camping is allowed by permit only. There are more than 200 primitive sites that can be reserved. One of the most beautiful and remote is Haynach Lakes Campsites, nearly nine miles into the backcountry via Green Mountain and Tonahuta Trails. There is a $15 backcountry camping fee. Call the Backcountry Office at 970-586-1242.

Cabins, Lodges and Hotels

There is no lodging in the park. There are hotels and lodges in Estes Park and Grand Lake. Stanley Hotel is in Estes Park. Rooms are available from $80-125 a night. If the hotel looks familiar, it may be because some of the film *The Shining* was shot here. For more information call 970-586-3371.

Picnic Areas

There are nearly 20 picnic areas in the park. Most picnic spots are off the main roads. Food and supplies are available in Grand Lake and Estes Park.

Restaurants

There is a snack bar at the gift shop at Fall River Pass.

Things to Do and See

Bear Lake Road. There is limited shuttle bus service on Bear Lake Road throughout the summer.

Moraine Park Museum. This museum features 3-D models and exhibits you can touch that illustrate mountain building, glacier movement and other aspects of the ecosystems at Rocky Mountain National Park. The museum is open May through October.

Never Summer Ranch. Visit this historical dude ranch from mid-June through Labor Day.

Scenic Drives. The park has 82 miles of paved roads and 28 miles of unpaved roads. Trail Ridge Road is a 48-mile road that crosses from Estes Park to Grand Lake. Eleven miles of the road, past Lava Cliffs, are above the timberline. The road crosses the Continental Divide at Milner Pass. There are scenic overlooks at Many Parks Curve and Rainbow Curve.

Fall River Road is a winding and narrow nine miles of gravel road that meets Trail Ridge Road at Fall River Pass. It is one-way and uphill. This road is open in July through mid-October if weather allows. Bear Lake Road is open year-round.

Hiking. The park has 355 miles of trails. Trailheads are off Trail Ridge Road and Bear Lake Road. To get a good look at the park's glaciers, walk the four-mile Andrews Glacier Trail. Cross the Continental Divide by taking the Flattop Trail between Grand Lake on the west and Estes Park. Other popular hikes are the Tundra Trail and the Colorado River Trail.

Fishing. The mountain streams and lakes have four species of trout: German brown, rainbow, brook and cutthroat. Don't expect big fish — the waters are too cold. Fishing is not permitted on Bear Lake at any time.

Horseback Riding. Check with a park ranger to find out which trails are closed to horses. Two stables at Moraine Park and Glacier Creek conduct rides in the summer.

Winter Sports. Cross-country skiing is increasingly popular in the park's lower valleys. Backcountry skiing is enjoyed in Hidden Valley, which is also a sledding area. Access roads from the east are kept open during the winter.

Mountaineering. There are many ascents to test your skill. A technical climbing school and guide service operates within the park. Call the Colorado Mountain School at 970-586-5758.

For More Information
Superintendent
Rocky Mountain National Park
Estes Park, CO 80517
Tel. 970-586-1206

The rare and venerable saguaro cactus, with its odd variety of all too human shapes, is indigenous to the arid Sonoran Desert of southern Arizona. Despite its unrelenting heat and lack of water, the homeland of the saguaro far surpasses all other North American deserts in its lushness and variety of plant and animal life.

During its first few years of life, the saguaro cactus will probably grow only four or five inches. It takes 30 years to grow two to three feet. But the plant doesn't really settle into its mature growth phase until the age of 75 or so.

When the saguaro has grown 15 to 20 feet tall, it develops branches, absorbing water through an elaborate underground root system. Sometimes called the king of the cacti, a fully mature saguaro can grow to a height of more than 30 feet and live as long as 170 years. One of these giant cacti might weigh anywhere from six to ten tons. One ton of that will represent the water reserves the plant has absorbed over its long life. The white blossom of the saguaro cactus is the state flower of Arizona.

Due to the intense desert heat, most of Saguaro National Park's wildlife is nocturnal. Deer, coyote, javelina, rabbits and squirrels come out in the cool of the evening to hunt or forage. Birds are also abundant in the park, with over 42 different varieties represented. Hikers and campers should be aware that this area is home to scorpions and rattlers.

Saguaro National Park was originally established as a National Monument in 1933, with the purpose of safeguarding these desert monarchs. The area was upgraded to National Park status only recently. It consists of two units on either side of the city of Tucson.

The much larger Saguaro East is five miles east of Tucson. The Eastern unit, also known as the Rincon Mountain Unit, has many large stands of mature saguaros, as well as many other varieties of plants and cacti. The 63,000 acre Rincon Unit is mostly wilderness, with very few roads. It attracts seasoned backpackers, who usually enter the park via the Douglas Spring Road. There are 77 miles of wilderness trails in the Rincon Mountain Unit and the elevation ranges from 2,800 feet to 8,666 feet at the top of Micah Mountain. Vegetation changes dramatically from the hot, dry, saguaro forest to the cool, moist, pine forests of the mountain. The eight-mile Cactus Forest Loop Drive runs through the park.

Saguaro West, also known as the Tucson Mountain Unit, is near the Arizona-Sonora Desert Museum, seven miles west of Tucson. The cacti of the western unit tend to be younger and smaller than their eastern cousins. The Tucson Mountain Unit has 21,000 acres of flatlands. It is crisscrossed by well-maintained dirt roads.

SAGUARO NATIONAL PARK

Arizona ◆ **Established 1994**

PLANNING YOUR VISIT

Park Open

The park is open year-round. Peak visitation is in March.

Seasons

May or early June is the best time of year to visit. This is when the desert is in bloom and the towering saguaros are topped with white flowers. High winds may be expected at any time. Summers are hot and clear in the daytime, with typical highs in the 90s and 100s and lows in the 80s. Late fall and early winter thunderstorms are common, accounting for half of the park's annual four inches of precipitation.

Entrance Fees

At the Rincon Mountain Unit:

Per vehicle..$4
Per individual $2

At the Tucson Mountain Unit:

No entrance fee.

Permits and Licenses

No off-road vehicles are allowed. Permits are required for camping at the Rincon Mountain District (Saguaro East). Free permits are available at the Rincon visitor center.

Access and Transportation

The park is in southeastern Arizona. To reach Saguaro West, take Speedway Road (becomes Gates Pass Road) or Ajo Way west of Tucson, then north of Kinney Road.

To reach Saguaro East, take Old Spanish Trail two miles east out of Tucson. Both Greyhound and Trailways serve Tucson as does Amtrak. Most major airlines serve Tucson, which is 16 miles from Rincon Mountain Headquarters and 20 miles from the Red Hills Complex in the Tucson Mountain District.

Special Needs

Both visitor centers and all restrooms are accessible. There are modified latrines at some picnic areas and a captioned audio-visual program for the hearing impaired. Short interpretive trails in both districts are accessible.

Amenities

Wildlife and bird watching ◆ Hiking ◆ Picnicking ◆ Photography ◆ Horseback riding ◆ Bicycling ◆ Scenic drives

Travel Advisory

Wear sturdy shoes and be on the look-out for rattlesnakes and scorpions. Carry plenty of water.

Emergency Information

First aid is available in both districts of the park. The closest hospital to the Rincon Mountain district is St. Joseph's Hospital, ten miles away. The closest hospital to the Tucson Mountain district is St. Mary's Hospital, 16.5 miles away.

Visitor and Information Centers

The Visitor Center and Park Headquarters in the Rincon Mountain District are two miles east of the Tucson City limits on Old Spanish Trail near Freeman Road. The Red Hills Visitor Center in the Tucson Mountain District is on Kinney Road, two miles west of the Arizona-Sonoran Desert Museum. Both facilities offer audiovisual programs, exhibits, nature walks and scheduled seasonal programs. Both are open daily from 8:30 a.m. to 5 p.m.

Camping and Lodging

Only backcountry camping is allowed in the Rincon Mountain District. There are some walk-in camps along backcountry trails such as Douglas Springs and Juniper Basin. However, you must apply for a permit before you visit. The most convenient developed campsites are the Gilbert Ray Campground near the Tucson Mountain District and Catalina State Park which is north of downtown Tucson.

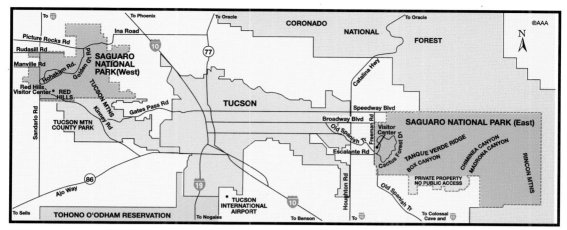

Park size: 84,000 acres

Picnic Areas

The Javelina Picnic Area is off the Cactus Forest Loop Drive. The Tanque Verde Ridge Trail begins here and leads to the Juniper Basin Campgrounds.

Cabins, Lodges and Hotels

There are no accommodations in the park. A variety of lodgings is available in Tucson.

Restaurants

There is no food service in the park. A variety of restaurants and grocery stores are available near both districts and in the Tucson basin.

THINGS TO DO AND SEE

Hiking. There are many short trails in Saguaro East and Saguaro West that can be reached from the eight-mile paved road running through the park. Some trails lead to scenic lookouts. In winter, rangers lead hikes that begin at the visitor centers and cover both sections of the park. The Desert Ecology Trail, in the Rincon Mountain District, is an easy, quarter-mile loop that is handicapped accessible. For more of a challenge, hikers can take the Douglas Springs Trail or Tanque Verde Ridge Trail into the backcountry, moving from desert to woodland. Many of the trails in Saguaro East intersect, so it is easy to choose the length and difficulty of hike that is right for you.

Arizona-Sonoran Desert Museum. This museum offers presentations that focus on desert plants and animals in simulated natural habitats.

For More Information

Superintendent
Saguaro National Park
3693 Old Spanish Trail
Tucson, AZ 85730-5699
Tel. 520-733-5100

SEQUOIA AND KINGS CANYON NATIONAL PARKS

California ◆ **Established 1890 (Sequoia)** ◆ **1940 (Kings Canyon)**

Sequoia and Kings Canyon were separate parks that unified in 1943. Many have compared this park favorably to Yosemite, noting that it is much less crowded but no less beautiful. Sequoia and Kings Canyon inspires superlatives. It contains the biggest tree in the United States. It also boasts the tallest peak, as well as part of the deepest canyon and a segment of the longest single continuous mountain range in the country.

The older of the two parks, Sequoia, is one of the few places on earth where its giant namesakes survive. There are 75 groves of Sequoias in the park. All but eight of them are south of Kings River.

The mighty Sequoias begin life as seeds the size of oat flakes. They require moderate temperatures, rain and fog and exactly the right soil to attain their mature growth. Their enormous size reflects the fact that they continue growing for as long as they live. They do not die of old age. Their unique chemistry helps them to fight off the ravages of fire, disease and insects. The real threat the Sequoias face is toppling.

Giant Forest, given its name by crusading naturalist John Muir, is home to four of the world's five largest trees. General Sherman, 275 feet tall, is the largest living thing on earth. The General's trunk weighs an estimated 1,385 tons. Its circumference at the ground is just under 103 feet. Its largest branch is almost 7 feet in diameter. The General Sherman Sequoia is believed to be somewhere between 2,300 and 2,700 years old.

The Grant Grove, in Kings Canyon, is home to the third largest sequoia, the General Grant. The General Grant has been officially designated the nation's Christmas tree and every year people gather under its boughs for a special holiday celebration.

Smaller but gem-like, Kings Canyon is north of the sequoia groves, cut by the south fork of the beautiful Kings River. At a point outside of the park the canyon reaches a depth of some 8,200 feet from river level up to the peak of Spanish Mountain. This makes it deeper even than the Grand Canyon. Kern Canyon is in the southern end of Sequoia National Park. Kern Canyon is 6,000 feet deep. Several other canyons are as deep as 4,000 feet.

A Few Tips

♦ *Park roads are steep and curvy. There is some roadwork underway in and around the park. Keep to the right, drive slowly and use lower gears even on automatic transmission vehicles to avoid overheating brakes and transmissions.*

♦ *For solitude, visit northern Kings Canyon. This area draws fewer tourists.*

♦ *Use extreme caution around rivers, especially in the early summer. They are swift, deep and very cold.*

The jagged peaks of the Sierra Nevada range tower over the canyons and sequoia groves to the east. The Sierra Nevada is the nation's longest continuous mountain range. Mount Whitney, at 14,494 feet is the highest peak in the continental U.S.

The tall trees and dense forests found in other parts of the park cannot tolerate the harsh climate that exists at elevations above 9,000 feet on the mountain.

The western foothills of the Sierra Nevadas have dry, hot summers, perfect for low-growing chaparral vegetation.

PLANNING YOUR VISIT

Park Open

The park is open year-round. Cedar Grove Highway (Kings Canyon) and Mineral King road (Sequoia National Park) are closed from November to April. Peak visitation is in August.

Seasons

Temperatures vary with elevation. Summer in the low elevations is hot and dry. In the middle elevations where the sequoias grow, expect warm daytime and cool evening temperatures with occasional afternoon thundershowers. Weather in the high elevations is pleasant with an occasional afternoon thundershower. Nighttime temperatures often drop to the low 30s and occasionally to the 20s. It can snow at any time. Winter weather at lower elevations is mild and wet with rain usually occurring from January to mid-May and averaging about 26 inches total. In the middle elevations, much of the 40-45 inches of precipitation comes in the winter and a deep blanket of snow covers the area from December to May.

Entrance Fees

Per vehicle...$10
Per individual $5
    Fees are valid for 7 days.

Permits and Licenses

Permits for wilderness camping are available at park headquarters or at any visitor center. Backcountry permits can be reserved up to three weeks before the start of your trip. A backcountry permit is required for all camping outside designated areas. California fishing licenses are required for people over 16 and are available at Lodgepole, Stony Creek, Grant Grove and Cedar Grove.

Access and Transportation

The park is located in central California. There are no roads into the park from the east and no roads over the Sierra Nevadas in the park. Two main roads enter the park from the west. Take Highway 180 for 55 miles east of Fresno to Grant Grove, continue 30 miles to Cedar Grove in Kings Canyon or south to Sequoia via the Generals Highway. You may also enter Sequoia by taking Highway 198 35 miles northeast of Visalia. In summer, the General's Highway connects the two roads, making loop trips possible.

Amtrak serves Fresno and Visalia via bus connection from Hanford. There is bus service to Fresno and Visalia. Rental cars are available in Fresno and Visalia. The closest airports are in Fresno and Visalia. Rental cars are also available in these locations.

In-Park Transportation

During the summer, a shuttle is available in Sequoia between Giant Forest, Lodgepole, Moro Rock and Crescent Meadow.

Special Needs

The park has handicapped accessible visitor centers, campgrounds and restrooms. Paved trails lead to General Sherman and General Grant trees. The Congress Trail and Trail for All People in Giant Forest are also paved. Picnic areas with modified tables are available at Ash Mountain, Hospital Rock and Big Stump.

Amenities

Scenic Drive ♦ Hiking ♦ Horseback riding ♦ Cave tours ♦ Motor tours ♦ Fishing ♦ Winter sports ♦ Naturalist programs ♦ Snowshoe walks

Travel Advisory

All vehicles are restricted to the developed roadways. Vehicles longer than 22 feet are not advised to drive General's Highway between Potwisha Campground

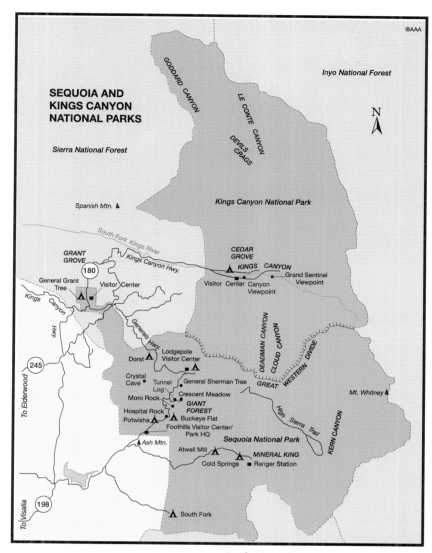

Park size: Sequoia; 402,482 acres
Kings Canyon; 461,901 acres

and Giant Forest Village in Sequoia National Park. Trailers are restricted to specific campgrounds. In winter, the General's Highway between Lodgepole and Grant Grove may be closed after heavy snows. Road construction between Ash Mountain and Lodgepole may add to your driving time. Traffic delays may also be caused by roadwork on General's Highway.

Emergency Information

Limited first aid is available inside the parks. The closest hospital to Kings Canyon National Park is in Fresno, 55 miles away.

The closest hospitals to Sequoia National Park are in Exeter, 46 miles away and from Giant Forest in Visalia, 48 miles away.

Visitor and Information Centers

There are five visitor centers. Foothills Visitor Center is also park headquarters. It is located at the southwest park entrance off Highway 198. The Ash Mountain and Grant Grove Visitor Centers are open year-round. The Cedar Grove Visitor Center, at the bottom of Kings Canyon, is open mid-May through September. The Lodgepole Visitor Center, in Giant Forest, opens mid-April through mid-October. It provides information, schedules, exhibits and audio-visual programs on the Sierra Nevada and sequoias. The Mineral King Visitor Center, in the southern part of Sequoia, is open June through Labor Day. Grant Grove Visitor Center provides Information, sched-ules and exhibits that explain the natural and human history of the area. There is a 10-minute slide program.

Campgrounds

There are 13 campgrounds in the park The Sequoia sites tend to fill up first. Campgrounds sometimes close for revegeta-tion or because bears are in the area. Campgrounds are available on a first-come, first-served basis. All campgrounds have tables and fire grills. Most have drinking water. Showers are available through a con-cessionaire. You can reserve a campsite at Lodgepole Campground (near a sequoia forest) by calling DESTINET at 800-365-2267. Camping fees vary with the time of year. Stays may be limited to 14 days.

Picnic Areas

There are picnic areas off the main park roads. One is in Grant Grove, three in Giant Forest and one north of Ash Mountain. In sum-mer, you can buy supplies in Giant Forest, Lodgepole, Stony Creek, Grant Grove and Cedar Grove. In winter, you can buy snacks in Wolverton. Outside the park, you can buy food and supplies in Fresno or Visalia.

Cabins, Lodges and Hotels

There are three lodges in the park. Giant Forest in Sequoia rents motel rooms in the summer. Grant Grove, in Kings Canyon, rents cabins year-round. Cedar Grove, also in Kings Canyon, rents motel rooms in the summer. To make reservations at any accommodation in the park, call 209-335-5500. Additional lodging is available outside the park.

Restaurants

Village Cafeteria in Giant Forest is open from mid-May through October. Grant Grove's restaurant is open year-round. Cedar Grove offers counter service from

May to September. You can buy fast food during the ski season in the Wolverton area of Giant Forest. Lodgepole Center sells sandwiches and pizza.

THINGS TO DO AND SEE

Crystal Cave Tour. Take a 50-minute guided tour of Crystal Cave, a marble cavern. You must buy your tickets at least an hour in advance at the visitor center at Lodgepole or Foothills. Tickets are not sold at the cave. The tour begins with a half-mile hike to the cave entrance. Tours run from mid-May through September. Admittance is $4 for adults and children 12 and older, $2 for children 6 to 11 and senior citizens. Kids five and under are free. Wear a light jacket.

Day Tours by Motorcoach. Day-long guided tours of Kings Canyon depart from Giant Forest and Grant Grove. Guided Giant Forest tours are one-and-a half hours in the morning and evening and include Moro Rock, the General Sherman Tree and Crescent Meadow. The tours stop frequently. Fees are charged. For more information call 209-565-3381.

Scenic Drives. The park's sequoia groves are the main attraction. Three of the most famous sequoias are General Sherman, General Grant and the Tunnel Log. Also of interest are Crescent Meadow and Moro Rock. Although much of the land is undeveloped, all of these areas can easily be reached by the one road that connects the two parks. The beautiful Sierra Nevada range, including Mount Whitney, its highest peak, can be viewed from many areas of the park. You can also see a good part of scenic Kings Canyon by driving along its rim.

The General's Highway and Kings Canyon Highway are the two main park roads. Both offer roadside pull-outs with scenic viewpoints including Canyon Viewpoint and Sentinel Viewpoint along the Kings Canyon Highway. The General's Highway connects the two parks in summer. In Grant Grove, you can also take a separate park road to Panoramic Point, offering a spectacular view of the High Sierra. In Giant Forest, the Crescent Meadow Road is a three-mile dead-end road beginning at Giant Forest Village and traveling past the Tunnel Log. (The tunnel is 17 feet high and eight feet wide.) Continue to Moro Rock and Crescent Meadow. In Cedar Grove, the Motor Nature Trail is a eight-mile rough dirt road providing a leisurely drive along the river in Kings Canyon.

Hiking. There are 750 miles of hiking trails in the park from easy paths to steep mountain trails. Short trails around Giant Forest include the two-mile loop Congress Trail through the heart of the sequoia forest and the Trail for All People, which circles Round Meadow and is surrounded by

sequoia forest. The Trail of the Sequoias in Giant Forest take you to some beautiful groves. The John Muir Trail runs 220 miles from Yosemite to Sequoia. Another strenuous but rewarding hike is the Copper Creek Trail, around Granite Pass at more than 10,000 feet.

Mountaineering. You must make reservations to hike to the summit of Mount Whitney. This walk looks deceptively simple but the altitude and weather conditions can make it very challenging.

Trail Rides. Horses, burros and llamas are allowed in the park. Corrals with horses for hire are open mid-May through September. For rates call High Sierra Pack Station at Cedar Grove (209-565-3464), Mineral King (209-561-3403), Grant Grove (209-335-2374) or Wolverton (209-565-3445). For trail rides in the high Sierras, call Pine Creek Pack Station/Sequoia Kings Pack Trail at 800-962-0775. This outfitter also offers day-long trail rides and guided pack trips.

Fishing. The park has more than 500 lakes that yield rainbow, brown, eastern brook and golden trout. Ask for a copy of fishing regulations, including information about seasons and limits at any visitor center. A California fishing license is required of people 16 and over.

Rafting. There are several independent outfitters that offer rafting expeditions, such as Kings River Expeditions (209-233-4881) and Sierra Whitewater (209-561-2401). Only experienced rafters should consider the Class IV and V Kaweah and upper Kings Rivers.

Winter Sports. Enjoy cross-country skiing and snowshoeing in the park from first snow through mid-April. Cross-country ski trails connect Giant Forest, Wolverton and Lodgepole. Ski trails in Grant Grove connect with trails in Sequoia National Forest. Maps are available at visitor centers. In Wolverton and Grant Grove, ski rental and instruction are available.

For More Information
Superintendent
Sequoia and Kings Canyon National Parks
Three Rivers, CA 93271
Tel. 209-565-3134

SHENANDOAH NATIONAL PARK

Virginia ♦ **Established 1935**

Long and narrow, the Shenandoah National Park is a natural corridor of valleys and ridges bisected by Skyline Drive, which runs for 105 miles along the crest of the Blue Ridge Mountains. The drive, constructed during the depression, is built on top of ridge trails first blazed by Native Americans thousands of years ago and later followed by pioneers and settlers in colonial times. Nearly 500 miles of trails crisscross Skyline Drive. Its entire length roughly parallels the famed Appalachian Trail.

To the west is the Shenandoah River, for which the park is named. The Piedmont Plateau is to the east. Massanutten Mountain lies between the north and south forks of the river. The parkland is full of beautiful hardwood forests, which blanket the Blue Ridge and the Shenandoah Valley.

Stretching out for miles, the rolling hills and slopes are laced with leaping streams and waterfalls and dotted with about 100 different species of trees. Pines, hemlocks, oaks and maples grow alongside of hickories, fir, black walnut and many other kinds of standing timber. The one

large open area in the park is Big Meadows, which is full of wildflowers, shrubs and blueberries.

The most frequently seen animals of Shenandoah are deer, chipmunks, raccoons, gray squirrels and opossums. There are even black bears which prefer the backcountry. The park is also the habitat of several species of salamander.

About 200 species of birds have been seen in the park. Grouse, various woodpeckers, junco and ravens are the most common. According to park rangers, fall brings raptors through the park on their migration south. Peregrine falcons have been reintroduced to the park.

In the spring, when the streams and waterfalls swell with meltwater, the park's scenery can be seen to its best advantage. Wildflowers like trillium and bloodroot come into bloom in April and May. You can watch the greening of the trees advancing up the slopes at a rate of 100 feet a day

throughout April. In the late spring, when the migratory birds start returning, the pink azaleas and mountain laurels flower. By late summer the open areas of the park are covered with later blooming wildflowers.

In the fall, the park's many trees put on an astonishing show as they change to vibrant shades of red, yellow and orange. The park's proximity to Washington D.C. and other eastern cities has made it a perennial favorite for motoring vacations and a destination sure to please riders and hikers.

PLANNING YOUR VISIT

Park Open

The park is open year-round.

Seasons

Mountain weather is unpredictable, but it can be cold and wet in any season. In summer the days are warm but the nights are cool. Fog is common. Overnight temper-

atures are lowest in the valleys. Winters are cold, with an average 36 inches of snowfall.

Entrance Fees

Per vehicle...$10
Per individual $5
Fees are valid for seven days.

Permits and Licenses

Permits are required for backcountry camping. Vehicles are restricted to public roads. Commercial trucking is restricted to park business. Bicycles and other vehicles are prohibited on trails. A Virginia state fishing license is required to fish in the park.

Access and Transportation

From Charlottesville, Virginia, take I-64 west. From Washington, D.C., take I-66 west and then follow U.S. 340 south to Skyline Drive. The North entrance is 24 miles south of Winchester. The Thornton Gap entrance is on U.S. 211 east of New Market or 80 miles southwest of Washington, D.C. The

Swift Gap entrance is on U.S. 33, 24 miles east of Harrisonburg or northwest of Ruckersville. The South entrance is on I-64, 91 miles west of Richmond or for 18 miles east of Staunton. The closest major airports are in Washington, D.C. and Richmond. All of the major bus companies and Amtrak serve Washington, D.C. and Richmond. Various bus companies serve Washington D.C. and Richmond. Rental cars are available at airports in Washington, D.C. and Richmond.

A Few Tips

♦ *Wear proper footgear. Rocks around waterfalls are slippery and dangerous.*
♦ *Pull completely off the road when stopping for a view.*

Special Needs

Restrooms, buildings and lodges at Skyland and Big Meadows and some campsites and toilets at picnic grounds are wheelchair accessible or accessible with assistance. Sign language interpreting is available for some activities. Written information on exhibits, interpretive booklets, or signs for self-guiding nature trails and printed scripts of the orientation films are available. Tapes of park information are available. The history handout and nature trail booklets are available in Braille.

Amenities

Scenic drive ♦ Hiking ♦ Fishing ♦ Horseback riding ♦ Ranger programs

Travel Advisory

Snow tires and chains are recommended in winter. Respect the rights of private landowners and take notice of posted signs.

Emergency Information

First aid is available inside the park. Hospitals are in Front Royal, six miles away and Luray, ten miles away.

Visitor and Information Centers

Park Headquarters is on U.S. 211. Dickey Ridge Visitor Center (mile 4.6) offers information, interpretive exhibits and illustrated programs. They are closed in the winter. Byrd Visitor Center at Big Meadows (mile 51) offers information, interpretive exhibits and illustrated programs. They are closed in the winter.

Cabins, Lodges and Hotels

There are hotels, cottages and cabins in the park. To make reservations at Skyland, Big Meadows and Lewis Mountains call 800-999-4714. There are also trail cabins for hikers.

Campgrounds

There are four developed campgrounds in the park at Mathews Arm, Big Meadows, Lewis Mountain and Loft Mountain. Woodfires are permitted only in fireplaces in developed areas and are prohibited in the backcountry. All campgrounds have a 14-day limit from June 1 to October 31. For reservation information, call 703-999-2282.

Nightly camping fees start at $8. Most of the park is open to backcountry camping.

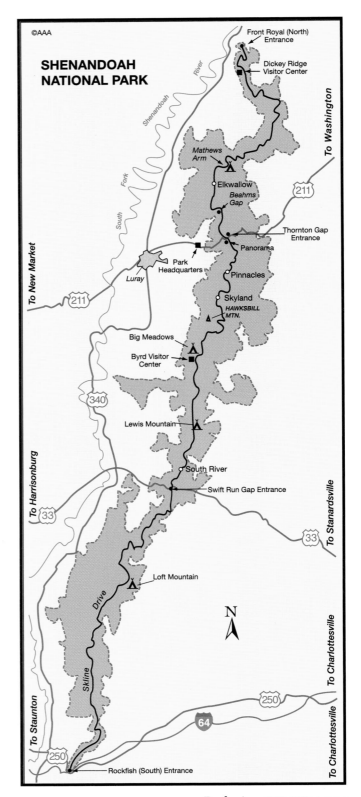

Park size: 195,382 acres

Picnic Areas

There are picnic areas in the park with tables, firepits, water and toilets. Picnic at Dickey Ridge (mile 4.6), Elkwallow (mile 24.1), Pinnacles (mile 36.7), Big Meadows (milepost 51), Lewis Mountain (mile 57.5), South River (mile 62.8) or Loft Mountain, (mile 79.5).

Restaurants

Dining rooms at Skyland, Big Meadows Lodge and Loft Mountain are open from April through October. There is a coffee shop and camp store at Big Meadows Wayside and a coffee shop at Loft Mountain Wayside.

Rock Tunnel at mile 32.4 goes through 600 feet of rock with a 13-foot clearance.

Hiking. There are 500 miles of trails in the park including a 100-mile section of the Appalachian Trail. The Whiteoak Canyon Trail leads to six waterfalls and an old-growth forest.

For More Information

Superintendent
Shenandoah National Park
Rt. 4, Box 348
Luray, VA 22835
Tel. 703-999-3500 (for a recorded message)

THINGS TO DO AND SEE

Trail Rides. There are guided horseback trips offered at Skyland. Pony rides are also available for children. Fees are charged.

Scenic Drives. The Skyline Drive, a winding 105-mile road, runs along the Blue Ridge for the full length of the park and provides spectacular vistas. Skyland is the highest point of the drive at 3,680 feet. Overlooks include the Shenandoah Valley Overlook (mile 2.8) with its sweeping view across the valley, Range View Overlook (mile 17.1) with an exceptional view of the Blue Ridge and Calf Mountain Overlook (mile 98.9) with a 300-degree view. Marys

THEODORE ROOSEVELT NATIONAL PARK

North Dakota ♦ **Established 1947**

Theodore Roosevelt National Park spans scenic badlands, buttes and mesas carved by wind, time and the Little Missouri River. It is also the site of a former president's ranch.

Roosevelt first visited the Dakotas in 1883 and returned to establish a cattle ranch. He carried his love of wild country and wildlife into his presidency, which began in 1901. He established national parks, forests, monuments and wildlife refuges, winning a reputation as the president most dedicated to conservation.

The park's river-sculpted tableland, gorges and valleys of shimmering color are divided into three units: South Unit, North Unit and Elkhorn Ranch. Grasslands surround canyons, cliffs and buttes, all whittled by the Little Missouri River. A mix of grasses includes needle-and-thread, which forms a critical habitat and a backdrop for a profusion of colorful wildflowers.

Wildlife in the park includes pronghorns, bison, wild horses, mule deer, prairie dogs, badgers and coyotes. Listen and you'll hear many songbirds among the 170 species of birds in western North Dakota. You may catch a glimpse of a golden eagle, or more likely, migratory waterfowl.

There are 85 miles of trails, many of them self-guided. In the South Unit, a petrified forest trail is a 16-mile round trip. In the North Unit, there are loop trails offering a close look at the badlands. Rangers lead guided walks and talks from June to mid-September.

PLANNING YOUR VISIT

Park Open

The park is open year-round. Some roads close in winter due to snow and ice.

Seasons

Summer highs are in the 90s. Lows are in the 50s. Summer storms can bring hail, lightning and lashing winds. Winter highs are in the low 30s and lows often reach below zero. The park gets about 30 inches of snowfall a year. Peak visitation is in July.

Entrance Fees

Per vehicle...$5
Per person...$3

Fees are only in effect from May to September and are valid for seven days.

Permits and Licenses

Free backcountry permits are available at the North and South Unit visitor centers.

Access and Transportation

The South Unit is on I-94 near Medora. The North Unit is accessible from Highway 85, heading north from the intersection of Highway 85 and I-94. The Elkhorn Ranch site is reached from South Unit on an unpaved road. You must ford the Little Missouri River to get to

Elkhorn. The road is impassable at times.

The closest airport is in Dickinson, North Dakota, 35 miles from the park.

Special Needs

An access guide is available at visitor centers. All three visitor centers, Cottonwood, North Unit Campground and Maltese Cross Cabins, are accessible. So are picnic areas and restrooms.

Amenities

Exhibits ♦ Guided walks ♦ Campfire programs ♦ Driving tours ♦ Trail tours ♦ Wildlife and birdwatching ♦ Backcountry hiking and camping ♦ Cabin tours

Travel Advisory

Get drinking water from approved sources. Rattlers and black widow spiders live in prairie dog burrows. Poison ivy grows in the wooded areas. Ticks are a problem in late spring and early summer.

Emergency Information

First aid is available in visitor centers. The hospital nearest to the South Unit is in Dickinson. The hospital nearest to the North Unit is in Watford City.

Visitor and Information Centers

The main visitor center is in Medora at the entrance of the South Unit. There are personal belongings of Theodore Roosevelt on display at this center. Seven miles east is Painted Canyon Visitor Center, which is closed fall to spring. The entrance and visitor center to the North Unit is 15 miles south of Watford City and 55 miles north of Belfield on Highway 85.

Visitor centers in the North Unit and South Unit are open daily except for Thanksgiving, Christmas Day and New Year's Day.

Visitor centers have bookstores, information for self-guided nature tours and directions to interpretive waysides along scenic drives.

A Few Tips

♦ *Climbing steep, barren slopes can be risky because the soft sediments may yield without warning.*
♦ *Do not feed or disturb wild animals. Look out for rattlers and black widow spiders. They often live in prairie dog burrows.*

Campgrounds

There are two campgrounds. Both are open year-round and charge $10 per night from May through September. Camping is free the rest of the year. Cottonwood is in South Unit and has 78 sites. The North Unit has 50 sites and a dump station.

Backcountry camping is allowed but you must have a permit. Group campsites are available in both units by reservation only. The cost is $2 per person per day with a minimum fee of $20 per day. There is a seven-day limit.

Picnic Areas

There are picnic areas at Painted Canyon and Peaceful Valley in the South Unit and in the North Unit. You may build fires only in the fire grates at campgrounds and picnic areas. Fires are prohibited in the backcountry. You may not gather firewood. Food and supplies are available in Medora, but can be limited in winter.

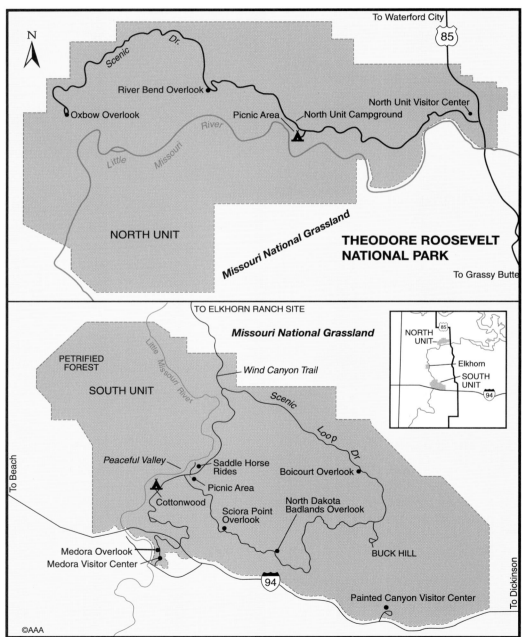

Park size: 79,000 acres

Cabins, Lodges and Hotels

There is no lodging in the park.

Restaurants

There is no food service in the park.

Things to Do and See

Historic Cabin Tour. The restored Maltese Cross Cabin which Theodore Roosevelt used is behind the Medora Visitor Center in the South Unit. From mid-June through mid-September, guided tours are regularly scheduled.

Scenic Drives. In the North Unit there is a 14-mile scenic drive from the entrance to Oxbow Overlook. There are turnouts and interpretive signs along the way. There are also trailheads off the road. In the South Unit, the 36-mile Scenic Loop Road has overlooks and signs that explain the park's history and natural phenomena. Boicourt Overlook has one of the best views of the badlands.

Hiking. There are 85 miles of trails off the main park roads. In the North Unit there are short, self-guided nature trails. In the South Unit, a 16-mile trail takes you to the heart of the park's petrified forest. A one-mile trail takes you past coal seams. You can climb Buck Hill, a 2,885-foot elevation.

Trail Rides. Peaceful Valley Ranch in South Unit offers trail rides. Call 701-623-4496. Little Knife Outfitters offers trail rides and overnight packtrips. Call 701-628-2747.

River Floating. You can float down the Little Missouri River, drifting past all three of the park's units in a canoe.

For More Information

Superintendent
Theodore Roosevelt National Park
Medora, ND 58654
Tel. 701-623-4466

VIRGIN ISLANDS NATIONAL PARK

U.S. Virgin Islands ◆ **Established 1956**

A FEW TIPS

◆ *High season is November through March. Off-season visits are cheaper and less crowded.*

◆ *Much of the land on the island is still private property. Permission is necessary to enter or use these areas.*

Virgin Islands National Park is one of the smallest in the National Park Service, comprising just over half of the island of St. John. The island of St. John, at 19 square miles, is the smallest of the three major islands that constitute the U.S. Virgin Islands. The park also extends to 5.,600 acres of offshore reefs.

Thanks to the presence of the park, St. John is the least developed of the Virgin Islands. Here the visitor will encounter high green hills with plants not seen anywhere else in the continental United States, turquoise bays, coral gardens and powdery white beaches shaded with palms and sea grape bushes. You will also find ruined plantations, with their echoes of slavery and of the sugar industry it once supported.

The clear tropical seas are normally placid and warm, ideal for swimming, sunbathing and snorkeling. St. John's densely wooded forests are excellent for hiking. There are moist, subtropical forests and protected valleys at the higher elevations and the trees have been flourishing again in land once cleared for sugar fields. At the lower elevations on the southern and eastern slopes, and at the less exposed coastal sites, subtropical dry forests and cactus scrublands appear.

The southern and eastern shores are almost desert-like. There are even cacti growing there.

The famous white sand beaches could not exist without the living coral growth that makes up the offshore reefs.

The reefs are a complex community of marine plants and animals. The hard corals are brilliantly colored and include brain, elkhorn, star, finger and staghorn coral. The soft corals are mostly sea whips and sea fan. There are more than 400 different species of fish swarming around the reefs, including angelfish, grunts, parrotfish and snappers.

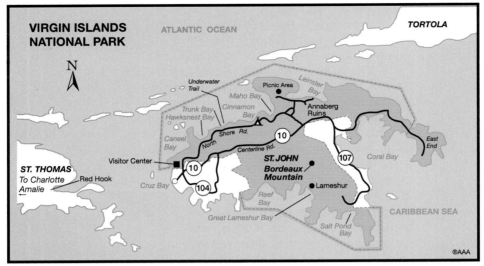

Park size: 14,688 acres

PLANNING YOUR VISIT

Park Open

The park is open year-round. Peak visitation is in March.

Seasons

The yearly temperature varies little between summer and winter. Temperatures rarely exceed 98° or fall below 65°. The rainfall generally comes in late afternoon or evening showers and averages 40 inches a year. Cooling easterly trade winds temper the summer's heat and keep humidity down.

Entrance Fees

There are no entrance fees.

Permits and Licenses

Persons returning to the U.S. mainland must go through Customs and Immigration at ports of entry. A special Department of Agriculture permit is required to exit with fruits, vegetables, plant cuttings or seeds.

Access and Transportation

From the mainland United States you can fly directly to Charlotte Amalie, St. Thomas or San Juan, Puerto Rico. You can also travel by ship. If you arrive in St. Thomas, taxis and buses can take you to

Red Hook, where a ferry operates daily to Cruz Bay on St. John.

The campground is 20 minutes by car or taxi from Cruz Bay. Jeeps and other vehicles may be rented, but reservations are necessary.

Special Needs

Check with park staff about accessible beaches. Annaberg Ruins, some campsites at Cinnamon Bay campground and ferries are accessible with assistance. There are ramps at Hawksnest Bay, Trunk Bay and wheelchair accessible restrooms at the visitor center.

Amenities

Swimming ♦ Snorkeling ♦ Scenic drives ♦ Hiking ♦ Fishing ♦ Boating ♦ Ranger-led activities

Travel Advisory

The speed limit is 20 miles per hour. Remember to drive on the left side of the road. Sound your horn on blind curves.

Emergency Information

First aid is available inside the park. The nearest clinic is at Cruz Bay, open Monday through Friday from 7 a.m. to 11 p.m. and on Saturday and Sunday from 8 a.m. to 11 p.m. Call 809-776-6400. A nurse and doctor are on call 24 hours a day at 809-776-6471 or 809-693-8900.

Visitor and Information Centers

Cruz Bay Visitor Center offers orientation talks and exhibits. Red Hook Contact Station is on St. Thomas.

Campgrounds

Camping is allowed only at the Cinnamon Bay Campground. It is five miles from Cruz Bay and has tent sites, pre-erected tents and cottage units with tables grills and water. Campsites can be rented with or without equipment, including tent, cots, bedding, cooking utensils and stove. There is a 14-day limit. For information and reservations call 800-539-9998.

Picnic Areas

There are several picnic tables scattered throughout the park.

Cabins, Lodges and Hotels

There are a number of accommodations on St. John. For a complete list, write the Virgin Islands Division of Tourism, Box 6400, St. Thomas, VI 00831.

Restaurants

There is one restaurant in the park. Tree Lizards Restaurant at Cinnamon Bay serves breakfast, lunch and dinner.

THINGS TO DO AND SEE

Scenic Drive. A 15-mile tour by taxi or auto over Centerline Road and back via the North Shore Road reveals spectacular scenery. Resident-guided taxi tours through the park are also popular. Tours typically take about two and a half hours. They depart from Cruz Bay.

Underwater Tour. For an underwater tour, start at Trunk Bay and dive in. There's a self-guided trail marked with etched glass plates ten feet under; perfect for snorkelers.

Annaberg Ruins. The park road and trails offer access to many of the island's most beautiful sights, including a ruined plantation. The partially restored ruins of the slave-run Annaberg sugar mill are above Leinster Bay on St. John's north shore.

Beaches. The island's clear, warm seas and sandy beaches are the park's main attraction. Trunk Bay has one of the best beaches in the world. Follow the underwater signs for a self-guided underwater snorkel trip. Lifeguards are on duty and snorkel equipment can be rented. Cinnamon Bay Water Sports Center offers scuba diving trips, wind-surfing lessons, sea kayak rentals and Hobie monohull sailboats. Other popular areas include Leinster Bay, Coral Bay, Lameshur Bay and Salt Pond Bay.

Hiking. There are 22 trails in the park and most lead to the beach. The Reef Bay Trail follows an old Danish road for two miles through the forest.

For More Information
Superintendent
Virgin Islands National Park
Box 710, Cruz Bay
St. John, VI 00830
Tel. 809-775-6238 or
809-776-6201

VOYAGEURS NATIONAL PARK

Minnesota ◆ Established 1975

"Voyageurs" refers to the French Canadian trappers and traders who traveled its network of lakes in birch canoes, transporting brown gold, as beaver fur was called in the 18th century. The waterways have been equally useful to loggers and bootleggers smuggling liquor from Canada during Prohibition. A 56-mile stretch of water highway the voyageurs once used forms the northern boundary of the park with Canada.

Today, the park is still best appreciated from the water. It is a haven for fishermen, boaters and winter sports enthusiasts. Kabetogama Lake, Rainy Lake, Crane Lake and Ash River are private communities through which you can enter the park.

There are about 25 miles of trails that wend through great stands of fir, aspen, spruce, pine and birch, reaching to the water's edge. Until recently, all trails were accessible only by boat. Now there are three trails you can approach on foot: Blind Ash Bay Trail, Echo Bay Trail and the Oberholzer Nature Trail, a self-guided, one-mile nature walk. The longest hiking trail is the Cruiser Lake Trail.

The park is alive with moose, wolves, deer, beaver, muskrat and bears and is also home to eastern timber wolves.

Anglers can pit their skills against pelicans, great blue heron, eagles and osprey, birds that also fish for the pike and bass in Voyageur's 30 lakes. You must stay at least a quarter of a mile away from the nests of bald eagles, osprey or great blue heron. There are also several species of ducks in the park.

PLANNING YOUR VISIT

Park Open

The park is open year-round. Access is limited during freeze-ups in November and ice-outs in April. The best time to visit is May to September. Peak visitation is in July.

Seasons

The park's many lakes draw swimmers, boaters water skiers and fishermen in the summer. Winter sports are also popular, especially cross-country skiing, snowmobiling, snowshoeing and ice fishing. A seven-mile ice road from Rainy Lake Visitor Center to Cranberry Bay creates a unique entrance to the park in the winter. Winter brings moderate snowfall, with occasional blizzard conditions and severely drifting snow.

Entrance Fees

There is no entrance fee and no camping fees. You may tow in your own water craft.

Permits and Licensing

There are no camping permits. Boats must be licensed in your state or Minnesota. A Minnesota fishing license is required. In adjacent Canadian waters, an Ontario license is required.

Access and Transportation

From Minneapolis. Take I-35 to Route 33. Then go 17 miles to U.S. 53 to a park entrance. There are four entrance roads into the park along U.S. 53. County Route 23-24 from Orr leads to Crane Lake. County Route 129 (also called Ash River Trail) leads to Ash River. County Route 122, gives access to Kabetogama Lake. County Road 11 goes from International Falls to Rainy Lake.

There is no train service. You may rent a car at International Falls airport. There are six miles of road in the park, but no roads beyond the edge of the park. Most of the park is accessible only by water.

You may enter the park by power boat, canoe, kayak, snowmobile and cross-country skis. The nearest airport is International Falls.

Special Needs

Three visitor centers are handicapped accessible. The trail at Rainy Lake Visitor Center is accessible for one-half mile. The visitor centers can provide a fact sheet on handicapped access. Braille park brochures and captioned park films are available upon request at all visitor centers.

Amenities

Boat and canoe rental ♦ Naturalist-guided boat tours and walks ♦ Boat launch ramps ♦ Fishing and boating guides ♦ Children's programs ♦ Free rowboats and canoes on small interior lakes

Travel Advisory

Voyageur's glacier-carved lakes are beautiful, but submerged rocks and stiff winds can make them hazardous waters. Small boats and canoes should wait out rough weather. Swimming from public docks or boat-launch areas is prohibited.

Emergency Information

First aid is available from park rangers. The nearest hospitals are in International Falls and Cook.

A Few Tips

♦ *Boaters should make sure their crafts are well-equipped and not overloaded.*
♦ *Keep an eye out for warning buoys and numbered channel markers. It is easy to unwittingly cross the border into Canadian waters.*
♦ *You need a permit to go ashore in Canada. You must report to customs offices when you return to the U.S.*

Visitor and Information Centers

There are three major visitor centers: Rainy Lake, Kabetogama Lake and Ash River. Rainy Lake is on Highway 11 at the northwest edge of the park. It is open daily, from May 1 to October 15. Call 218-286-5258.

Kabetogama Lake is on Road 122 at the southwest edge of the park. It is open daily, mid-May through September 30. Call 218-875-2111.

Ash River is on the southeast edge of Kabetogama Lake. It is open mid-May to Labor Day.

Campgrounds

Voyageur has 150 backcountry campsites. These are tent sites only with no showers. Many of the campsites are along major lakes. Most have a 14-day limit. Sites are reserved on a first-come, first-served basis. There are also houseboat sites. Private campsites with tent and RV

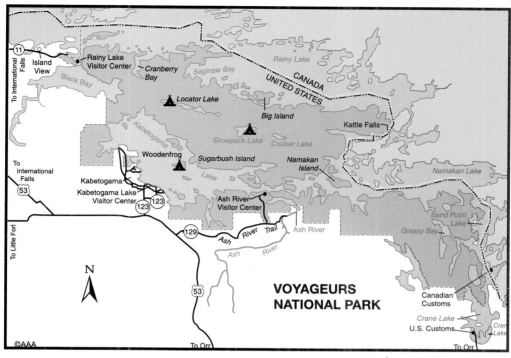

Park size: 218,035 acres

sites are located near the park. Several sites have bear-proof food storage lockers or poles. You must use only dead and downed wood for campfires. Remove all trash from the park.

Picnic Areas

You may picnic at designated areas along Voyageur's lakes. However, be aware that there are private cottages within the park and resort areas adjacent to the park that are also privately owned. Buy food and supplies in International Falls, Orr and in the resort areas.

Cabins, Lodges and Hotels

Park headquarters can provide a full list of accommodations in the four resort communities adjacent to the park.

Kettle Falls Hotel. Open from mid-May to September 30 and January 1 through March 15, the hotel has 12 rooms with shared baths for $45 per person. This historic hotel has been in business since 1910. It is accessible only by water, boat service is available. Call 888-KF-HOTEL.

Holiday Inn. On U.S. Highway 71, the hotel has 126 units for $67. There is also a restaurant. Call 218-283-4451.

Island View Lodge. On Rainy Lake, the lodge has nine rooms for $60-65 and 11

cabins with kitchenettes for $95–195. There is also a restaurant. Call 218-286-3511.

Thunderbird Lodge. On Rainy Lake, the lodge has 15 rooms for $50–68 and ten cabins with kitchenettes for $90–175. It also has a restaurant. Call 218-286-3151.

On Lake Kabetogama:

North Star Resort. The resort has seven cabins with kitchenettes for $410–680 per week. They are open mid-May to Labor Day. Call 218-875-2175 for reservations.

Rocky Point Resort. This resort has eight cabins with kitchenettes for $180–600 per week, two lodge rooms for $15 per person and a restaurant. Call 218-875-2411.

Voyageur Park Lodge. There are 11 cabins with kitchenettes for $267–$1,135 per week and five rooms with shared bath (winter only) for $60–76 per person. Call 800-331-5694 for reservations.

Restaurants

There is a restaurant in the Kettle Falls Hotel. You can buy food and supplies in International Falls, Ray and Orr.

THINGS TO DO AND SEE

Kabetogama Lake. There is a weekly, full-day tour of Kabetogama Lake that departs from the Kabetogama Lake Visitor Center. The boat docks at La Bontys Point, where you begin a two-mile hike that takes you past a beaver lodge. You can complete your exploration of the lake by canoe.

Boat Tours. There are daily boat tours to observe park scenery and wildlife, including bald eagles and loons. Trips vary from a half-hour to day-long trips.

Exploring. You get around the park by concession boat tours, water taxi or in your own boat. Two trails are accessible by water. The Locator Lake Trail is a two-mile hike into a chain of four lakes. Canoes and rowboats are available on loan but must be reserved. The nearly ten-mile Cruiser Lake Trail traverses the Kabetogama Peninsula.

Kettle Falls Historic District. You can look south into Canada from the international boundary and visit the dam and Kettle Falls Hotel. The flower beds and rock sculptures of Ellsworth Rock Gardens make this spot popular for picnics.

Little American Island. Experience the Rainy Lake Gold Rush of the 1890s by visiting Little American Island. Exhibits describe the once active mine as you walk back in time.

Near Voyageurs National Park

Chippewa National Forest. The 661,161-acre forest in Cass Lake is a breeding ground for bald eagles. The lake provides opportunities for boating, fishing and skiing. Hunters and hikers make camp here from mid-May through mid-September. The national forest is about 85 miles from Voyageurs on U.S. 2.

For More Information

Superintendent
Voyageurs National Park
3131 Highway 53
International Falls, MN 56649-8904
Tel. 218-283-9821

WATERTON-GLACIER NATIONAL PARK

Alberta, Canada ♦ *Montana* ♦ **Established 1932**

I n 1932, the United States and Canada combined Waterton Lakes National Park (founded in 1895) and nearby Glacier National Park (founded in 1910), forming the world's first international peace park. Under this unique arrangement, each country administers the park lands on its own soil but cooperates in the areas of visitor services, scientific research and wildlife management.

The park land on both sides of the border has many resources in common. Of course the wildlife of the region is indigenous to both countries. Therefore, in order to see all the sights, visitors are permitted to pass over the international boundaries at certain border crossings.

Waterton-Glacier National Park offers an astounding diversity of natural grandeur. Contemplating its jagged mountain peaks, deep green forests, pristine lakes and streams and meadows full of wildflowers, naturalist John Muir called this country "the best care-killing scenery on the continent."

There are more than 200 bodies of water in the park. Lake McDonald, with its cascading waterfall, is the largest. Other small lakes called tarns dot the mountain slopes. There are more than 50 glaciers within the park. The area that became the Waterton-Glacier National Park is really their creation. Today's glaciers are a mere 4,000 years old. Sperry Glacier, the largest of them, moves only about 30 feet a year. This is a snail's pace when measured against the speed of the great glaciers of the last ice age.

The park lands have been completely covered over at

A FEW TIPS

♦ *Never climb or hike alone.*
♦ *Avoid steep snowfields.*
♦ *Wear layered clothing. The weather is apt to change suddenly.*

least four times during the last three million years. As the icy juggernauts advanced and retreated over the land, their passage sculpted the spectacular topography of today's park. Narrow glens were widened into U-shaped valleys. Long deep basins were carved out of mountain sides and round peaks were cut into sharp ridges.

Retreating glaciers sometimes left debris in their wake, blocking a stream of meltwater. The beautiful lakes and streams of today are the result.

Waterton-Glacier National Park straddles the Continental Divide. The eastern and western areas of the park are separated by the Rocky Mountains. Consequently, the two areas are completely dissimilar in climate.

The western side, which is moister, is forested with ponderosa pine, Douglas fir, hemlock, larch and even a few 500-year-old red cedars. The drier eastern side's trees are shorter and include sub-alpine fir, lodgepole pine and Engelmann spruce. The park's meadows come into bloom all too briefly, but there are gorgeous displays of wildflowers.

The park is unusually rich in wildlife. Park rangers are currently tracking two different packs of wolves. There are also grizzlies, ptarmigan, bald eagle and moose. Each spring, mountain goats return to an exposed riverbank cliff. The cliff contains mineral salts. As many as a dozen goats at a time can be seen taking advantage of this natural salt lick.

The park is the ancestral homeland of the Native American Blackfoot people.

Many sites in the park were once associated with the Blackfoot religious tradition of the spirit quest. The eastern part of the park was formerly reservation land until the tribe sold it in 1896. Many members of the tribe still make their home in this area. The park lands remain sacred to them.

PLANNING YOUR VISIT

Park Open

The park is open year-round. Most roads are closed in winter. Peak visitation is in July.

Seasons

Weather is unpredictable. Rain, hail or snow may occur at any time of the year. High temperatures in the summer are usu-

ally in the upper 70s, with lows in the 40s. Winter highs are in the 40s with lows in the teens.

Entrance Fees

Per vehicle $10
Per individual...$5
Fees are valid for 7 days.

Permits and Licenses

Free permits are required for overnight stays in the backcountry. Permits are available at Apgar and St. Mary visitor centers.

Vehicles on Going-to-the-Sun Road between Avalanche Point and the Sun Point Parking Area are limited to 21 feet in length, including bumpers and eight feet in width, including mirrors. Bicycles are not allowed on portions of Going-to-the-Sun Road during peak travel times. Bicycles and other vehicles are not allowed on trails or off the roads.

Access and Transportation

The park is in northwest Montana along the Canadian border.

From Columbia Falls. The west entrance is on U.S. 2, 34 miles east of Kalispell, Montana. The east entrance is via U.S. 89 and 2.

The closest airport is Waterton-Glacier International Airport at Kalispell. There is a regularly scheduled commercial bus from Waterton-Glacier International Airport to West Glacier. Call 406-752-4022 for schedule and cost information. Rental cars are available at the airport and in Lethbridge and Calgary, Alberta, Canada.

Special Needs

The park's wheelchair accessible sites include the Apgar and St. Mary visitor centers, the Trail of the Cedars, the evening slide and campfire programs in the campgrounds and the asphalt Apgar bike path. Texts and written descriptions of walks and talks are also available. Limited sign language interpretation is available. Also, some tactile exhibits and interpretive programs are available. For the visually impaired, a tape recording of the park brochure is available.

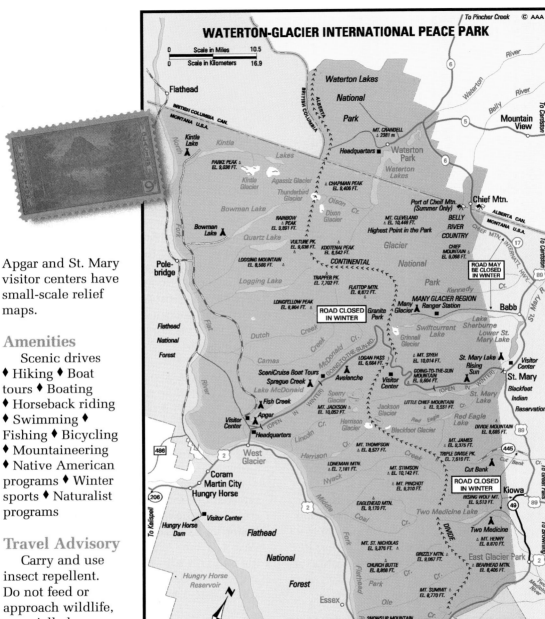

WATERTON-GLACIER INTERNATIONAL PEACE PARK

Park size: 1,013,572 acres

Apgar and St. Mary visitor centers have small-scale relief maps.

Amenities

Scenic drives
◆ Hiking ◆ Boat tours ◆ Boating ◆ Horseback riding ◆ Swimming ◆ Fishing ◆ Bicycling ◆ Mountaineering ◆ Native American programs ◆ Winter sports ◆ Naturalist programs

Travel Advisory

Carry and use insect repellent. Do not feed or approach wildlife, especially bears.

Emergency Information

First aid is available in the park. The nearest hospitals are in Cardston, Alberta, Canada (35 miles) and Whitefish, Montana (24 miles).

Visitor and Information Centers

Park headquarters is just inside the west entrance. There are three visitor centers in

the park. Apgar Visitor Center, in Apgar Village, is closed mid-December to mid-May. St. Mary Visitor Center at the east entrance to the park, is closed mid-October to mid-May.

Logan Pass Visitor Center, at the summit of Going-to-the-Sun Road, is closed from mid-September to mid-June.

Campgrounds

There are 15 campgrounds in the park. Most are open from June through September. Campsites are available on a first-come, first-served basis. The camping fee is $10 a night. Apgar, Bowman Lake, Cutbank, Kintla Lake, St. Mary and Two Medicine are open for primitive camping in winter. Backcountry camping is allowed with a permit, available from a visitor center or headquarters.

Picnic Areas

Picnic areas are located off the main roads.

Cabins, Lodges and Hotels

Visitors can choose between lodges, hotels, inns and chalets in the park. Most are open from June through September. Call Glacier Park, Inc. at 406-226-5551 for more information and reservations. In Apgar, stay at Apgar Village Lodge or the Village Inn Motel. On Lake McDonald, the Lake McDonald Lodge offers cabins and motel rooms. Many Glacier Hotel is in St. Mary and so is the Rising Sun Motor Inn, which also rents cabins. Swiftcurrent Motor Inn has motel rooms and cabins. Granite Fork and Sperry Chalets rents backcountry chalets.

Restaurants

There are restaurants and coffee shops at the Rising Sun Motor Inn, Many Glacier Hotel and Swiftcurrent Motor Inn. Both the Lake McDonald Lodge and Many Glacier Hotel have cocktail lounges. In Apgar, Eddie's Restaurant is open May through September and the Cedar Tree Deli is open June through September.

THINGS TO DO AND SEE

Lake Tours. From June through September, the Glacier Park Boat Company offers narrated tours of Lake McDonald. Tours depart from the lodge boat dock, lake side. Tours of St. Mary Lake depart from the Rising Sun boat dock. Swiftcurrent and Josephine Lake Tours depart from the Many Glacier Hotel dock, lakeside. The Two Medicine Lake tour departs from the Two Medicine Lake boat dock. Fees are charged. For information on these tours, call 406-732-4480.

Backcountry Tours. Guided backcountry tours are available. Fees are charged. For more information call Glacier Wilderness Guides at 406-8885466 (summers) or 406-862-4802 (winters).

Scenic Drives. The 50-mile Going-to-the Sun road is one of the most spectacular drives on the continent. It is the only road that crosses the park, traveling from St. Mary at one end, across the Continental Divide and on to West Glacier. Logan Pass (elevation 6,680 feet) is the high point. Because of the narrow mountain roads,

plan on taking between one and a half to three hours to make the journey from one end of the park to the other. Check with the headquarters staff for current vehicle length restrictions. Going-to-the-Sun Road is closed in winter. There are several other beautiful roads. Camas Creek Road runs ten miles through forests of different ages and offers frequent roadside exhibits. Chief Mountain International Highway takes you to Waterton Lakes National Park in Canada and offers a clear view of the Chief Mountain. Two Medicine Road and Many Glacier Road also offer many scenic vistas.

Hiking. There are more than 700 miles of trails in the park. Boulder Pass Trail is 37 miles. The Continental Divide National Scenic Trail takes about ten days.

Trail Tours. From June through September, guided trail tours, from a few hours to a few days, are available. Tours depart from Apgar Corral, Lake McDonald Corral and Many Glacier Corral. For more information, call Glacier Park Outfitters at 406-732-5597.

Glacier Institute. The Glacier Institute offers a wide range of courses, ranging from ecology to photography workshops. For more information write to The Glacier Institute, Box 1457, Kalispell, MT 59903.

Near Waterton-Glacier National Park

Flathead National Forest, Kalispell, Montana. This 2,346,000-acre spread of mountains, lakes and wild and scenic rivers has 400 campsites that are open all year. The visitor center is on U.S. Highway 89 at Hungry Horse Dam, about seven miles from Waterton-Glacier National Park. Visitors can enjoy hiking, boating, horseback riding, hunting, climbing, scenic drives, picnic areas and winter sports. For more information call 406-755-5401.

Lewis and Clark National Forest, Great Falls Montana. This national forest adjoins Waterton-Glacier National Park on the south. The forest is in two regions separated by plains. The Rockies region has steep terrain with parts of two wilderness areas. The Jefferson region has gentler peaks, broad plateaus and rolling hills.

The forest is home to a large herd of bighorn cattle. The national forest is 1,843,000 acres, with 278 campsites and five winter cabins. Reservations are required. Visitors can enjoy hiking, boating, horseback riding, hunting, climbing, scenic drives, picnic areas and winter sports. The park is open year-round. Campsites are open late spring to fall. For more information call 406-791-7700.

For More Information
Superintendent
Waterton-Glacier National Park
West Glacier, MT 59936
Tel. 406-888-5441

GRIZZLY BEARS OF WATERTON

They roamed North America in the tens of thousands in the middle 1800s. The Blackfeet people called them the Real Bears. An adult male can weigh twice as much as a black bear, 400 to 600 pounds and yet a grizzly can sprint at speeds of 35 m.p.h. Intelligent and unpredictable, the grizzly of myth is a ruthless, vicious killer.

In fact, man is the real predator. Today there are perhaps 900 grizzlies in the lower 48 states, their numbers reduced by hunters, ranchers and a vanishing wilderness. There may be as many as 50,000 grizzlies worldwide, mostly in Alaska and Canada.

Grizzlies feed on grass, berries and roots. Unfamiliar with the scent of humans, the great bears will generally shy away, avoiding all contact with the interlopers. In days gone by, the threat to humans from grizzlies was caused by careless garbage disposal. In 1967 two campers in the park were fatally mauled by grizzlies who had become accustomed to feeding on garbage. Since then safeguards have been put in place. Overly bold or aggressive bears have been shot, or tranquilized and relocated to distant wilderness areas, far from human habitation. The danger from the bears is minimal but they should always be given a wide berth. All food should be disposed of properly at campground dump sites.

WIND CAVE NATIONAL PARK

South Dakota ♦ **Established 1903**

There are really two parks at Wind Cave, one above ground and one below.

Above are rolling grasslands, forests and hills. The elm and burr oak of the eastern forests, the yucca and cactus of the southwest deserts and the ponderosa pines and juniper of the Rockies coexist here. So do herds of elk, deer, pronghorns and bison. Badgers, coyotes and prairie dogs make their home on these Dakota plains too.

Under the prairie there is cool, dark world. An 80-mile network of limestone passages runs below the 28,295-acre park. Guided tours of the cave travel only a few of the 80 miles of passages that have been explored and mapped.

Wind Cave has been 60 million years in the making. Limestone cracked and allowed water to seep through and dissolve the stone, carving out the passages. The wind can be heard at the cave's only natural opening, caused by differences in the atmospheric pressure above and below ground. The sound actually led to the discovery of the cave by two brothers in 1881 and accounts for its name.

The cave has a unique display of stone filigree called boxwork. Thin calcite fins form these fantastic honeycomb patterns on ceilings and walls. This boxwork was created when groundwater full of dissolved calcium carbonate seeped through the earth. It eventually crystallized into calcite, which hardened to form popcorn, frostwork and other boxwork. Wind Cave has the greatest display of boxwork in the world. The only other major caves in the national park system, at Carlsbad Caverns, boasts only stalagmites and stalactites.

The park has 30 miles of hiking trails, including part of the South Dakota Centennial Trail. Two backcountry roads make this park one of the most accessible national parks. Backpacking and overnight camping are allowed on the Centennial Trail.

PLANNING YOUR VISIT

Park Open

The park is open year-round. There are fewer cave tours off-season. Peak visitation is in July and early August.

Seasons

Spring and fall are recommended times to visit Wind Cave, but the weather is variable. Fall is warm and clear with cold nights. Spring, a short but beautiful season on the Dakota plains, brings wildflowers but can also bring wet snows. Summer lasts

A FEW TIPS

♦ *Watch for poison ivy.*
♦ *Rattlesnakes often reside in the burrows of prairie dogs.*
♦ *Cave tours are less crowded before 11 a.m.*

through August and daytime temperatures can top 100 degrees, though nights are much cooler. During summer afternoons, thunderstorms with violent lightning and hail can strike. Winter is mild with little snow though the temperature occasionally dips below zero.

Entrance Fees

There are no entrance fees. There are fees for cave tours and camping. Cave tours range from $4 to $15 per adult. Children between 6 and 16 pay reduced prices. Children five and under are free.

Permits and Licenses

Permits are required for backcountry camping. Overnight backcountry campers can obtain free permits at the visitor center.

Access and Transportation

The park is in southwestern South Dakota, about 60 miles south of Rapid City, off U.S. 385. It is just seven miles north of Hot Springs, on U.S. Route 385. There are three entrances.

From the Northeast. Take I-90 at Rapid City, South Dakota and exit onto U.S. Route 79 South. Follow U.S. Route 79 for 50 miles

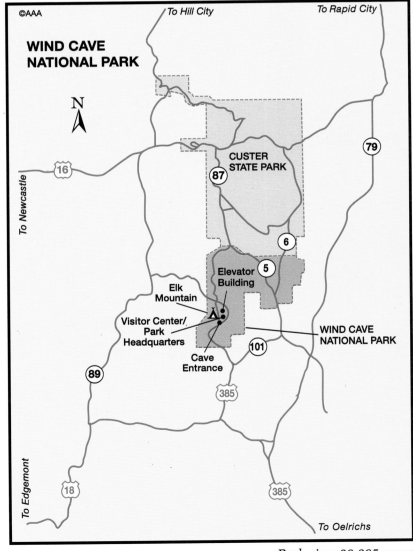

Park size: 28,295 acres

to U.S. Route 18. Turn right onto U.S. Route 385 North which takes you into the park. Follow signs to the visitor center.

From the South. Take U.S. 385 for seven miles north of Hot Springs.

From the Northwest. Take U.S. 385 for 21 miles south of Custer. To reach the North entrance, take Highway 87 from Custer State Park.

The closest airport is in Rapid City.

Special Needs

The exhibit rooms and restrooms of the visitor center are accessible. One campsite and campground restrooms are accessible.

Amenities

Cave tours ♦ Special needs tours ♦ Displays and exhibits ♦ Self-guided nature trails ♦ Bookstore ♦ Junior ranger program

Travel Advisory

The cave may only be visited as part of a tour led by rangers. Touring the caves requires bending due to low ceilings and also requires climbing stairs. If you do plan to enter the cave, wear sturdy, low-heeled shoes that will not slip on cave trails.

Emergency Information

First aid is available in the park. The closest hospital is in Hot Springs

Visitor and Information Center

The visitor center is open daily except Thanksgiving and Christmas Day. Hours vary with the season. Two exhibit rooms highlight cave exploration and history, wildlife and the prairie. A bookstore sells maps, postcards and tapes about the park. The visitor center has complete information about cave tours. Cave tours run daily except Thanksgiving and Christmas Day. The schedule is limited in the off-season.

Campgrounds

Elk Mountain Campground. This campground is near the visitor center. It has 75 sites available from April to October. The site has flush toilets and water only. There are no showers, dump stations or electrical hookups. Sites are available on a first-come, first-served basis. Costs are $10 a night; $5 a night for off-season.

To reserve group campsites call 605-745-4600.

Other camping is available in federal, state and private campgrounds.

THE GHOST DANCERS

In 1890, Sitting Bull was visited by a brave who brought news of the Ghost Dance religion. A Paiute holy man taught that Christ had returned to earth as an Indian. The Red Messiah promised to render the white man's bullets powerless. Christ had shown the Paiutes a mystical dance which would hasten a great flood, a cataclysm which would sweep all the white people off the face of the earth. Then, dead Indians would be reborn and the buffalo and antelope would return to the plains. Sitting Bull was skeptical, but the new religion gave his people hope. Indian agents were horrified and asked for troops. A list of "fomenters of disturbances" was forwarded to Washington. Sitting Bull's name headed the list.

On December 15 of that year, Indian police arrested Sitting Bull. Catch-the-Bear, a Ghost Dancer, believing himself invulnerable to bullets, shot an Indian policeman. Another tribal policeman, Red Tomahawk, killed Sitting Bull. The shots prompted Sitting Bull's horse to launch into a dance routine learned during their days with Bill Hickock's Wild West show. To bystanders, it seemed the horse was performing the ghost dance.

Ghost dancers fled the reservations and agencies only to be surrounded by the 7th U.S. Cavalry, Custer's old regiment. The troopers fired on the encampment, killing more than 300 people. Survivors were carried to a makeshift infirmary in the Episcopal Mission at Pine Ridge, where a Christmas banner proclaimed, "Peace on Earth, Good Will To Men."

Picnic Areas

There are markets in Hot Springs (seven miles from the park) and Custer State Park (12 miles from the park).

Cabins, Lodges and Hotels

There is no lodging in the park. There are accommodations in Hot Springs and Custer, South Dakota and in Custer State Park.

Restaurants

From May through October, there is a vending area at the visitor center that offers limited snacks and beverages. There are restaurants in Hot Springs, Custer and Custer State Park.

THINGS TO DO AND SEE

Cave Tours. In the summer there are five types of cave tours. They are scheduled every 20 minutes starting at about 8:40 a.m. until 6:30 p.m. They include an exploration of passages that were discovered more than 100 years ago and major sights such as the Garden of Eden, Natural Entrance and Fairgrounds. (An elevator returns you to the surface at the end of your tour.)

Tour schedules are more limited off-season. Cave tours often sell out during the summer. A one-hour wait is not unusual during peak season, which runs from mid-June to Labor Day.

Reservations are taken for two special tours: a caving tour and a candlelight tour. Minimum age for the caving tour is 16.

Minimum age for the candlelight tour is eight. Both tours are limited to ten people. You may make reservations a month in advance and these reservations must be confirmed two days before your scheduled tour.

Group tours of the caves can be arranged but are limited to 40 people. These tours are scheduled between 8 a.m. and 11:30 a.m. only. Reserve a group tour three weeks in advance by calling 605-745-4600.

Hiking. There are 30 miles of trails in Wind Cave National Park. Two trails, the Rankin Ridge Trail and Elk Mountain Trail, are self-guided nature trails with trail booklets. One of the prettiest views of the park is from the Rankin Ridge Fire Tower. Get a topographic map at the visitor center. There is no bicycling or horseback riding allowed on the trails.

For More Information
Superintendent
Wind Cave National Park
Route 1, Box 190 — WCNP
Hot Springs, SD 57747-9430
Tel. 605-745-4600

WRANGELL-ST. ELIAS NATIONAL PARK

Alaska ♦ **Established 1978**

This mountain kingdom is the largest of all national parks. Some of the most beautiful mountain wilderness in the world is in Wrangell-St. Elias National Park, where the Wrangell, St. Elias and Chugach Mountains and the eastern end of the Alaska Range meet. Nine of the sixteen highest peaks in the United States are located here. Mount St. Elias, at 18,008 feet, is the second highest peak in the country. Mount Wrangell is an active volcano.

The high country in the park is covered with snow all year. This snow creates more than 100 massive glaciers and icefields that cover a good deal of the park's interior. The park has the largest collection of glaciers in North America. Malaspina, a glacier that flows out of the St. Elias Mountains, is larger than the state of Rhode Island. You will recognize Malaspina, even from the air, because it has a distinctive, black and white striped pattern. Wrangell-St. Elias is also the site of the largest subpolar ice field in North America, the Bagley Icefield.

The land here is criss-crossed with streams and rivers flowing from the glaciers. The Chitina River travels from the Chitina and Logan glaciers on the park's eastern boundary to the Copper River. The Copper is the largest river in the park. It runs along the park's western border and empties into the Gulf of Alaska.

Roads do lead into this huge park because this area once had two booming mine towns. The discovery of copper deposits in the Chitina River valley lured people to the town of McCathy and later to the town of Kennicott. From 1911 to 1938,

ore was extracted from these rich mines and a railroad was built in the valley to transport the copper. Eventually, the ore deposits were depleted and the miners moved on. The ruins of Kennicott mining town are now on the National Register of Historic Places.

Although the icefields and glaciers may make the land appear barren and empty wildlife thrives in the park. If any single species symbolizes the hearty animals who make Wrangell-St. Elias their territory, it is the Dall sheep. At least 13,000 Dall sheep, the largest population in all Alaska, live in the interior highlands. The mountains are also home to caribou and mountain goats, who make their way along the cliffs with amazing ability. Grizzlies, brown and black bears are also in the park. Moose can also be sighted, foraging in the coastal bogs. Salmon spawn in the waters and sea lions and harbor seals also live in the coastal areas.

A FEW TIPS

♦ *Pack good rain gear.*
♦ *In the backcountry, you must be self-sufficient and well supplied. Assistance may be days away.*
♦ *Remember there are private areas in the park. Check maps and respect property owners' rights.*
♦ *Sport hunting is prohibited in the park. Subsistence hunting is done by residents in the fall.*

Native American populations also live in this area. Copper Center, Chitina, Gulkana and Chistochina were the homes of the Athabaskans. Yakutat, located on the coast, is a traditional Tlingit fishing village. The park still has residents who hunt and fish its lands as their ancestors did. Their property rights should be respected when visiting the park.

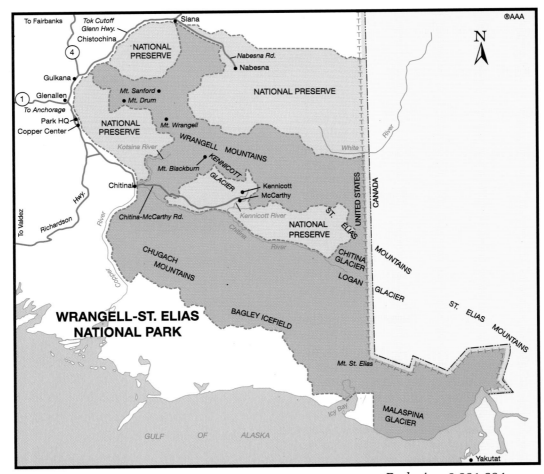

Park size: 8,331,604 acres

PLANNING YOUR VISIT

Park Open
The park is open year-round.

Seasons
Summers are cloudy and clear. Hot days are typical of July, the warmest month. August and September are cooler and wet, but with fewer mosquitoes. Average summer temperatures range from the 50s to 70s. Fall is delightfully clear but the season is short. Winter is cold and dark with temperatures dipping down to minus 50°. Average snow cover is two feet and days are often clear. Spring brings clear skies and warming temperatures.

Entrance Fees
There is no entrance fee.

Permits and Licenses
An Alaska fishing license is required.

Access and Transportation
The park is reached via the Glenn Highway from Anchorage to Glennallen and the Richardson Highway, which skirts the park's western boundary and Edgertown Highway. The Tok Cutoff south from the Alaska highway borders the northwestern corner of the park.

Access into the central portion of the park by road is through the community of Chitina. Take the 60-mile Chitina-McCarthy Road up the Chitina River Valley. This follows the historic route of the Copper River and Northwest Railroad. At the river you must take a foot bridge across the river to McCarthy. The privately owned Kennicott mining complex can be reached by van (for a fee). The Nabesna Road, from Slana on the Tok Cutoff, extends 45 miles to Nabesna, an inactive, privately owned mining community.

In the summer, buses run between Anchorage and Whitehorse, with stops in Glennallen. Charter flights to the park are available from Anchorage, Fairbanks, Northway, Glennallen, Cordova, Valdez, Tok and Yakutat. Rental cars are available in Anchorage and Fairbanks.

Special Needs
The park headquarters and the ranger station at Slana are accessible.

Amenities

Backcountry camping ♦ Kayaking ♦ Rafting ♦ Lake fishing ♦ Cross-country skiing ♦ Mountaineering ♦ Flightseeing

Travel Advisory

Road conditions can deteriorate quickly, making roads impassable to all but four-wheel drive vehicles.

Emergency Information

First aid is not available in the park. The nearest clinic is in Glennallen.

Visitor and Information Centers

Park headquarters is located at mile 105 Old Richardson Highway near Copper Center. There are ranger stations at Slana, Chitina and Yakutat with small exhibits and informational displays.

Campgrounds

There are no campgrounds maintained in the park. However, there are 23 state campgrounds in the Copper River region. These sites are open in the summer and have toilets, drinking water, picnic tables, fire pits and many can accommodate RVs. No reservations are required. For a complete listing of Alaska State Parks call 907-745-3975.

There are two private campgrounds on McCarthy Road. You may camp in a tent within the park except on private property. Backcountry campers must be self-sufficient and well-supplied.

Picnic Areas

There is a market in Glennallen and Tok. Limited supplies are available in Chitina and Slana.

Cabins, Lodges and Hotels

Lodging is available in Copper Center, Glennallen and McCarthy. Most lodges are open from Memorial Day through mid-September.

Ultima Thule Cabins. This fly-in lodge is on the Chitina River. There are five cabins and a dining room. Call 907-258-0636 for information.

McCarthy Lodge. This is a hotel in the McCarthy/Kennicott area. McCarthy Wilderness B&B is a bed and breakfast with rustic cabins. For more information, call 907-277-6867.

Kennicott Glacier Lodge. This is a hotel in the McCarthy/Kennicott area. Call 907-258-2350 for reservations.

Silvertip Lodge. This lodge rents bunkhouses and cabins on Nabesna Road. Call 907-337-2065 for reservations.

Devil's Mountain Lodge. They also rent bunkhouses and cabins on Nabensa Road. Call 907-822-3426 for reservations.

Rustic accommodations are also available at fishing camps and guide cabins in various parts of the park.

Restaurants

There are restaurants at McCarthy and Kennicott.

THINGS TO DO AND SEE

Tours. The park headquarters and visitor center can provide a list of tours and classes. Activities include mountaineering lessons, glacier walks, rafting trips, extended backpack trips into the wild and guided tours of the historic Kennicott mines.

Hiking. There are no maintained trails in the park. Hiking here can be much more difficult than on other terrain. What looks like scrub grass may be knee-deep water. Hikers must be familiar with safe techniques for crossing rivers and streams — many are impassable here.

Boating. The Copper and Chitina Rivers are great sites for rafting. The 77-mile trip down the Copper River from Chitina to the Gulf of Alaska takes rafters through rugged but beautiful terrain. Ocean kayakers can explore the bays, inlets and coast in the Yakutat and Icy Bay areas. Rafters can choose between the Chitina River or the Kennicott through Nizina River Canyon.

Mountaineering. The park's glaciers, icefields, rivers and steep rocks present a variety of challenges to mountaineers who visit the park from all over the world. Climbing expeditions scale Mounts Drum, Sanford, Blackburn and St. Elias. Mountaineering is best from April through June.

Fishing. You must have an Alaska fishing license and should also check with the park for catch limits. The lakes yield grayling, Dolly Varden trout, rainbow trout and lake trout.

Skiing. Cross-country skiing is best in March and April. This is after the severe cold has passed but when lowlands are still snow-covered.

Near Wrangell-St. Elias National Park

Kluane National Park Reserve. Adjacent to the Wrangell-St. Elias National Park is this 6.6 million acre Canadian park in the southwestern corner of the Yukon Territory. Canada's tallest mountain, Mount Logan, is here. You can reach the park via the Alaska Highway to Haines Highway. For more information call 403-634-7250.

For More Information

Superintendent
Wrangell-St. Elias National Park
PO Box 439
Copper Center, AK 99573
Tel. 907-822-5234

YELLOWSTONE NATIONAL PARK

Wyoming ◆ Montana ◆ Idaho ◆ Established 1872

Yellowstone is both the largest park in the continental U.S. and the oldest. President Ulysses S. Grant signed the Park Bill in 1872 and the next March, Yellowstone National Park became the world's first federally protected recreational area.

Yellowstone straddles the Continental Divide, spanning parts of Wyoming, Montana and Idaho. The Central Rockies offer unforgettable landscapes. Yellowstone's 2.2 million acres include the 110-mile shoreline of North America's largest mountain lake, Lake Yellowstone. There are more than a thousand miles of wilderness trails to ride, walk and ski.

There is more geothermal activity at Yellowstone than anywhere in the U.S. The park has more than 300 geysers (which expel water) and fumaroles (which expel gases), as well as colorful hot springs and mud pots. The most famous geyser is Old Faithful, which sends a huge plume of water more than 100 feet in the air roughly every 79 minutes.

Yellowstone is home to a great variety of wildlife, including grizzly bears, mountain lions, mink, moose, coyotes, bison, beavers, bighorn and pronghorn. There is an effort underway to bring wolves back to Yellowstone. The area is a great site for bird-watching. Be on the look out for great gray owls, trumpeter swans, eagles, osprey and white pelicans.

Plan on spending at least three to five days to do Yellowstone National Park justice. There are nearly 350 mile of paved roads in the park. Major scenic attractions are around

A FEW TIPS

the Grand Loop Road, a figure-8 shaped circuit at the center of the park. You can drive the 142-mile Grand Loop in a day, but road conditions are sometimes bad and traffic can be heavy.

Park activities include hiking and backpacking, fly-fishing (with permit), boating, wildlife and wildflower viewing, cross-country skiing, snowmobiling (in restricted areas), horseback riding, scenic drives and snowshoeing. Rangers lead campfire programs, hikes and walks.

Certain areas in the park have been designated Bear Management Areas because of the higher-than-average concentration of bears. Hikers and campers do not have access to these areas. Check at ranger stations and visitor centers for more information.

Wildfires in 1988 affected half the park. Lightning caused initial fires and a carelessly discarded cigarette caused more fires a month later. Evidence of these blazes today serves as a reminder to protect the beauty of the wilderness during your visit.

♦ *Enjoy the show from the safety of the boardwalk. Jets of scalding water can injure you and you could stray to unstable ground.*
♦ *The spectacle of steam rising from the geothermal areas is most dramatic in cooler weather.*
♦ *Photograph the geysers using a fast shutter speed. Remember to wipe down the camera lens (and eyeglasses!) after leaving the area.*

PLANNING YOUR VISIT

Park Open

Nearly 50 percent of Yellowstone's visitors arrive in July and August, but the growing popularity of winter sports, especially wilderness cross-country skiing, is making the park a more popular year-round destination. If you plan to camp, make reservations up to two years in advance.

In winter, only one main road is open. It runs from the north entrance in Gardiner, Montana, to the northeast entrance and on to Cooke City, Montana.

WHEN DOES OLD FAITHFUL ERUPT?

Old Faithful is so consistently spectacular that park rangers can usually predict the time of the next eruption within ten minutes. Eruptions begin with a few sputters and splashes and grow into a fountain that shoots into the air for about five minutes.

Yellowstone's landscape has been shaped by volcanoes dating back 55 million years. Although there are now no volcanoes on the surface, hot molten rock remains in the interior of the earth. This molten rock is closer to the surface at Yellowstone than anywhere else on Earth.

As water seeps through cracks and faults in the earth's crust, it finds its way to an area of extreme heat and pressure. Water under pressure has a higher boiling point and this water may reach 400°F. As the hottest water rises, it begins to bubble up to the surface, growing in pressure until you see a geyser like Old Faithful explode with great plumes of water.

Seasons

Temperatures drop quickly and dramatically at Yellowstone. Warm days can turn into surprisingly cold nights. The coolest temperatures are typically in December to January (high 20s to low 30s). Subzero nights are common. The warmest temperatures are typically in July and afternoon thundershowers are common. Fall and spring are cool, but night temperatures can drop to the teens.

Entrance Fees

Fee per private vehicle
(any number of passengers) $20
Fee per person
(if arriving by other means) $10
Visitors under 17 ....FREE
Fees are valid for seven days and include entrance to Grand Teton National Park.

Permits and Licenses

Permits are available at ranger stations or visitor centers. They are required for backcountry camping, fishing, boating and certain day hikes. Ten-day permits for non-motorized boats are $5; for motorized boats

it's $10. Fees are charged for horseback riding, boat and bus tours, stagecoach and snowcoach rides.

Access and Transportation

The park has five entrances. The three Montana entrances are Gardiner (north), Cooke City (northeast) and West Yellowstone (west). The two Wyoming entrances are through Grand Teton National Park, Jackson (south) and Cody (east).

Main roads are open May through October. In winter, only one road is open to automobiles: the north entrance at Gardiner, Montana to Mammoth Hot Springs and Cooke City, Montana. Snowstorms can close roads at any time.

In summer, you can reach the western part of the park via Greyhound Bus or major airlines. There is an airport in West Yellowstone, Montana (summer only). Rental cars are available. There is no train service.

Special Needs

A *Guide to Accessibility for the Handicapped* is available from the park.

Amenities

Post offices ♦ Photo shops ♦ Slide shows ♦ Tour buses ♦ Religious services ♦ Boat rentals ♦ Laundries ♦ Horse rentals ♦ Interpretive campfire presentations

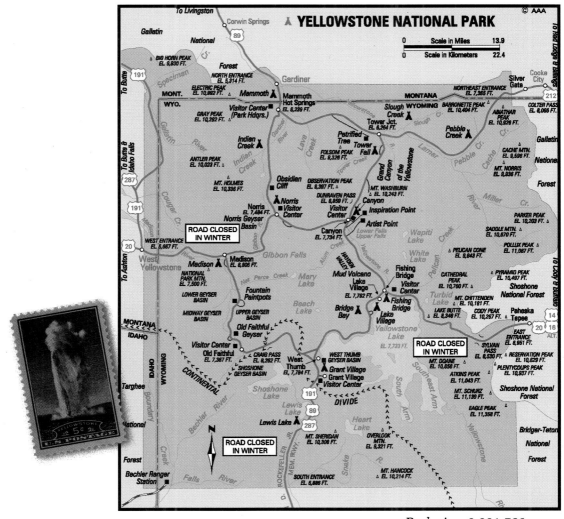

Park size: 2,221,766 acres

Travel Advisory

People with respiratory or cardio-vascular conditions should consult a physician before ascending to higher elevations. Park elevations range from 5,300 feet to more than 11,000 feet at Eagle Peak.

Stop in at ranger stations or visitor centers before hiking. Maps are highly recommended and you should check on trail conditions and restricted areas.

Emergency Information

There are three medical facilities in the park: Lake Hospital, Mammoth and Old Faithful Clinic.

Visitor and Information Centers

The visitor center at Mammoth Hot Springs is open daily, year-round. Old Faithful Visitor Center is open May to October and mid-December through mid-March. Canyon Visitor Center at the center of the park, Fishing Bridge and Grant Village Visitor Center (on Yellowstone Lake) are open May through September.

Campgrounds

There are 12 campgrounds in the park but you must reserve a spot — even years in advance. A national telephone reservation system has the most up-to-date information about schedules and camping fees. Call 307-344-7311 for complete information about RV sites, campgrounds and lodgings in the park.

Picnic Areas

Picnic areas are located off the park roads and most have tables and pit toilets.

You may only build a fire in fire grates. Use fuel stoves where no grates are available.

Food and supplies are sold at Lake, Fishing Bridge, Canyon, Tower-Roosevelt, Tower Fall, Mammoth Hot Springs, Grant Village and Old Faithful.

Cabins, Lodges and Hotels

There are nine major accommodations in the park, ranging from rustic cabins to modern hotels with a touch of frontier elegance. Most are open from May through October. Grant Village, the park's newest facility, is AAA Rated. For information about the availability and price range of various lodgings, call 307-344-7311.

Restaurants

All nine of the accommodations operate restaurants in the park. They are at Old Faithful Inn, Old Faithful Lodge, Grant Village, Lake Yellowstone Hotel, Lake Lodge, Roosevelt Lodge, Mammoth Hot Springs Hotel. Canyon Lodge features a cafeteria and snack bar, as does Lake Lodge. Mammoth Fast Foods operates during the summer.

THINGS TO DO AND SEE

Boating. Motorboats are allowed on Yellowstone Lake and Lewis Lake. Other lakes are limited to hand-propelled craft. Rivers and streams are closed to all boats. Sightseeing and fishing boats operate from Bridge Bay Marina.

Trail Rides. Trail rides start at Mammoth Hot Springs, Canyon and Roosevelt Corrals. Independent outfitters will also plan horseback excursions. A stagecoach outing is available through Roosevelt Corral.

Thermal Features. The park's most famous attractions are Old Faithful Geyser and the geysers and hot springs at Mammoth Hot Spring Terraces, Norris Geyser Basin and Black Sand Basin. Be prepared to do some hiking to get the best views. Maps of the geyser basin are available in the park.

Near Yellowstone National Park

Yellowstone is undeniably scenic, but can be over-crowded, especially during the peak summer season. Five national forests border the park and wilderness areas in Montana and Wyoming offer acres of stark beauty with smaller crowds. However, these areas are rugged. Inexperienced hikers and campers would be better off within the park.

For More Information

Superintendent
Yellowstone National Park
PO Box 168
Yellowstone National Park, WY 82190
Tel. 307-344-7381

Grand Prismatic Springs is the biggest and most beautiful hot spring in the park. Its shimmering colors are caused by algae and bacteria thriving at different water temperatures and minerals dissolving in the heated water.

From the main road you can also access Fountain Paint Pot, a mud pot of boiling pink mud.

Yellowstone Lake, Canyon & River. This is a half-day trip of nearly 40 miles. The falls at Yellowstone River are nearly twice as high as Niagara. The surrounding canyon walls are yellow and orange due to the heat and a chemical action on the brown rhyolite rock.

Grandview Point offers one of the best views of the park, as does the Brink of the Falls Trail, which is paved, but a strenuous hike. The river flows out of Yellowstone Lake at Fishing Bridge. A little farther east is Pelican Valley, where you may see pelicans as well as moose and bison.

Specimen Ridge. In the Northern Range is a large fossil forest of redwoods. The rest of the Northern Range is a series of grassy valleys where large animals spend the winter.

Norris Museum. The museum displays exhibits on thermal features and geysers. Also at Norris is the Museum of the National Park Ranger, dedicated to the park professionals dating back to 1916. Both museums are open only in the summer.

YOSEMITE NATIONAL PARK

California ◆ **Established 1890**

The mighty glaciers that crept down from the central Sierra Nevada mountains took millions of years to sculpt the seven mile long, one mile wide Yosemite Valley. Receding, they left a pristine High Sierra wilderness of 748,542 acres in their wake, an unforgettable panorama of scenic grandeur roughly the size of Rhode Island.

Unlike other North American mountain ranges, the Sierra Nevadas are not a chain of separate mountains. Severe and barren, they are a solid spine of granite thrust up from the earth's crust. The summit of Mount Lytell, the highest mountain, towers 13,110 feet into the sky. The Yosemite Valley, a grassy meadow corridor, is nestled between the sheer granite walls of the 7,500 foot El Capitan and the slopes of the 8,800 foot tall Half Dome.

The tree most associated with Yosemite is the sequoia. The park boasts three world-famous groves of giant sequoias: Mariposa, the largest, Tuolumne and Merced. You can walk in the deep shadows of living giants that pre-date the arrival of Christopher Columbus. One tree, the Grizzly Giant, is thought to be 2,700 years old.

Mule deer are the most commonly seen animal, but chipmunks, bobcats, coyotes and black bears also make their homes in the park.

PLANNING YOUR VISIT

Park Open

The park is open 24 hours a day, year round. The Tioga Pass, Glacier Point and Tuolumne Grove roads usually close in late November and open in late May. May and June are the best months for viewing the waterfalls. The park's peak visitation month is August. To enjoy winter sports, visit the Badger Pass ski area between Thanksgiving and mid-April. Reserve accommodations before coming for an overnight visit.

Seasons

Yosemite's elevation brings rapid changes in precipitation and temperature. Summer is usually warm and dry. Daytime temperatures in Yosemite Valley sometimes reach 100° but nights are cool. Temperatures in the Tuolumne Meadows are usually in the 70s during the day and the 30s at night. Winter is relatively mild, with moderate snowfall between November and March.

A Few Tips

♦ *See the park during the off-season if possible. Yosemite draws 14,000 visitors a day at the peak of the summer season.*

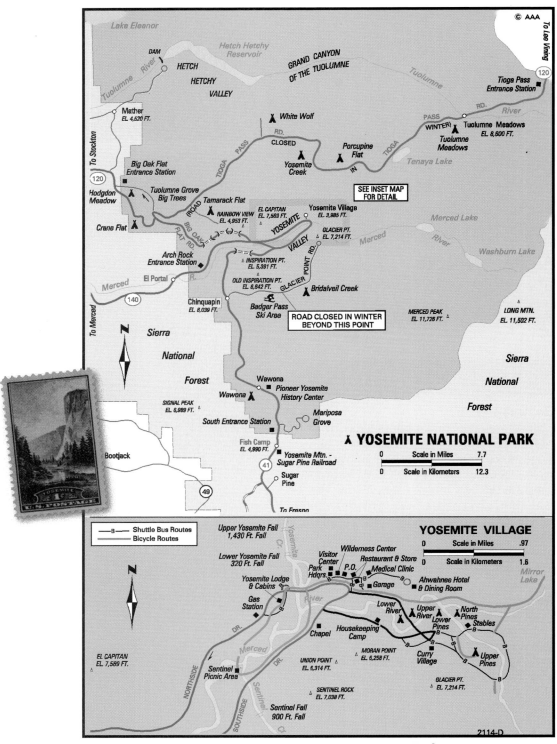

YOSEMITE NATIONAL PARK

0	Scale in Miles	7.7
0	Scale in Kilometers	12.3

YOSEMITE VILLAGE

0	Scale in Miles	.97
0	Scale in Kilometers	1.6

— B — Shuttle Bus Routes
——— Bicycle Routes

2114-D

Park size: 748,542 acres

Entrance Fees

Fee per vehicle..$20
Fee per individual $10

Fees are valid for seven days.

Permits and Licenses

Backcountry wilderness camping permits are available upon written application to the backcountry office, Wilderness Permit Reservations, PO Box 577, Yosemite, CA 95389, between March 1st or May 31.

Fishermen should check current catch and release information at park information stations. A California fishing license will also be required.

Access and Transportation

There are four entrances to Yosemite. The South Entrance is 63 miles from Fresno on Highway 41. The Southwest Entrance is 71 miles east of Oakdale on Highway 140. The West Entrance is 71 miles east of Oakdale on Highway 120. The East Entrance is 12 miles west of Lee Vining on Highway 120.

The nearest airports are in Fresno (63 miles from the park) and San Francisco International (183 miles from the park). There is a small airport in Merced with flights to San Francisco.

Rental cars are available at the airports. All vehicles must stay on surfaced roads. The Greyhound line serves Merced and Fresno. Transportation to the park is also available from Yosemite Gray Line or VIA Bus Lines. Amtrak serves Merced (70 miles from the park) and Fresno (63 miles from the park.)

In-Park Transportation

Yosemite operates its own transportation system. Call 209-372-1241 for schedule information. A valley shuttle runs between visitor centers and many other stops in the

YOSEMITE'S WORLD FAMOUS WATERFALLS

Yosemite National Park boasts some of the highest waterfalls in the United States. The falls are at their most impressive in the spring when melting snow transforms slow moving streams into turbulent displays of rushing water.

Yosemite Falls, the highest falls in the country and is probably the park's best known landmark. Seen from below, it appears to be one continuous waterfall. Actually, it descends in two levels. The Upper falls drops 1,430 feet. The Lower Falls drops another 320 feet. Yosemite Falls feeds into the river that awestruck Spanish explorers dubbed El Rio De Nuestra Señora De Merced, today known as the Merced River.

At 1,612 feet, Ribbon Fall is the largest single waterfall in the park. Bridalveil Fall is 620 feet high.

eastern valley. Explore the Valley on the open-air tram tour, which is particularly lovely on moonlit nights.

Special Needs

Three of the ten shuttle buses are wheelchair accessible and two have tie downs. Yosemite Valley's visitor centers, restaurants and shops are all wheelchair accessible. Campgrounds, restaurants, lodging and trails are connected by eight miles of paved bicycle paths, which make excellent thoroughfares for wheelchair users.

The Badger Pass ski area has a "sit-ski" program, which teaches individuals with lower body paralysis to ski, using a kayak-like device. For information about this program, call the Yosemite Ski School at 209-373-1330.

To request the free brochure on accessibility and special programs, call the Yosemite Access Coordinator's Office at 209-372-0200.

Amenities

Bike rental ♦ Skiing and mountaineering instruction ♦ Bus tours ♦ Nature walks ♦ Exhibits and displays ♦ Natural history presentations ♦ Showers ♦ Service stations ♦ Repair garage ♦ Shuttle bus ♦ Recreational equipment rental.

Travel Advisory

Never swim or wade in streams above waterfalls or in cascade areas.

Store food properly to protect it from bears and other wildlife.

Emergency Information

Yosemite Medical Group provides 24-hour emergency care. The nearest hospitals are in Merced, Fresno, Bridgeport, Mariposa and Sonora.

Visitor and Information Centers

Yosemite Valley Visitor Center is open daily, year-round. The center offers a range of historical and natural history exhibits presentations.

Campgrounds

There are 12 campgrounds at Yosemite but because of flooding in 1997, some campgrounds are not open to the public. For the most up-to-date information about campground availability, reservation guidelines and camping fees call 800-436-PARK.

Picnic Areas

Picnic areas and campgrounds have tables, fire pits and grills. You can buy supplies at the Yosemite Store.

Cabins, Lodges and Hotels

If you plan to stay at one of the five lodgings inside the park, you must make reservations well in advance. Book all accommodeations in Yosemite Valley by calling 209-252-4848.

Restaurants

There are nine restaurants in Yosemite and two snack bars. Most restaurants are open for breakfast, lunch and dinner. Dinner reservations are recommended. You should also make reservations for the Wawona Hotel's popular Sunday brunch.

THINGS TO DO AND SEE

Tram/Bus Tour. Daily open-air tram and bus tours stop at major points of interest. A two-hour tour runs during the summer. In winter, heated motor coaches tour the Yosemite Valley. One-hour snowmobile tours from Badger Pass offer dazzling views of the Sierra Nevadas. For information on fees and schedules call 209-372-1240.

Exhibits. The Yosemite Valley Visitor Center features historical and nature displays. The Indian Culture Exhibit showcases Miwok and Paiute cultures. The Village of the Ahwahnee leads you down a trail that passes a reconstructed Native American village. The Ansel Adams Gallery is nearby. The Pioneer History Center is staffed by volunteers in period costumes. The Mariposa Grove Museum and Happy Isle Nature Center feature natural history exhibits.

Changing Yosemite. This one-mile hike begins near the visitor center and winds through the Mariposa grove of giant sequoias. Other easy hikes include the John Muir Trail, which starts at Happy Isles and winds through the Tuolumne Meadows and along the Sierra Crest. Check current trail conditions at park information stations before setting out. Detailed maps and hiking guides are on sale at visitor centers.

Saddle Trips. Guided saddle trips, from two hours to day-long excursions, depart from four locations in the park: Yosemite Valley, Wawona, White Wolf and Tuolumne Meadows. Reservations are highly recommended. Call 209-372-1248.

Mountaineering. The season runs from mid-April to mid-October. Climbers should contact the Yosemite Mountaineering School at the park.

Skiing and Snowshoeing. Snow conditions are often favorable for skiing and snowshoeing in the sequoia groves of Mariposa and Tuolumne, in Crane Flat and at the Badger Ski Area. Ranger-led snowshoe walks depart from Badger Pass. Visitor centers sell ski maps. Ski lessons and equipment rental are available at Badger Pass. Call 209-372-1244.

Near Yosemite National Park

There are two national forests and one national monument near Yosemite.

Stanislaus National Forest. A high sierra forest in Sonora adjoins Yosemite National Park on the north and east. There are 1,143 campsites. It offers white water rafting on the Tuolumne river, trout fishing and off-road vehicle routes. For more information call 209-962-7825.

Devils Postpile National Monument. This Mammoth Lakes site is off California Highway 203 about 40 miles from Yosemite. It has 23 campsites. See the spectacular 60-foot high basalt columns formed by volcanic activity and carved by glaciers. Enjoy hiking and fishing. There is a shuttle bus available. It is open July through October. For more information call 619-934-2289.

Sierra National Forest. This area adjoins Yosemite at Mariposa and California Highway 49. There are 1,500 campsites. Experience the rugged backcountry, white-

water rafting and giant sequoias. For more information call 209-966-3638.

For More Information

Superintendent
Yosemite National Park
PO Box 577
Yosemite National Park, CA 95389
Tel. 209-372-0200

ZION NATIONAL PARK

Utah ♦ **Established 1919**

It is easy to see why this other-worldly landscape of cliffs, buttes and mesas was a sacred place to the Paiutes. Today it still inspires visitors with its towering sandstone cliffs reaching 3000 feet, yet in places barely 18 feet apart. A climb to the top of any of Zion's higher points will reward you with a sunrise or sunset you will never forget.

Some of the highlights of this beautifully carved rock garden are West Temple, Towers of the Virgin, the Great White Throne, the Great Organ, Angels Landing, the Temple of Sinawava, Weeping Rock and Emerald Pools. At Checkerboard Mesa you can study the intriguing pattern of cracks and grooves etched on a sandstone mountain.

Although this is semi-desert country, parts of the park are lush with box elders, ashes, willows and cottonwood. The Virgin River flows through the red rock canyons of Zion. During flash floods, this peaceful river has tossed trees and boulders across the canyon.

The forests provide shelter for mule deer, mountain lions, porcupines and more than 200 species of birds, including the golden eagle. Nine hundred species of wildflowers blossom in spring.

There are 55 miles of hiking trails at Zion. To the northwest, Kolob Canyons has backpacking trails along a creek bordered with pink sands. There you can see the Kolob Arch. It spans 310 feet, making it the largest free-standing natural arch in the world. In nearby Kolob Terrace and Kolob Finger Canyons, iron-capped rocks look like enormous, petrified mushrooms.

You can enjoy most of Zion's spectacular landscape from your car if you're willing to brave the narrow, winding and sometimes very steep roads. The Zion Canyon Scenic Drive follows the river along the floor of the canyon. There are two narrow tunnels that RVs and buses are too large to pass through without an escort. A $10 fee is charged for this service.

Planning Your Visit

Park Open

The park is open year-round. Both visitor centers are closed Christmas Day.

Seasons

Visit in late spring or fall. In summer you'll face 100-degree temperatures. From May to October, temperatures routinely rise to 105 degrees. Thunderstorms are common. Peak visitation to Zion is in August. Winters are mild, with highs of about 40 degrees. There is little snow and humidity is very low most of the year.

Entrance Fees

Per vehicle
(per passenger).....................................$10
Per individual..$5
Fees are valid for 7 days.

Permits and Licenses

Backcountry permits are required for overnight trips. Permits are also required for all hikes through the Virgin River Narrows. Apply 24 hours in advance at park headquarters. The number of permits is limited. Permits cost $5 per person per night.

Access and Transportation

From the East. Take Highway 9 west, approximately 20 miles off Utah 89.

From the West. The park is about 40 miles from St. George. Exit I-5 onto Highway 9 at St. George.

Rental cars are available in St. George and Cedar City.

The closest airport is in St. George, 46 miles from the park.

A Few Tips

♦ Check in with a park ranger before setting out on backcountry trails.
♦ Stay out of drainage areas. Thunderstorms can come up suddenly.
♦ Be alert for rockfalls and landslides.

Special Needs

The Zion Canyon Visitor Center and Kolob Canyons Visitor Center are accessible. Zion Lodge is also accessible. There are accessible campsites at South Campground. The one-mile Riverside Walk that begins at the north end of Zion Canyon Drive is paved and the new two-mile Pairus Trail is also accessible. Park headquarters can provide a brochure, *Access to Zion for People with Disabilities.*

Amenities

Films and exhibits ♦ Tram tour ♦ Nature center for children ♦ Telephones ♦ Picnic areas with fire grates and table ♦ Religious services ♦ Sanitary disposal station ♦ Horseback trips

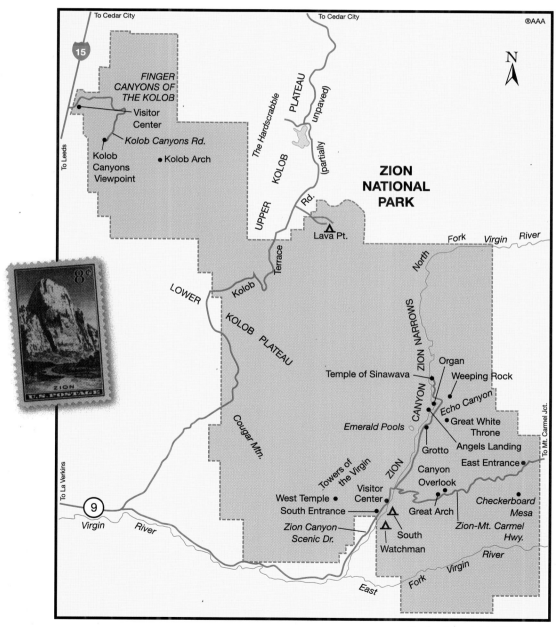

Park size: 146,598 acres

Travel Advisory

This is wild country and there is a risk of landslides and falling rocks. Do not hike, climb or camp alone. Stay on designated trails.

Emergency Information

First aid is available in the park. The nearest hospitals are in Kanab (42 miles from the park) and St. George (46 miles from the park).

Visitor and Information Centers

The visitor center at Kolob Canyons is accessible via Exit 40 from I-15. It passes west of the park and connects with Utah 9 and 17 leading to Park U.S. 89. The Zion Canyon Visitor Center is a short distance from the park's south entrance, adjacent to Springdale.

Campgrounds

Two major campgrounds have a total of 340 sites in the canyon and along the river.

Campsites are available on a first-come, first served basis for $10 per night. Stays are limited to 14 days. They fill up in summer. Group camping requires reservations. Kolob Arch requires a 14-mile round trip hike. This is a primitive site with no facilities. No fires are allowed. There is a stream nearby. There is no fee but a backcountry permit is required. Lava Point has six primitive sites.

Picnic Areas

There are picnic areas in the park. Food and supplies are available in nearby Springdale, located south of the park and Zican at the park's boundary.

Cabins, Lodgers and Hotels

Zion Lodge has cabins and motel rooms. It is open all year. Call 303-297-2757 for reservations. There are 12 motels and eight bed and breakfasts in Springdale. For information on accommodations call 801-772-3757.

Restaurants

There is a dining room in Zion Lodge. There are also shops and restaurants in Springdale, near the south entrance to the park.

Angels Landing. This is a good challenge for experienced hikers, but the last portion of the trail is extremely steep. The West Rim Trail is a good overnight trip.

A concession-operated service shuttles hikers to and from back-country trailheads.

Hike the Narrows. This is a strenuous hike. You'll wade through chest-deep water for 16 miles but you'll see fern waterfalls and side canyons you would miss otherwise. You need 10 hours, good boots and a walking stick. You must pick up a permit 24 hours in advance at park headquarters. The hike is only permitted when river flows are low and flash flood danger is minimal.

Climbing. Technical climbing is permitted, but do not climb alone. The rock at Zion is soft sandstone that does not hold pitons. The visitor centers can provide a climbing guide. Never roll or throw things from high places. The trails below are full of hikers.

THINGS TO DO AND SEE

Trails. There are 122 miles of hiking trails in the park. Most trails are closed to horses, so if you plan to ride into the park, consult the park before you arrive.

Tram. Open-air trams run several times during the day throughout the summer. Make your reservations at Zion Lodge.

Naturalist Programs. From late March to November rangers conduct nature hikes and talks. There are also evening hikes and campfire programs. Check with a visitor center for schedules.

Hiking. The least challenging hikes are the short trek to Weeping Rock and the two-mile trek to Emerald Pools. Other popular trails are Canyon Overlook and the Riverside Walk.

For More Information

Superintendent
Zion National Park
Springdale, UT 84767
Tel. 801-772-3256

PHOTO CREDITS

p. ii, first: ©1997 Carol Lee

p. ii, second: Photo courtesy the Utah Travel Council

p. ii, third: Image ©1997 PhotoDisc, Inc.

p. ii, four: Image ©1997 PhotoDisc, Inc.

p. iii: Photo courtesy Alaska Division of Tourism

p. v, top: Image ©1997 PhotoDisc, Inc.

p. v, bottom: Photo courtesy of Oregon Tourism Commission/Gary Wilson

p. vi: Image ©1997 Corel

p. vii: Photo courtesy Alaska Division of Tourism

p. 2–3: ©Drinker/Durrance Graphics, Inc. 1997

p. 2, inset: Photo courtesy of National Park Service/Richard Frear

p. 3, silo.: ©1997/Stephen Bicknell photograph/from the collection of the Abbe Museum, Bar Harbor, Maine

p. 5, top: Image ©1997 Corel

p. 5, inset: Photo courtesy of Rushing & Associates Design

p. 6: Photo courtesy of National Park Service/Richard Frear

p. 7: Photo courtesy of National Park Service/Richard Frear

p. 8–9: Photo courtesy of American Samoa National Park/Chris Stein

p. 9, inset: Photo courtesy of National Park Service

p. 9: Image ©1997 PhotoDisc, Inc.

p. 10, both photos: Courtesy of National Park Service

p. 12–13: © Drinker/Durrance Graphics, Inc. 1997

p. 12, silo.: Photo Courtesy of Rushing & Associates Design

p. 14, both photos: Images © 1997 Corel

p. 15: Image ©1997 Corel

p. 16: Image ©1997 Corel

p. 17, silo.: Photo courtesy of Badlands National Park

p. 18–19: ©1997 F. Sieb/H. Armstrong Roberts

p. 19, inset: ©1997 J. Irwin/H. Armstrong Roberts

p. 21: Image ©1997 PhotoDisc, Inc.

p. 22–23: ©1997 J. Buehner/H. Armstrong Roberts

p. 23: Photo courtesy of National Park Service/Fred E. Mang, Jr.

p. 23, silo.: Photo courtesy of Big Bend National Park

p. 25: ©1997 Joura/H. Armstrong Roberts

p. 26: ©1997 T. Algire/H. Armstrong Roberts

p. 28–29: ©Drinker/Durrance Graphics, Inc. 1997

p. 28, silo.: Photo courtesy of Rushing & Associates Design

p. 29, inset: Image ©1997 PhotoDisc, Inc.

p. 30: Photo courtesy of Florida Department of Commerce Division of Tourism

p. 31: Photo courtesy of Florida Department of Commerce

p. 32, top: Photo courtesy of Florida Department of Commerce, Division of Tourism

p. 32, bottom: ©1997/Jeff Foott/Adventure Photo & Film

p. 33: Image ©1997 PhotoDisc, Inc.

p. 34: Image ©1997 Corel

p. 34, silo.: Photo courtesy of Bryce Canyon National Park

p. 35: ©Drinker/Durrance Graphics, Inc. 1997

p. 36: Photo courtesy of the Utah Travel Council

p. 37: Image ©1997 Corel

p. 38: Image ©1997 Corel

p. 39, both photos: Images ©1997 Corel

p. 40–41: Image ©1997 Corel

p. 40, silo.: Photo courtesy of Rushing & Associates Design

p. 42: Photo courtesy of the Utah Travel Council/Frank Jensen

p. 44: Image ©1997 Corel

p. 45: Photo courtesy of the Utah Travel Council/Frank Jensen

p. 46: Image ©1997 Corel

p. 47, silo.: Image ©1997 PhotoDisc, Inc.

p. 47: Photo courtesy of the Utah Travel Council/Frank Jensen

p. 49, both photos: Images ©1997 Corel

p. 50: Image ©1997 Corel

p. 51, both photos: Images ©1997 Corel

p. 52: © Drinker/Durrance Graphics, Inc. 1997

p. 53, silo.: Photo Courtesy of Rushing & Associates Design

p. 53: Image ©1997 Corel

p. 55–57, all photos: Images ©1997 Corel

p. 58–59: Photo courtesy of National Park Service/T. Pedroga

p. 58, silo.: Photo courtesy of Rushing & Associates Design

p. 59, inset: Image ©1997 PhotoDisc, Inc.

p. 60, inset: Photo courtesy of National Park Service/Tim Hauf

p. 61: Image ©1997 PhotoDisc, Inc.

p. 62: Image ©1997 PhotoDisc, Inc.

p. 64: Photo courtesy of National Park Service

p. 65: Photo courtesy of Oregon Tourism Commission/Steve Terrill

p. 65, silo.: Photo courtesy of Rushing & Associates Design

p. 66–67: Photo courtesy of Oregon Tourism Commission/Craig Tuttle

p. 69: Image ©1997 PhotoDisc, Inc.

p. 70: ©1997/Vern Clevenger/Adventure Photo & Film

p. 71, top: Image ©1997 PhotoDisc, Inc.

p. 71, silo.: Photo courtesy of Rushing & Associates Design

p. 73: ©1997/Anne Marie Weber/Adventure Photo & Film

p. 74: Image ©1997 PhotoDisc, Inc.

p. 75: ©1997/Vern Clevenger/Adventure Photo & Film

p. 76: Image ©1997 Corel

p. 77: Image ©1997 PhotoDisc, Inc.

p. 77, silo.: Photo courtesy Clairette T. Murray

p. 79, top: Photo courtesy of National Park Service?

p. 79, bottom: Image ©1997 PhotoDisc, Inc.

p. 80: Image ©1997 PhotoDisc, Inc.

p. 81: Image ©1997 PhotoDisc, Inc.

p. 82, silo.: Photo courtesy of Rushing & Associates Design

p. 82–83: Image ©1997 PhotoDisc, Inc.

p. 83, inset: Image ©1997 PhotoDisc, Inc.

p. 84: Image ©1997 PhotoDisc, Inc.

p. 85, both photos: Images ©1997 PhotoDisc, Inc.

p. 86–87: ©Drinker/Durrance Graphics, Inc. 1997

p. 86, inset: Image ©1997 PhotoDisc, Inc.

p. 86, silo.: Photo Courtesy of Rushing & Associates Design

p. 88: Photo Courtesy of National Park Service/Richard Frear

p. 89: Photo Courtesy of National Park Service/Richard Frear

p. 89, inset: Image ©1997 PhotoDisc, Inc.

p. 90, top: Image ©1997 PhotoDisc, Inc.

p. 90, bottom: Photo courtesy of National Park Service/Cecil W. Stoughton

p. 91: Image ©1997 PhotoDisc, Inc.

p. 92, silo.: Image ©1997 PhotoDisc, Inc.

p. 92–93: Photo courtesy of Alaska Division of Tourism

p. 93: Image ©1997 PhotoDisc, Inc.

p. 94, top: Image ©1997 PhotoDisc, Inc.

p. 94, bottom: Photo courtesy Alaska Division of Tourism

p. 95–96: All photos courtesy Alaska Division of Tourism

p. 98, silo.: Photo courtesy of Rushing & Associates Design

p. 98–99: Photo courtesy Alaska Division of Tourism

p. 99, inset: Image ©1997 PhotoDisc, Inc.
p. 101, both photos: Images ©1997 PhotoDisc, Inc.
p. 102, both photos: Courtesy Alaska Division of Tourism
p. 103: Photo courtesy Alaska Division of Tourism
p. 104, silo.: Photo courtesy of Grand Canyon Association
p. 104–105: ©Drinker/Durrance Graphics, Inc. 1997
p. 105, inset: Image ©1997 Corel
p. 106–109, all photos: Images ©1997 Corel
p. 110: Image ©1997 PhotoDisc, Inc.
p. 111: Image ©1997 Corel
p. 112, silo.: Photo courtesy of Rushing & Associates Design
p. 112–113: ©Drinker/Durrance Graphics, Inc. 1997
p. 113, inset: Image ©1997 PhotoDisc, Inc.
p. 114: Photo courtesy of National Park Service
p. 115: ©1997 R. Kord/H. Armstrong Roberts
p. 116: ©Drinker/Durrance Graphics, Inc. 1997
p. 116, inset: Image ©1997 PhotoDisc, Inc.
p. 117: Image ©1997 PhotoDisc, Inc.
p. 118: Image ©1997 PhotoDisc, Inc.
p. 119: ©1997 J. Blank/H. Armstrong Roberts
p. 120, both photos: Images ©1997 PhotoDisc, Inc.
p. 121: Image ©1997 PhotoDisc, Inc.
p. 122–123, all photos: Courtesy of Great Basin
    National Park
p. 124: Photo courtesy of Great Basin National Park/
    Fred R. Bell
p. 126: Photo courtesy of Great Basin National Park
p. 127: Photo courtesy of Great Basin National Park
p. 128: ©Drinker/Durrance Graphics, Inc. 1997
p. 129: ©1997 W. Metzen/H. Armstrong Roberts
p. 129, silo.: Photo courtesy of Great Smoky Mountains
    National Park
p. 130: Image ©1997 PhotoDisc, Inc.
p. 131, top: Photo Courtesy of National Park Service/
    Richard Frear
p. 131, bottom: Image ©1997 PhotoDisc, Inc.
p. 132: Photo Courtesy of National Park Service/
    Richard Frear
p. 134: ©1997 Wyman Meinzer
p. 135: ©1997 T. Algire/H. Armstrong Roberts
p. 135, silo.: Image ©1997 PhotoDisc, Inc.
p. 137: Photo courtesy of National Park Service/
    Richard Frear
p. 137, inset: ©1997 Wyman Meinzer
p. 138: ©1997 Wyman Meinzer
p. 140–141: ©Drinker/Durrance Graphics, Inc. 1997
p. 140, silo.: Photo courtesy of Rushing & Associates Design
p. 141, inset: Photo courtesy of Hawaii Visitors and
    Convention Bureau
p. 143, top: Photo courtesy of Hawaii Visitors and
    Convention Bureau/Anthony Anjo
p. 143, inset: Image ©1997 PhotoDisc, Inc.
p. 144: Photo courtesy of Hawaii Visitors and
    Convention Bureau/Brian Powers
p. 145: Image ©1997 PhotoDisc, Inc.
p. 146–147: ©Drinker/Durrance Graphics, Inc. 1997
p. 146–147, silo.: Photo courtesy of Rushing &
    Associates Design
p. 147, inset: Photo courtesy of Hawaii Visitors and
    Convention Bureau/Greg Vaughn
p. 148: Photo courtesy of National Park Service/Butterfield
p. 149, top: Image ©1997 Corel
p. 149, inset: Image ©1997 PhotoDisc, Inc.
p. 150: Photo courtesy of Hawaii Visitors and Convention
    Bureau/Peter French
p. 151: Both photos courtesy of Hawaii Visitors and
    Convention Bureau/Peter French

p. 152–156, all photos: Courtesy of Hot Springs Advertising
    & Promotion Commission
p. 157: Photo courtesy of the Michigan Travel Bureau
p. 158: Photo courtesy of the Michigan Travel Bureau
p. 159: Image ©1997 PhotoDisc, Inc.
p. 160: Image ©1997 Corel
p. 161: Photo courtesy of the Michigan Travel Bureau
p. 162, silo.: Photo courtesy of Rushing & Associates Design
p. 162, inset: Image ©1997 Corel
p. 163: ©1997/Brian Bailey/Adventure Photo & Film
p. 165: Image ©1997 Corel
p. 166: ©1997/Greg Epperson/Adventure Photo & Film
p. 167: Image ©1997 Corel
p. 168–169: ©1997 T. Dietrich/H. Armstrong Roberts
p. 168, silo.: Photo courtesy of Rushing & Associates Design
p. 169, inset: ©1997 PhotoDisc, Inc.
p. 170: Photo courtesy of Alaska Division of Tourism/
    Ernst Schneider
p. 170, inset: Photo courtesy Alaska Division of Tourism
p. 172: Photo courtesy Alaska Division of Tourism
p. 173: ©1997 R. Krubner/H. Armstrong Roberts
p. 174, top: Image ©1997 PhotoDisc, Inc.
p. 174, silo.: Photo courtesy of Rushing & Associates Design
p. 175: Photo courtesy of Alaska Division of Tourism
p. 176: Image ©1997 PhotoDisc, Inc.
p. 177: Image ©1997 PhotoDisc, Inc.
p. 178: Photo courtesy of Alaska Division of Tourism
p. 179: Image ©1997 PhotoDisc, Inc.
p. 180: Photo Courtesy of National Park Service
p. 181: Photo courtesy Alaska Division of Tourism
p. 182–183: Photo courtesy of Alaska Division of Tourism
p. 182, silo.: Photo courtesy of Rushing & Associates Design
p. 183, inset: Image ©1997 PhotoDisc, Inc.
p. 185: Image ©1997 PhotoDisc, Inc.
p. 186: Both photos courtesy Alaska Division of Tourism
p. 187: Photo courtesy Alaska Division of Tourism
p. 188, top: ©1997 E. Cooper/H. Armstrong Roberts
p. 188, silo: Photo courtesy of Rushing & Associates Design
p. 189: ©1997 H.G. Ross/H. Armstrong Roberts
p. 191: Photo courtesy California Division of Tourism/
    Robert Holmes
p. 192: Photo courtesy of National Park Service
p. 193: Image ©1997 PhotoDisc, Inc.
p. 194: ©1997 D. Muench/H. Armstrong Roberts
p. 195, top: Image ©1997 PhotoDisc, Inc.
p. 195, silo.: Photo courtesy of Rushing & Associates Design
p. 196: Image ©1997 PhotoDisc, Inc.
p. 198: Image ©1997 PhotoDisc, Inc.
p. 199, silo.: Image ©1997 PhotoDisc, Inc.
p. 200–203, all photos: Images ©1997 Corel
p. 204: ©1997 R. Kord/H. Armstrong Roberts
p. 205–206, all photos: Images ©1997 Corel
p. 207, silo.: Photo courtesy of Rushing & Associates Design
p. 207–211, all photos: Images ©1997 Corel
p. 212: ©1997 Joura/H. Armstrong Roberts
p. 213, silo.: Photo courtesy Rushing & Associates Design
p. 213–215, all photos: Images ©1997 Corel
p. 216: Photo courtesy of National Park Service/
    M. Woodbridge Williams
p. 218, silo.: Photo courtesy Rushing & Associates Design
p. 218–219: ©Drinker/Durrance Graphics, Inc. 1997
p. 219–220, bottom: Images ©1997 Corel
p. 222: Image ©1997 PhotoDisc, Inc.
p. 222–223, bottom: Images ©1997 Corel
p. 224–225: ©1997 T. Algire/H. Armstrong Roberts
p. 224, silo.: Photo courtesy of National Park Service
p. 226, both photos: Images ©1997 Corel
p. 227, both photos: Images ©1997 Corel

p. 228, inset: Image ©1997 Corel
p. 229, top: Photo courtesy of National Park Service/
   Richard Frear
p. 229, bottom: Image ©1997 Corel
p. 230–231: ©1997 D. Muench/H. Armstrong Roberts
p. 231: Photo courtesy of the National Park Service
p. 232, silo.: Image ©1997 PhotoDisc, Inc.
p. 232: ©Drinker/Durrance Graphics, Inc. 1997
p. 233: Image ©1997 Corel
p. 235: Image ©1997 Corel
p. 236, both photos: Images ©1997 PhotoDisc, Inc.
p. 237: Photo courtesy of the National Park Service
p. 238: ©1997 P. Degginger/H. Armstrong Roberts
p. 239, silo.: Photo courtesy Rushing & Associates Design
p. 239–243, all photos: Images ©1997 Corel
p. 244, silo.: Photo courtesy Rushing & Associates Design
p. 245: Image ©1997 PhotoDisc, Inc.
p. 246: ©1997/MacDuff Everton/Adventure Photo & Film
p. 247: Image ©1997 PhotoDisc, Inc.
p. 248: ©1997 C. Bryant/H. Armstrong Roberts
p. 249, silo.: Photo courtesy Rushing & Associates Design
p. 249: Image ©1997 Corel
p. 250: Photo courtesy of the National Park Service
p. 252, top: Image ©1997 Corel
p. 252, bottom: Photo courtesy of the National Park Service
p. 253: Image ©1997 Corel
p. 254: All photos courtesy of the National Park Service
p. 255, silo.: Photo courtesy Rushing & Associates
p. 255: Virginia Travel Corporation/Jack Hollingsworth
p. 256–257: ©1997 George Hunter/H. Armstrong Roberts
p. 257: Photo courtesy Virginia Travel Corporation/
   Richard Nowitz
p. 259: Photo courtesy Virginia Travel Corporation/
   Buddy Mays
p. 259: Virginia Travel Corporation
p. 260–261: ©1997 T. Algire/H. Armstrong Roberts
p. 262, silo.: Photo courtesy Rushing & Associates Design
p. 262–265, all photos: Images ©1997 Corel
p. 266–267: ©1997 Carol Lee
p. 267, silo.: Photo courtesy Rushing & Associates Design
p. 267: ©1997 Carol Lee
p. 269: ©1997 Carol Lee
p. 270: Photo courtesy of the Minnesota Office of Tourism
p. 271, silo.: Photo courtesy Rushing & Associates Design
p. 271, inset: Image ©1997 Corel
p. 272: Photo courtesy of the Minnesota Office of Tourism
p. 273: Photo courtesy of the Minnesota Office of Tourism
p. 274, both photos: Courtesy of the Minnesota Office of
   Tourism
p. 275, top: Image © 1997 Corel
p. 275, silo.: Image ©1997 PhotoDisc, Inc.
p. 276–277, all photos: Images ©1997 Corel
p. 279: ©1997 J. Blank/H. Armstrong Roberts
p. 280: Image ©1997 Corel
p. 281: ©1997/Kennan Ward/Adventure Photo & Film
p. 282, silo.: Photo courtesy Rushing & Associates Design
p. 282–283: Photo courtesy National Park Service/
   W. S. Keller
p. 283: Photo courtesy Wind Cave National Park
p. 285–287, all photos: Images ©1997 Corel
p. 288, silo.: Photo courtesy Rushing & Associates Design
p. 288–289: Photo courtesy Alaska Division of Tourism
p. 289: Photo courtesy Alaska Division of Tourism/
   William Keller
p. 290–293: All photos courtesy Alaska Division of Tourism
p. 294, silo.: Photo courtesy Rushing & Associates Design
p. 294–295: ©Drinker/Durrance Graphics, Inc. 1997

p. 295, bottom: Image ©1997 Corel
p. 296: ©1997 R. Kord/H. Armstrong Roberts
p. 299, top: Image ©1997 Corel
p. 299, bottom: Photo courtesy Rushing & Associates Design
p. 300, silo.: Photo courtesy Rushing & Associates Design
p. 300–301: ©Drinker/Durrance Graphics, Inc. 1997
p. 301: Image ©1997 Corel
p. 303–306: All photos, Images ©1997 Corel
p. 307: ©Drinker/Durrance Graphics, Inc. 1997
p. 307, top: Image ©1997 PhotoDisc, Inc.
p. 308, silo.: Photo courtesy Rushing & Associates Design
p. 310, both photos: Images ©1997 Corel